WELL-BEHAVED
TAVERNS
SELDOM MAKE HISTORY

PENNSYLVANIA PUBS WHERE
RABBLE-ROUSERS AND RUM RUNNERS
STIRRED UP REVOLUTIONS

M. DIANE McCORMICK

To the tavern!
M. Diane McCormick

SUNBURY
PRESS
Mechanicsburg, PA USA

Continue the Enlightenment!

For Marc, because he kept a light burning
when I came home late. Also because he fed me.
Food just appeared every night. Magic.

CONTENTS

INTRODUCTION
"Diseases, vicious habits, bastards, and legislators"

Pubs are educational. There's so much to learn. Such as: Hitting your head on a stone ceiling hurts. A Colonial "bar and grill" was, literally, a grill made of bars, protecting liquor from theft and flying chairs. Ghost cats are a thing. A tunnel, a hose, or a child was handy to have during Prohibition. Rebellions run on rum.

It struck me over a burger and Sly Fox O'Reilly Stout at the Jean Bonnet Tavern, a haven of stone and brick and long verandas near Bedford, that Pennsylvania taverns seem to specialize in starting rebellions, uprisings, and insurrections fueled on rum (or whiskey, or applejack, or Madeira wine in unfathomably vast quantities). Linger at the Jean Bonnet, and you still seem to hear 500 infuriated farmers flocking in protest—please let them be waving pitchforks—and on their way to launching the Whiskey Rebellion.

In early America, only two community places hosted public gatherings. Drinking, dancing, carnal relations, frontier justice, politicking, and other unsavory acts were frowned on in churches, so people gravitated to the other option—their local taverns. Where people gathered, they aired their gripes. Add booze, and the flame torch was lit.

After all, taverns came highly recommended by none other than John Adams, who said, "Here the time, the money, the health, and the modesty, of most that are young and of many old, are wasted; here diseases, vicious habits, bastards, and legislators, are frequently begotten."

Why spend my time anywhere else? Could I find more rebellion-forward pubs like the Jean Bonnet Tavern—still standing, still serving good food and drinks, maybe still smelling of wood smoke?

I could, and they spanned from the American Revolution to Prohibition. Generous owners and proprietors opened their doors, and I got to ask the nosy questions. I peeked in the corners. I sampled the food, sipped the spirits, and swilled the beer (well, not exactly swilled, but indulge me the alliteration).

This is a guide to 12 taverns—their histories as rebellious hotspots, and their culinary and beverage scenes today. They introduced me to the great cauldrons of American upheaval and the people who stirred the pots. I mean, I met Thomas Jefferson. In the flesh. I was dumbstruck. Okay, he was a TJ impersonator, but see how quickly your brain functions when the Declaration of Independence author pops up in front of you.

Every age has reason to rebel. Like the Muppets traveling by movie map, I toured via taverns through the American Revolution, the Whiskey Rebellion, and a woozy, boozy uprising known as Fries Rebellion. I saw where canal diggers died and Molly Maguires plotted. In Gettysburg, two inns safeguard tales of the Underground Railroad and the tumultuous days of battle. Our sepia-toned ancestors thumbed their collective nose at the silliness of Prohibition by slipping into neighborhood speakeasies as easily as we stop at a Sheetz or a Wawa (and yes, I visited a few of those on this magical history tour. The Hamburg Wawa off I-78 saw a lot of me.)

May I add that the owners of our misbehaving pubs exhibit their own brand of defiance? As steely-eyed as any Founding Father, they have stared down red tape and sinking floors, sagging ceilings and beehives, redevelopers and doubters. Almost all have a story that begins with a touchup and ends with major reconstruction. They all recognize the tradition they carry on from the earliest innkeepers. Each swears it's the history of the place that keeps him or her going.

Belly up to the bar, and I'll share tales of rebellions and hangings, battles and bullet holes, murder and hostage-takings, flirtation and smuggling, lawsuits and disease, rum-running and autopsies. Many are true. As for the rest—let's just say that legends get burnished over the years. If it's a fun story, I tell it, along with a tip that this might or might not be factual. I simply wanted to stand at the intersection of liquor and history and, from there, share the intrigue that you don't find on the back of the menu.

So here's to the rogues, rapscallions, ne'er-do-wells, scalawags, ruffians, rebels, patriots, and scoundrels who stirred up trouble in, from, and around Pennsylvania pubs. Pursuing happiness as they interpreted it, some were right, and some were wrong, and many were both. Some rumbled over questions that still rankle today. Listen closely, and their voices urge us to keep up the fight. Question authority. Defy tyranny. Repair the lingering injustice.

And do it all over the lobster mac 'n cheese or peanut-butter burger, the homemade cheesecake, and the local beer or house-specialty cocktail that our rebellious forebears would be glad to share.

City Tavern entrance

City Tavern rear and side alley

I.

CITY TAVERN
Philadelphia, Pennsylvania

Epicenter of revolt

Misbehavior makes history: City Tavern

■ Plot a revolution in public, and you're courting a date with the hangman. City Tavern was literally made to order for rebellion, a sanctuary for surreptitious talks.

■ Within these walls, John Adams and Thomas Jefferson swapped ideas for their new republic. Adams sized up his fellow provocateurs as "very sensible and learned" or "not very promising." Here, George Washington met the dashing Marquis de Lafayette, whose zeal would keep the revolutionary fires burning.

■ Insurrect hard, play hard. When the cares of the world are on your shoulders, let's have another round tonight—say, a pour from one of the 522 bottles of Madeira ordered for a single banquet.

■ Your meal today brims with the revolutionary concept that 18th-century dishes had flavor.

■ Today's scene: City Tavern is a reconstruction, but it is more real than real, ceding little to the present and lingering with the spirit, and spirits, of '76.

Built: 1773, by an investor group. Razed 1854. Rebuilt 1976.

Meet the chef

We are in 1948, a long way from 1773, but a crucial year to City Tavern. On a visit to Philadelphia, President Harry Truman found little more than neglect and disuse in the city's historic center, the linchpin of the American Revolution. The irony of having just fought a world war for freedom from oppression must

5

have been searing. That year, Congress authorized the creation of Independence National Historical Park, with Independence Hall as the centerpiece.

Terrific, said historians, but the park needed an essential addition. They told Truman, "You've got to rebuild the tavern." (The quote belongs to Chef Walter Staib, who was telling me the story). City Tavern was demolished in 1854, they said, but its spirit was inextinguishable.

"It's because George Washington met John Adams in here," Staib was saying. "Jefferson was here. Hamilton was here. The Marquis de Lafayette, August 5th, 1777, upstairs was where he first got introduced to George Washington with a commitment of support from the king of France. There were so many firsts that happened here. When Washington got elected as president of the United States, he had a bigger going-away party here than his actual inauguration in New York."

I was glued to this tale of revolution and revival. I picked up a beer on my flight of Ales of the Revolution—I think it was the Thomas Jefferson's 1774 Tavern Ale—and Chef Staib clinked my glass with his Riesling.

"Salut," he said.

This is City Tavern, the granddaddy of misbehaving pubs, where rebellion-minded patrons shook the world to its core. Long after the demolition of the original City Tavern, its lingering essence of righteousness and genius and towering egos drove the National Park Service to rebuild in exacting detail. Research into the details of every brick, corner, and room would take more than 25 years. The recreated City Tavern opened in 1976, just in time for the Bicentennial.

"They did a beautiful job in restoring it," Chef Staib said, "but they forgot one thing."

What?

"Food."

Oh, that.

"They cooked somewhere else. It was all heated up in a steam table. They had a company that served airline snack bars."

Right. Because airline snacks are everyone's favorite. At least the second vendor converted the kitchen to gas, but the food remained so horrid that City Tavern closed for a year in the early 1990s. Then a friend suggested that Chef Staib consider stepping in. He flinched. He had eaten here once before. It was "horrendous."

The author with Chef Staib and Thomas Jefferson impersonator Steve Edenbo

But he said he'd look into it "because the place was big," and a second kitchen would provide space for researching recipes.

The federal government's regulatory minefield also gave pause, but on a flight from Tokyo to Chicago, he reached for the National Park Service's history of City Tavern and culinary trends of the 18th century. He was hooked. His proposal for a menu based on authentic recipes won congressional approval in 1994. He invested in a pastry chef's kitchen, complete with baking stone because "you couldn't cook bread in a convection oven." He converted the basement from storage to lower-level dining rooms, staged to look like larders and wine cellars of the past.

The relaunched City Tavern opened in 1994, and Chef Staib has been here since. While he changed the building, the building also changed him. Before 1994, he had "very little interest in American history." He was born to cook. Third-generation restaurateur. Founder and president of the global consulting firm Concepts by Staib, Ltd. Winner of prestigious cooking, hospitality, and leadership awards.

But he walked into City Tavern, and revolutionary history grabbed him by the chef's jacket.

7

"Something to remember," Chef Staib told me as we sat in that basement, watching the passing feet of tourists through the windows. "This place was the place to be. It was built by people who knew what was going to happen. They knew the Continental Congress was going to be coming here in 1774. They knew things were coming around. This revolution didn't just come overnight."

All these important visitors would need a base of operations. City Tavern opened in late 1773. The First Continental Congress arrived as expected. John Adams met George Washington in this tavern, "and the rest is, if you will, history."

City Tavern intrigued Chef Staib's Old World sensibilities. Growing up in Germany, he cooked and baked, gardened and preserved, just like the Colonials. Eighteenth-century Germans and French and other immigrants made Philadelphia "this great culinary melting pot." He was fascinated to learn that French royal refugees, fleeing to America in order to keep heads attached to shoulders, settled in this part of town, just past the harbor where they stepped off the boats.

"The French people called it 'Le Petit Champs Élysées,'" he said. "Everything from here to Christ Church was French. Ice cream shops, chocolate shops, jewelry shops." In the heart of it, City Tavern "was a very sophisticated place. It was a very expensive place."

I asked Chef Staib how he has managed to maintain his place at City Tavern for 24 years and counting.

"We're here every day," he said. "We're like Disney. Every day, same thing." The tavern closes only a couple of days a year. Otherwise, open, including the President's Day when I visited and was tongue-tied at meeting President Thomas Jefferson, who looked good for someone approaching 275 years old (in the form of remarkably look-alike impersonator Steve Edenbo).

Even if you're more interested in history than food, you're welcome to wander in. "A lot of people just want to walk through and feel it," Chef Staib said. "You don't need to come here and eat. We don't force you."

But if you want to eat—and I highly recommend that you do— City Tavern "does not shortcut the 18th century," he said. All recipes are researched, approved by the National Park Service, and offered without catchy names like "Poor Richard's Hot Dog."

"Everything is made from scratch. Everything. Everything. Everything," he said. "Everything. Every oyster you eat is breaded by one guy that breads them in cornmeal before frying. Every vegetable gets cut. Everything. Everything."

I was surprised to learn that finding 18th-century recipes was "very easy." Many were inspired by cookbook writer Hannah Glasse and her 1745 "The Art of Cooking Made Plain and Easy," so influential that everyone from average families to Thomas Jefferson dined on its dishes. Others came from Martha Washington's compilation of recipes. When Chef Staib finally got to hold Martha's original cookbook in his hands, the pages obligingly opened to the chocolate mousse cake that is a City Tavern staple.

The challenge, actually, was learning to recreate recipes with such directions as "boil the Peeling of the Apples, and the Cores in some fair Water, with a Blade of Mace, till it is very good."

"Hannah Glasse tried to organize a little bit, but by far, you'd have to be a very professional chef to understand those recipes and recreate them," Chef Staib said. He applies a very light hand to adapting for health consciousness and modern tastes—no more lard or the goose fat known as "schmaltz"—but as you eat his dishes, you realize that 18th-century diners knew the true meaning of flavor when unmasked tastes were free to linger on the tongue.

I asked how he makes sure his dishes are something that today's diners will eat.

"I don't care," he said. "Don't care. They're loving it. My portions are too big, and I know that. My market is very sophisticated people that understand. They read about it. They heard about it."

Chef Staib can't tell you what George Washington ate here, because even the most distinguished guests ate *table d'hote*, or what we would call family style. There might be 18 dishes on the table, and that was just one course.

"Eighteenth-century food was all fresh," he said. "It was from farm to table. It wasn't just a cliché. If your name was Thomas Jefferson, you would stop at nothing to get the best. If your name was George Washington, you really didn't care. He was a soldier."

As host and executive producer of the Emmy Award-winning PBS show "A Taste of History," Chef Staib has cooked in the kitchens or estates of the first five presidents. Even cooking consistently with 18th-century equipment, including Thomas Jefferson's stew stove for making delicate sauces and custards that would have been impossible on open fires, has never been a challenge.

"I have outside help," he said. "Meaning, I get funneled from the spirits. I pick where we're filming, and many times I have no idea where it ends up. I cannot tell you right now where we're going to start season 10. It comes, but different directions come, and change comes. It's really weird. There's no set course."

Which led me to a question. Early in our conversation, Chef said that he sometimes feels as if he were here back in the 18th century. I pointed to the floor and said, "Like *here?*"

Yes, *here.* Operating City Tavern is "not about dollars and cents. It's about being pure to history and celebrating history."

"This place to me is like a sanctuary," he said. "When you come up here, it takes you away. We don't have a sound system. We don't have television. We don't have T-shirts. We don't have peanuts on the floor. We don't have taco Tuesday or Miller Lite. Honestly, we carved our niche, and I will never change anything. And all my people know it, and the cooks know it. Everybody knows it's what we do. Just strive forward."

A City Tavern tour

Are we creatures of our time, or can we feel at home in another century? City Tavern proves there's a place for us in the center of a revolution.

The Cincinnati Room: In an age of low ceilings and small rooms, dimensions mattered, especially if your name was George Washington, you were about 6 foot 2, and you regularly traveled with an entourage of 18 or so.

George Washington was such a frequent guest at the spacious City Tavern that it's easy to imagine him greeting staff by name as they escort him to his regular table. Longtime rumor holds that he sat in the rear corner of the second-floor Cincinnati Room, back to the wall, at a table by the window. He could see the courtyard. He could see the door. If an assassin were to lunge, the large man known for his graceful dance moves would have time to react.

"He'd like to have his eyes and ears on the access point of the room so nobody could sneak up on him," Jonathan Jones, Staib's aide, told me as we toured City Tavern. "He could sit here and be able to see what was going on in the courtyard and the garden and make sure he's perfectly aware of whoever comes and goes."

The Cincinnati Room is named for the Society of the Cincinnati, Pennsylvania Chapter, formed by Revolutionary officers in City Tavern in 1783. Their direct descendants helped refurbish the space in 1975. The Roman leader Cincinnatus was Washington's idol, and as war general and as president, Washington plotted strategy and held court in this room. He and his staff would headquarter at City Tavern before heading out to a devastating defeat at Brandywine. That loss would open Philadelphia to British occupation, putting City Tavern in British hands while the Continental Army huddled in Valley Forge and Washington strategized his next steps away from the warm fire and friendly greeting he left behind.

The Long Room: This second-floor room spans much of the width of City Tavern. It was a room for public meetings. And it was a room for banquet after banquet. Insurrectionists loved their banquets, overflowing with food and booze. Congress held its first Fourth of July celebration here. On Washington's way to New York for inauguration in 1789, Philadelphians cheered the procession taking him to a City Tavern bash featuring music and fireworks. Washington's farewell tour before retiring to Mount Vernon in 1797 included a City Tavern stop for a banquet with Philadelphia friends.

At the end of the Constitutional Convention, the party thrown for Washington by the Light Horse of Philadelphia, stalwart veterans of the Delaware River crossing and Valley Forge, has been

The Long Room

called an "epic bender." Imagine "55 gentlemens," as the bill stated, downing 54 bottles of Madeira, 60 bottles of claret, 22 bottles of porter, 12 bottles of beer, eight bottles of cider and seven large bowls of punch. There was food, thank goodness. The nine musicians and seven waiters imbibed an additional 21 bottles of wine.

That party looks Spartan next to the 1778 blowout sprung at City Tavern by local soldiers celebrating the election of Pennsylvania's chief executive. The bill of £2,995 for 270 dignitaries and other guests covered only £500 worth of food. Most of the rest was for "522 bottles of Madeira, 116 large bowls of punch, nine bottles of toddy, six bowls of sangria, twenty-four bottles of port, and two tubs of grog, a rum-and-water concoction, for artillery soldiers," according to "The City Tavern Cookbook." Hardly a surprise, but the bill also charged for 96 broken plates and glasses, and five broken decanters.

The Charter Room and Courtyard: Membership has its privileges. The 53 investors who combined in 1773 to finance construction of City Tavern could get clubby in their exclusive space, now called the Charter Room. It had one thing that even George Washington lacked in the Cincinnati Room—a door to the balcony. On a steamy summer day, members could step outside, a pint of beer or glass of Madeira in hand, and catch a breeze.

In the courtyard below, they could watch the servants doing the day's baking in the outdoor oven. Maybe in the distance, they could see ship masts bobbing in the harbor.

Harbor? What harbor? This is the place to realize that even geography can change. Step onto the balcony today, and get an eyeful of the 21st century. Movie theater across the street. Highrises in the distance. But in the 18th century, that area was all water, since filled in. That cinema is where boats docked. Ship crews arriving with spices from the Spice Islands, or mangoes from Jamaica, or oranges from Seville, or Nurnberg gingerbread from Germany, would bring their goodies straight to City Tavern.

"They would knock on the door and say, 'Chef, do you know what this is?'" Jonathan told me. "Chef would say, 'Nope. Let's figure out what it is and play with it.' So, we were like the test kitchen of the New World."

Today's courtyard beckons with greenery in warm weather. Flowers bloom. Shrubs blossom. Trees arc overhead. Diners laze away the evening under a canopy. A resident hawk named Spartacus does what hawks do to survive. "It's like a little Nat Geo

Madeira storage

down here watching him take down some squirrels," Jonathan said.

Coffee and Subscription Rooms: City Tavern was rebuilt according to painstaking, meticulous research, but a few details have changed. The front and back coffee rooms are dining areas today, adjoining the main entrance hallway. In 1789, these two rooms became headquarters for the Merchants' Coffee House and Place of Exchange. Here, merchants conducted business over coffee or another beverage of choice. Today's wall between the rooms would have actually been a partition, presumably to keep discussion free and flowing.

The barroom

Across the hallway, in the front, is the Subscription Room. The tavern subscribed to everything that could shed light on the affairs of business or revolution—newspapers, magazines, ships' manifests, letters of decree. Twice a day, the newspaper would be read out loud, for the benefit of anyone, literate or not, interested in current events.

Barroom: I'd invite you to belly up to the bar, but this isn't that kind of bar. The City Tavern bar has always held liquor, but it's more like a cage. It's a typical design of the time, with a divided wooden grill on sliders at the doorway. There was good reason for that. Say they're partying like it's 1799, carousing in a gala involving 522 bottles of Madeira. Into the third or fourth hour, someone says, "Your mother wears army boots." The guy with the mother says, "By the way, your sister left her corset at my place last night." You know. Party talk. Then fists smash into jaws. Chairs crack over heads.

Where's the barkeep while plates fly? Locked in his cage—his "bar and grill"—where he and the valuable liquor avoid breakage until it's safe to emerge.

Cellar: George Washington and John Adams probably never gave much thought to the basement, but the cellar held the

The cellar

beating heart of City Tavern. Fresh food was brought to the front entrance, but casks, barrels, and boxes came to the rear, off the cobblestone alley, and went into the cellar. Pumps on the street provided water for dishwashing. Bulk staples such as flour were stored in the rear. The larder could have held pickled meats and preserved fruits. Here in the kitchen, staff prepared the food that fueled revolutionary fervor.

SECTION II

The history of City Tavern: Breaking free

They wanted to break from Great Britain, but they sure missed its comforts, its elegance, its proprieties. In a city of 40,000 residents—the largest in the colonies and second-largest in the British empire—the only tavern choices were rough and disreputable places for merchants doing business over pints of ale.

So 53 Philadelphians ponied up £25 each toward construction of a refined place, modeled after the taverns of London. The investors were Quakers and gamblers, lawyers and judges, future governors and future signers of the Declaration of Independence. They contracted an experienced British innkeeper named Daniel

Smith because colonial innkeepers with polished hospitality skills were scarce.

The doors opened in December 1773. A few months later, the persnickety John Adams proclaimed City Tavern "the most genteel one in America" and lauded a supper "as elegant as ever was laid on a table."

But beneath the veneer of gentility, treasonous talk rumbled.

The teakettle boils over: In May 1774, a ruddy, muscular man dismounted his horse after a breakneck, 345-mile sprint from Boston. Silversmith Paul Revere's sideline as patriotic provocateur was taking most of his time these days.

Today, Revere barged into City Tavern—already the stew pot for simmering revolution—with momentous news. The British had closed Boston Harbor, punishing those audacious Bostonians for dumping 342 chests of tea into Boston Harbor in December 1773. Colonists waving fists in anger was one thing. Causing losses to the British East India Tea Company, granted a monopoly on trading with the colonies, was quite another.

The harbor closing was just one retaliatory act. Parliament clamped down throughout the colonies. Any British officials who committed capital crimes on Colonial soil would be shipped to England for trial, presumably by sympathetic juries. British troops could demand barracks and supplies from Colonial authorities, taking over public houses and unoccupied buildings.

The British called their response the "Coercive Acts," meant to squeeze recompense from the colonies for the sodden tea. Colonists called them the "Intolerable Acts." Revere's dash to Philadelphia was part of a multi-city tour, delivering an urgent plea that merchants boycott British goods. Would they do it? Several hundred Philadelphians crammed into City Tavern's Long Room, debated the question, and declined to boycott. They weren't ready for a trade war.

But the city crafted an alternative response, one that would make Philadelphia and City Tavern the epicenter of revolution. Philadelphia's Committee of Correspondence—throughout the colonies, these were local governing bodies that were becoming the building blocks of revolt—called for "a general Congress of Deputies from the different Colonies, clearly to state what we conceive our rights and to make claim or petition of them to his Majesty, in firm, but decent and dutiful terms." New York followed suit, and then other colonies. The wheels were turning toward the creation of the First Continental Congress, and it would convene in Philadelphia.

First and Second Continental Congress: Eavesdrop at City Tavern, said a delegate to the First Continental Congress, and you learn more than you would from a session at the State House.

Of course, "eavesdropping" could be another word for "spying." Here, after a day of legislating in the Pennsylvania State House, sidebar meetings convened over soup and fish and meat and Madeira, hammering out the details of an uprising.

"The revolution, literally, by everyone's account, was finalized right in these very walls," said Chef Staib.

The First Continental Congress would meet in—Carpenters' Hall. Not Independence Hall, not yet. That building was the Pennsylvania State House then, and the Pennsylvania provincial assembly was using the space. Luckily, the Carpenters' Company—master builders who had already designed and constructed many prominent city buildings—offered their newly built headquarters.

Would it suffice? The delegates couldn't know until they saw the space, so they rendezvoused at nearby City Tavern. In the preceding days, City Tavern was the place where many delegates met in person, attaching faces to names for the first time.

At these City Tavern get-togethers, John Adams assessed New Jersey's William Livingston as "a plain man," with "nothing elegant or genteel about him. They say he is no public speaker, but very sensible and learned, and a ready writer." The elder Mr. Rutledge, on the other hand, was "not very promising. There is no keenness in his eye, no depth in his countenance; nothing of the profound, sagacious, brilliant, or sparkling, in his first appearance."

On that first Continental Congress session day, delegates strolled from City Tavern to Carpenters' Hall and deemed the space "a good room, and the question was put, whether we were satisfied with this room? and it passed in the affirmative," said Adams.

With a little boost from City Tavern, the First Continental Congress had a productive session. Hope for reconciliation with Great Britain lingered. Once, invited to a "most elegant entertainment" at City Tavern by members of the Pennsylvania House of Representatives, delegates heard a toast: "May the sword of the parent never be stained with the blood of her children."

Even amid "nibbling and quibbling as usual," in the words of John Adams, the First Continental Congress produced a statement of grievances, delineated the rights of colonists, and launched a boycott of British goods. They made plans to reconvene, in case their demands failed to win repeal of the Intolerable Acts. Their business concluded, they held a big bash at City Tavern.

They did reconvene, of course. By May 1775, reconciliation seemed a moot point. The Second Continental Congress was now managing a war that started that April when British troops fired at Minutemen trying to prevent the arrest of Patriot leaders at Lexington and Concord. The Second Continental Congress created an army, appointing George Washington as supreme commander. Members would sometimes come to City Tavern to record the day's proceedings or meet in committee. Then they would sit down to eat, debates finagling the fine points of revolution around tables filled with the best food and drink in Philadelphia.

"Tolerably disciplined": Compared to the highly trained, even brutal troops of the British army and their Hessian mercenaries, Continental troops could hardly be called crack soldiers. But as British troops were landing in the Chesapeake Bay, the 16,000-strong Continental Army put on a show with a march through Philadelphia. They appeared "extreamly well armed, pretty well cloathed, and tolerably disciplined." Orders that anyone breaking ranks receive 39 lashes might have had something to do with it. Then again, George Washington himself was known to break ranks, "not above stopping for refreshments with his entourage at the City Tavern," in the words of historian Edward G. Lengel.

The first Fourth: 1776, and City Tavern's congenial atmosphere offered relief from frigid relations with Great Britain. In Congress, Richard Henry Lee of Virginia stepped forward to introduce a resolution declaring the 13 colonies "free and independent states." Since British citizens and potential allies might like an explanation, a committee was formed to write a declaration. Thomas Jefferson and John Adams had spent many evenings at City Tavern, discussing the soul's hunger for liberty over meals of salmon or turkey, chased with Madeira.

Now at the head of the declaration committee, Jefferson turned to Adams and said, "You should do it." Adams said no. For what reasons, Jefferson asked?

"Reason first, you are a Virginian, and a Virginian ought to appear at the head of this business." Adams was thinking politically, because "independence" was a fraught word in most colonies except his own, ardent Massachusetts. "Reason second, I am obnoxious, suspected, and unpopular. You are very much otherwise. Reason third, you can write ten times better than I can."

Who could argue? "Well, if you are decided," Jefferson conceded, "I will do as well as I can." Whenever he looked up from his pen long enough to realize that he was hungry, he usually dined at City Tavern.

On July 4, 1776, the Second Continental Congress approved a Declaration of Independence. That the signers would "pledge to each other our lives, our fortunes, and our sacred honor" was not an idle statement. This was treason. They could hang. Their families could suffer. The revolution had to succeed and the republic gain a foothold, or their lives were sacrificed.

On July 4, 1777, even while British troops maneuvered to capture the Colonial capital of Philadelphia, the city held a great celebration of the first anniversary of independence, creating a model that has stood for more than 240 years. Parades marched. Fireworks sparkled. Thirteen-gun salutes reverberated from a naval review. Inside City Tavern, delegates to Continental Congress toasted the anniversary. Outside, a Hessian military band captured in Trenton provided music.

British occupation: The euphoric mood turned grim by September 1777. British troops under Gen. William Howe had made their way to Philadelphia. Congress, still hanging together instead of hanging separately, fled to York, Pennsylvania. Anyone branded as a Patriot took to the road, and the city was in chaos. Wagons thundered through the streets. Horses galloped. Women ran, and children cried. The scene, said the wife of a prominent merchant, showed "altogether the greatest consternation, fright & terror that can be imagined."

In City Tavern's short life to this point, you have to wonder what innkeeper Daniel Smith thought of his traitorous patrons. No doubt, Smith pleased his employers, and padded their profits, by attracting the upper crust of Colonial society with the finest food and service. But qualified innkeepers for high-toned establishments were rare in the colonies, and Smith had come from Britain. Even in the belly of the rebellion, he remained a Tory. Did it rancor to kowtow to these ingrates?

"It wasn't easy, because depending on who you were, you didn't know what cards to play," Chef Staib told me.

Smith flung open the doors when British troops marched into Philadelphia on September 26, 1777, and commandeered City Tavern for officer recreation. At the same tables where Washington, Jefferson, Adams, and their co-conspirators talked treason, British officers masked the taint of occupation with a genteel veneer. Supplies were scarce. Continental troops held two key forts on the Delaware River, choking supply lines into the city. Soldiers and civilians suffered, but Smith must have scrounged the necessities of daily life and the luxuries for weekly balls hosted at City Tavern, where young officers danced the minuet and flirted with the eligible daughters of Philadelphia's prominent Tory families.

By springtime 1778, it was clear that Howe's decision to occupy Philadelphia gave the British no military advantage. In June, the British left Philadelphia for New York. Three thousand Tories evacuated by water, escaping the clutches of angry Philadelphians pouring back into their city. Now, Daniel Smith was the one fearing for his life. He boarded a ship—maybe in view of City Tavern?—and sailed back home to England.

One more word on those officers' balls, that hollow attempt at decorum in a scene of deprivation and hunger. Loyalists who enjoyed their brief time in the sun faced a social reckoning. In 1780, the elite Philadelphia Dancing Assembly, which held weekly cotillions in City Tavern, branded the Tories as "either too detestable or too insignificant for Whig society. The company of those who were so insensible of the rights of mankind and of personal honour, as to join the enemies of their country in the most gloomy moment of the Revolution, cannot be admitted."

Lafayette, he is here: Marie Joseph Paul Yves Roche Gilbert du Motier, Marquis de Lafayette, was dazzled by the world-famous man he was now meeting at City Tavern. "Although he was surrounded by officers and citizens," Lafayette would recall, "it was impossible to mistake for a moment his majestic figure and deportment; nor was he less distinguished by the noble affability of his manner."

Many revolutionaries had their first meetings at City Tavern. The moment on August 5, 1777, when Marquis de Lafayette met George Washington ranks among the most pivotal. Lafayette's native France was intrigued by the idea of joining the fight against the British—as they say, the enemy of my enemy is my friend—but still needed convincing.

In the meantime, the young, orphaned, wealthy, royally connected, and British-hating Lafayette hankered to jump in the fight. Lafayette bought his own ship and, carrying other French officers, landed in South Carolina in June 1777. From there, he sailed to Philadelphia, where he invited the Continental Congress delegates to an elaborate lunch on board. Lunch became dinner. A happy Congress commissioned Lafayette as a major general in the Continental Army. After all, he was French nobility and volunteering to help lead the fight without pay.

Washington traveled to Philadelphia and met Congress for a City Tavern dinner and war briefing. Lafayette, with no military experience, had been a major general for one week. The ebullient, 20-year-old orphan and the 45-year-old general clicked immediately. Washington surprised Lafayette with an invitation to tour Philadelphia's defenses the next day. Soon, Lafayette was a key figure in Washington's staff and on the battlefield.

"It was with such simplicity that two friends were united whose attachment and confidence were cemented by the greatest of causes," said Lafayette. He would follow Washington from City Tavern to Brandywine, Valley Forge, and Yorktown, charging into battle until the day the revolution and independence were won.

SECTION III

Touch history

The National Park Service's precise reconstruction of City Tavern puts history in every glance and at your fingertips.

The bells, bells, bells: I was standing in the entrance hallway, my eyes on a metal contraption hanging high on the wall. Then, movement.

"There it goes!" I said. This was exciting. The tiny brass bell went "ding-ding-ding" from its curlicue spring connected to a wire emerging from the wall. The person doing the ringing, Jonathan Jones, was out of sight on the second floor, demonstrating City Tavern's bell system.

Of all the innovations introduced here, the mechanical bell system may have been the most marvelous. It was the first in the colonies. In the basement where staff congregated, a bell hanging on a board—"Downton Abbey" fans know all about this—would announce the need for someone to, say, carry out an overnight guest's chamber pot. This is what you did when you were an

Mechanical bell

indentured servant, probably Irish, who had signed away about seven years of your life in exchange for transport to the New World.

On the upper levels, ringing bells announced that dishes were ready in the kitchen, assuring timely service of hot dishes to City Tavern's discriminating guests.

Still today, the bells serve a purpose. Say a party of nine is waiting to be seated. A bell rings. The host says, "Let me show you to your table." That bell signaled to the host that the nine-top in the Long Room was ready.

Founding Foodies: Don't tell Walter Staib that 18th-century dining was dull and flavorless.

"They were very innovative. They were very smart people," he said. "They knew what was in the world. What you could buy. What you could cure."

If you were poor, you ate "a lot of potato and starches. A lot of green. A lot of oats. They were all like vegetarians, not by design but by no choice. They couldn't get regular meat."

Ah, but City Tavern catered to the wealthy, accustomed to life's finer things.

Chef Staib marvels at the attention paid to food by men and women otherwise busy plotting a revolution and running a new nation. Households kept "harvest manuals," planning the arrival and use of each season's bounty. When the cabbage ripened, they would determine that "so many heads can be sold and so many heads, we've got to store for ourselves in the root cellar."

"They would do the same for rutabaga and carrots," he said. "They kind of knew what they needed for the whole household to make the winter. We don't even think about it. Just imagine how sophisticated in that period."

Chef Staib called his time at City Tavern "an eye-opener" about the ingenuity of people we might think of as rustic or unsophisticated. When the Colonial elite wanted something exotic from overseas—cocoa from Caracas, lemons from Seville, dried grapes from Nurnberg—they would write the lists themselves. There was no delegating. Even William Penn sent exact specifications for a kitchen house to be built at Pennsbury Manor, his country home on the Delaware River (see it in use, Season 9, "A Taste of History." On the menu—cabbage savoy, clafouti with blackberries, and cream of chicken persimmon soup featuring persimmons picked fresh by the crew on the estate's orchards).

Bisected windows: Either the builders made a terrible mistake, or there's a good reason that the City Tavern windows are basically cut in half by the stair landings.

There is a reason, good or not. You can always spot a Georgian-style building by its symmetry. Front door in the center, balanced by an equal number of windows on each side, and all ruler-straight. As Jonathan explained to me, "exterior symmetry was more important than interior functionality." From the outside, those windows must be in perfect order, even if they don't line up perfectly with the stairs inside. "The windows were all divided a bit," he said, "but they do line up sill to sill on the outside."

Maps: Look at the décor, and you think that someone sure liked maps and geographical drawings. Perhaps someone did, but for early City Tavern guests, maps and diagrams served a vital purpose. Many guests were merchants and sea captains, stopping here to do business over a grog or two. They might be plotting their next voyage, or explaining the origins of their cargo. By pointing to a map on the wall, they instantly made their points.

Any ghosts? Chef Staib doesn't have time to entertain paranormal investigators, but he can tell you a story or two. Early in his tenure, there was the whiff of air that would blow past when he walked the steps. Nothing he paid much attention to, until one particular morning.

The first thing to know is that this government-owned building is "controlled like you have no idea," Chef Staib said. Leave or enter when it's vacant without calling a special number, and find yourself faced by "a bunch of guys with guns drawn on you. Nobody can come into the building. No way. Impossible."

So, one night, he left as usual, following protocol for alerting the Park Service that the building was now vacant. The next morning, he was first in, "and I see all the place settings switched around. There's no way. It would take too long. So I figure the ghost made a joke on me."

It's said that a waiter was stabbed to death in a drunken brawl on January 3, 1781, and the killer, a Col. Craig, escaped prosecution due to his elevated standing. It's also said that a bride who perished from an errant candle torching her dress might photobomb the wedding photos of today's living brides.

The food scene: At City Tavern, authenticity meets fine cuisine meets history. No other tavern in America can match it, said Chef Staib.

"Everything happened here and everything was discussed in here, and everything was cemented in here," he said. Dedicated researchers and designers and craftspeople reproduced the tavern in meticulous detail. With equally meticulous care, he created a historically based menu to complete the equation.

Each recipe that Chef Staib researches and tests must be approved by the National Park Service before it goes on the menu. "It took me like five years to get French fries on the menu, even though everybody knew Thomas Jefferson took his chef all the way to France to teach him how to make *pommes frites*."

Choose the mushroom toast as your appetizer—and believe me, you cannot say you've lived a fulfilling life until you've tried it—and you've hit on another Thomas Jefferson favorite. These sautéed Pennsylvania mushrooms are served on toasted Sally Lunn bread and sprinkled with a bit of Bearnaise.

Like all the breads here, the Sally Lunn bread, named after the 18th-century British baker whose rich, buttery bread predated Auntie Anne's pretzels by only about 200 years, is made on site. The sweet potato butter pecan biscuit, another heavenly morsel, was another personal favorite of—need I say his name? Thomas Jefferson's presence is so vivid here that Chef Staib calls him "one of my mentors."

City Tavern dishes

George Washington, enduring the winter in Valley Forge, instructed his cook to serve his shivering troops the same West Indies Pepperpot Soup. It was so good that I ate it as if I hadn't eaten in days. Enslaved people "from the islands, could be Barbados, Jamaica, nobody knows exactly where they were from" cooked the recipes from their native lands. The soup is spicy and beefy and satisfying. After long, frigid days, this must have warmed Washington's soul, notwithstanding how deeply he searched that same soul over the dichotomy of fighting for freedom while enslaving others.

On the entrée menu, it's amazing how 18th-century dishes can get dressed up for a night on the town in 21st-century style. Colonial Turkey Pot Pie recalls the bounty brought to Philadelphia by Pennsylvania Dutch farmers, prepared with fat turkeys then roaming the forests. Roasted Duckling gleams with a clover-honey glaze and mango chutney. Chicken Breast Madeira features the ubiquitous wine—ubiquitous because the island of Madeira, 400 miles off the coast of Portugal, was a popular stopover along Colonial trade routes, and ships would stock large quantities in their holds for ballast.

Think of a meat and a seafood or two, and it's on the menu— pork, venison, lamb, rabbit, steak, chicken, trout, Chef Staib's homemade sausage, tofu.

Yeah, right. Eighteenth-century tofu. Good one. Except that Benjamin Franklin wrote a letter in 1770 instructing the recipient how to make tofu. So, vegetarians rejoice. Immerse in the atmosphere of City Tavern without skipping the entree. The Fried Tofu is served breaded with Sally Lunn bread, plus spinach, seasonal veggies, sautéed tomatoes and herbs, and linguine.

Let's talk desserts. I conveniently forgot until my visit to City Tavern was over that I give up sweets for Lent. While it slipped my mind—I swear—I met Pastry Chef Diana Wolkow. She is the maker of City Tavern's wildly popular fresh fruit cobbler, vanilla bean crème brûlée, and Martha Washington's chocolate mousse cake. Plus, she creates her own versions of classic treats, all emerging from the pastry kitchen Chef Staib added in his vision for City Tavern's rejuvenation.

Diana joins him on episodes of "A Taste of History," preparing desserts based on her research into ingredients and recipes of the past.

"It's fascinating to understand what they were capable of back then even without modern equipment and methods of transferring ingredients," she told me. "It's very impressive, and I just try to bring that through myself and my own creative spins."

Plus, she noted, "back then, without modern refrigeration or freezing or anything like that, everything was what was local, was fresh. And what's happening currently?"

Oh, what's that phrase so popular today? Something about farms and tables.

"It's funny to see the two come together, so I certainly try to stick by that, as well," she said. "We won't have peach cobbler in the middle of winter, because there's nowhere to get peaches. We can get them from Mexico, but they would not, so I'm not going to do it, either."

I tried: Did I mention the mushroom toast? Yes, I did, but sweet heaven, I can now die happy. I also tried the luscious cornmeal fried oysters with herbed remoulade and the delectable basil shrimp, prepared with apple-wood smoked bacon and horseradish barbeque sauce. That sweet potato biscuit was like a dessert in itself. The sweet and sour red cabbage was perfectly *al dente*, French-style, served with a light, flavorful sausage made by Chef Staib himself. The spicy pepperpot soup brimmed with beef and callaloo, which I learned is the taro root's leafy top.

City Tavern desserts

Then Chef Staib offered an entrée. I had to beg off. I literally could not eat another bite. Until they offered dessert. In the interest of research, you know. Diana was just unveiling her new carrot cake which, Chef Staib noted, "is more like a carrot tea cake, not the like current carrot cake." She found the recipe—originating from Fraunces Tavern in New York City, another historic watering hole with revolutionary roots—in a book written by a friend of Chef Staib's, and then put her own spin on it by roasting the carrot. Like he said, it was "almost like a pudding, almost like a cake," flavored in a delicate manner by cinnamon and nutmeg.

I cannot tell a lie. Martha Washington's chocolate mousse cake was also on the table. It was flat-out the best chocolate dessert I've ever had—smooth and light, without the in-your-face attitude of some others. There's no death by chocolate here because you want to stay alive long enough to have another piece and another. That, and the mushroom toast.

The beverage scene: How does one describe the General Washington's Tavern Porter?

"Kind of like your morning cup of coffee, or your morning chocolate milk," Jonathan explained. Of course, beer was the colonial beverage of choice for breakfast, and lunch and dinner. Which might explain why most of the "Ales of the Revolution," created by

27

Ales of the Revolution

Yards Brewing Company in conjunction with City Tavern, have direct ties to their Founding Father namesakes:

■ *General Washington's Tavern Porter:* George Washington had a taste for Philadelphia-style porters, especially those made by a brewer just a few blocks from the current Yards site. He detailed his molasses-based recipe in a wartime letter to his officers, and this version is created from a recipe in the New York Public Library's Rare Manuscripts Room.

■ *Thomas Jefferson's 1774 Tavern Ale.* Medium-bodied, light in color, and fashioned from an original recipe of Jefferson's. Though he was a famous wine lover, Jefferson brewed beer twice a year.

■ *Poor Richard's Tavern Spruce.* Between flying kites, printing almanacs, and wooing the French to the cause of American liberty, Ben Franklin found time to write a beer recipe. Made with minimal hops and local, organic blue spruce clippings, this version finishes dry.

■ *Alexander Hamilton's Federalist Ale:* A pale ale made for the common man.

Like the food, the featured drinks of City Tavern are based on meticulous research, and available along with the bar selections we expect with fine dining today. In Colonial days, a "shrub" was a liquid resulting from preserving fruits in vinegar, suitable for cocktails or salad dressings. City Tavern's martini version mixes its raspberry shrub with Philadelphia Distilling's Penn 1681 Vodka. The Champagne shrub is like a colonial Kir Royale. Even kids can have a taste of the colonies, spiking their drinks with soda water for a sort of shrub Shirley Temple.

Wine lovers can sip like Jefferson did, with the same B&G wines that he ordered from the finest winegrowing regions of France. Before signing into law an 1807 European trade embargo to protest English and French meddling with U.S. ships and goods—a harsh measure domestically that got him called "the damdest fool that God put life into"—President Jefferson stockpiled the White House wine cellar with B&G wines.

For the true Colonial experience, wine lovers can also try Madeira. It was affordable, and it was everywhere, thanks to a royal marriage between King Charles II and the daughter of the Portuguese king that gave England a dominant position in the Madeira trade. And if you think King George III was a tyrant, his father, King George II, banned the importation of any other wine into the colonies.

I tried: I was debating my choice of beers when Chef Staib said, "The best way is to have all four." Well, when in Rome. Each one delivered as promised. Just like George Washington, I'm partial to porters, and this one was rich and tasty. Poor Richard's Tavern Spruce was a surprise. I never knew I would like drinking pine needles. The Hamilton was lively and light. The unfiltered Jefferson had a nice, strong body.

No, I didn't drain every glass, and I was taking the train, so when Chef Staib said, "Bring her a shrub," I had to try in the name of research. Jonathan took the initiative to bring me the Champagne shrub, "because you look like a lady who likes Champagne." However did he guess? And it was so good. Sparkly and fruity and tangy, all at once.

PLAN YOUR VISIT

City Tavern
138 South 2nd Street at Walnut Street
Philadelphia, PA 19106
www.citytavern.com, (215) 413-1443

WHAT'S NEARBY

Birthplace of independence: What's not nearby? Stroll around Independence National Historical Park, and City Tavern comes into context. Marvel at this compact community where daring men, their lives on the line, argued heretical points, hammered out compromises, and then ate and drank so they could do it over again the next day.

For me, this was a chance to visit the landmarks that I have never seen, despite all my years in Pennsylvania. Independence Hall, a 15-minute tour of two rooms, reminds us that big things can happen in small spaces. In the Assembly Room—thank you, Pennsylvania Assembly, for loaning out for the Second Continental Congress and the Constitutional Convention—I was transfixed by the Rising Sun Chair.

It wasn't called the Rising Sun Chair until the Constitutional Convention in 1787. It was just the chair that seated George Washington as he presided over battles as crucial as any fought between armies, as delegates from the states hammered out the details of a constitution in only four months—four stinking hot Philadelphia summer months. Though they would leave the question of slavery for another generation to settle over arms and cannons, Washington called the result "little short of a miracle." The chair with the sun carved in its crest rail became the Sun Chair when delegates were signing the final document, and Ben Franklin turned to James Madison and said he had often "looked at that behind the President without being able to tell whether it was rising or setting: But now at length I have the happiness to know that it is a rising and not a setting Sun." And then the Constitutional Convention adjourned to City Tavern for a banquet. With lots of Madeira.

At the Liberty Bell Pavilion, weave through exhibits showing the bell's significance as a symbol for all forms of freedom-fighters, from suffragists to Civil Rights protestors. Finally, you encounter the massive hulk proclaiming "LIBERTY Throughout All the Land Unto All the Inhabitants thereof." When I got to the bell, a young couple from Asia were taking photos of each other with their kids. I pantomimed an offer to photograph them together. I don't know how much English they knew, but they said, "Thank you," and I said, "You're welcome." The Liberty Bell speaks a universal language, and I like to think that photo of the family together is a cherished memento of a pilgrimage to the place where citizen-driven government—as flawed as the bell would become, but still the framework for something unheard of—had its birth. (www. nps.gov/inde/index.htm)

Morris House Hotel: Ten years after the colonies declared independence, Philadelphia physician William Reynolds built a rowhome in perfect Georgian style. Unfortunately for Dr. Reynolds, this new age of freedom didn't bring prosperity, or else his money management skills were lacking, because he lost the house in a sheriff's sale within a decade. For 120 years, the Morris family lived here, so prominent that they bought and de-molished all the neighboring rowhomes. For a taste of Colonial life, but with much nicer mattresses, and air conditioning, and wireless internet, and 24-hour concierge service, stay at the beautifully restored Morris House Hotel. It's a boutique experi-ence in a National Register property. In the afternoon, raise a glass of complimentary wine in honor of Captain Samuel Morris, ancestor of the Morris family and officer of the Philadelphia Light Horse, the troop that served as George Washington's bodyguard and threw that "epic bender" in their commander's honor at City Tavern. (www.morrishousehotel.com)

2.

GENERAL WARREN
HISTORIC HOSPITALITY

Malvern, Pennsylvania

Espionage afoot

Misbehavior makes history:
General Warren Historic Hospitality

■ A Tory-leaning sanctuary for British officers—and their spies. Two years before his doomed date with Benedict Arnold, John André made this his headquarters for gleaning intelligence from local Loyalists.

■ Possible planning place of the Paoli Massacre, a murderous British victory that turned Pyrrhic when enraged Patriots rallied under the cry, "Remember Paoli!"

■ Post-Revolution, shunned by locals for its Tory legacy until the proprietor took paint to the signboard and recast the original namesake, British hero *Admiral* Warren, as dashing American martyr *General* Warren.

■ Still crazy after all those years—a 1960s biker bar in a law-enforcement no-man's land.

■ Today's scene: Dine on the classics or quick bites, over a white tablecloth or patio high-top. In food and lodging, 18th-century atmosphere meets 21st-century lifestyles.

Built: 1745

Meet the proprietor

How many years in its history, I asked Patrick J. Byrne, has the General Warren been an inn and a tavern?

"Hoo boy," he said. "Give me a paper. I'll give you a rough estimate. This is not an exact science."

He started scribbling on a piece of notepaper cut from an old wine list. By the end of my visit, I would have six or so notes with maps and lists in Byrne's handwriting. It's easy to see the world through his eyes. He pens his thoughts on notepaper or a handy napkin. He shares the story behind every item. He even admitted to a personal failing—that he didn't pay attention to the General Warren's history when he arrived in 1987.

"I was just a chef here," he said. "I could show you my grades from high school in history."

I half expected him to produce his report cards.

"Now I understand," he continued, "how it's important to my business. It makes us unique. There's tons of restaurants out there. We live in such a great culinary time. But I've got a hook, and my hook is history. I've got good food, a good product, and we maintain our heritage."

Ah. "Maintain our heritage." The past has its commercial advantages, but it's more than that. Patrick caught the fever. As the steward of the General Warren's history, he recognizes his spot as a mere blip in a timeline extending—so far—two and a half centuries.

Back to those scribbles on the General Warren's time as a tavern. Ownership transferred from a William Penn grandson to a Pennsylvania German businessman, and then to a strict teetotaler who put an end to liquor sales. No shocker, but that temperance bit ended the taverning from the 1840s to 1903. Then came time as a restaurant, rest home, and a biker bar—more on that later—until the General Warren's resurrection as a fine dining establishment in 1980.

You get the sense that Patrick is detail-oriented, but in a way that people appreciate, because he doesn't tell. He shares. We were standing by a table in a meticulously set dining room when I asked about the days leading to the Battle of Paoli. He said, "We're gonna go to graphics here." In a move that probably exasperated some poor server, he rearranged bread plates, salt and pepper shakers, and vase into a sort of diorama representing Philadelphia, this region known as the Great Valley, and the British landing spot in the Chesapeake Bay.

"So they need to get from here to here," he said, pointing from the bay (a water glass) to the Warren (flowers). "They came up

Front entrance to the General Warren

through the Brandywine and Great Valley. There were a lot of battles. There was the Battle of Brandywine. There was the Battle of Wawaset. There was the Battle of the Clouds. You can look this up. This was three days before the Paoli Massacre."

The Battle of the Clouds, he explained, was a clash interrupted by a nor'easter. "Everyone went back to their encampments. Unfortunately, Washington's powder got wet, so he had to go to Warwick Furnace, which was a two-day drive to the north, to get dry powder. By then, the British had blown through town. They had the Battle of Paoli and moved on to Philadelphia."

The British colonizing this new land had a proprietary interest in building taverns, Patrick told me. Coming by sea, it was easy to occupy the coastline, but that wasn't why they were here. They wanted the riches of the interior.

"They had to figure out how to get people inland so they could get more raw material and food and stuff," Patrick said. And how could they do that?

I saw this coming.

"Booze. Booze and food, so they built these inns as a natural magnet to draw commerce inland."

34

Proprietor Patrick Byrne diagramming the Battle of Paoli

When we first met, Patrick was carrying a plastic quart container—the kind that Chinese takeout soup comes in—filled with red paint. He told me he was going to change hats—the figurative kinds that inn proprietors juggle. We went to the inn's General Paoli Suite, and he invited me to have a seat because he needed "to touch up this one last thing before the people check in."

While I sat on a love seat, he knelt and painted a fireplace surround. The fireplace had been installed that morning. A portable fan whirring away helped speed it dry.

"I am on deadline every day, but I love it," Patrick said as he brushed. "It'll be a 15-hour day before I get home today. We'll get done what we need to get done, and we'll pull it off. We will create the magic."

Magic is the common thread weaving through the fabric of the General Warren. The stone exposed by chipping away stucco in the terrace bar. The spring house converted to seating. The patio lights. The hickory flooring handmade by Amish craftsmen.

"It's all an illusion," Patrick said. "We're nothing but smoke and mirrors in our industry. We're just creating a buzz and a feel."

If you want to find Patrick Byrne on your visit to the General Warren, look for the man holding that paintbrush. In a banquet room, he told me a door was propped open because he had painted it that morning.

"I had black paint on a brush today, and by God, I'm not gonna let anything black that needs a touch-up go," he said. "My staff sees me walking around with a paintbrush, and they ask what color, so they know not to touch anything in that color."

Then he adjusts the window shades. Mentions that he planted the trees outside the window so diners wouldn't have to look at the parking lot. He admits to being "a fusser. I guess it's a curse, but it's a blessing because I want it to look nice for the customers."

Some things around here never change because, well, they can't. The joys of an old building. The size of the kitchen "has stayed the same from incarnation," Patrick told me. "It's always been a tight fit. But we make it work. We adapt."

Other things don't change because that's the sign of a well-run inn. Sure, he adapts the menu to today's dining trends—light bites along with the fine-dining classics—but he strives to maintain continuity in personnel, "and the formula's really simple. I have their back. I'm gonna be here every day, making sure that the rooms are ready, the bills are paid, the electricity is flowing, and that I'm booking parties to keep them going so they've got a job that is going to be good."

Staff continuity assures that guests "are greeted by someone you know, and they know us, and we can custom design their dining experience." It's all part of running "a place of safety, comfort, and warmth."

Every new hire gets introduced to the front door. Really. The front door. It might look like nothing more than a glass-paned door, he tells them, but customers walk through it, and "this is who we work for."

"They're stepping across that threshold for hospitality, and people have been doing that for 273 years. When you look at it from that perspective, it really floors you. You go through the motions. You walk into the door. You turn on the light. You turn on the heat, the air conditioning. You turn on the TVs and unlock the beer taps. You do all those mechanical things. But think about the real mission statement."

He conceded that "mission impossible" is more like it. A server walked past with a tray of cosmopolitans. "Are they for me?" he

General Ladies Suite

asked. But whenever he looks at the tavern, he said, he sees the original, three-story structure. Upstairs, it housed guests. Downstairs, it offered food and drink.

"The thing I'm most proud of is that we've come full circle," he said. "That's how it was built—tavern, restaurant, lodging. We're still doing that today."

A General Warren Historic Hospitality tour

Like any respectable historic tavern, the General Warren looks compact from the outside but is a maze inside. And that doesn't include the outdoor dining area. It's all about settling into the atmosphere that suits your mood.

The Warren Tavern: Step through the foyer and to the right, and time tumbles back centuries. The tavern is a single space renovated most recently in 2015, but the air bristles with 18th-century tavern aura. The original layout offered two small rooms with five-stool bar and three booths. We modern diners might have popped in for a pre-dinner cocktail, but not to linger.

The Warren Tavern

Today, the 18-seat, horseshoe bar is topped in charmingly imperfect soapstone, a nod to local quarries that produced the materials for Colonial Philadelphia's windowsills and thresholds. Two columns rising from the end of the bar mark the spot of the pre-renovation wall. The floors, also part of the rehab, are Amish-crafted from hand-hewn hickory. Windows remained their original single-pane glass secured with putty—not in the least energy-efficient, but oh-so atmospheric.

While the original tavern hosted wagoners, coach passengers, and soldiers, today's bar hosts weekday business travelers and weekend regulars, Beverage Manager Tom Poiesz told me.

"We try to make it a little more of a comfort zone," he said. "We specialize in getting people together, networking. You're here. You're by yourself. We're aware of that. We make sure nobody bothers you if you don't want, but if there's somebody interested in sitting next to you, we're gonna introduce you."

That Friday evening, Tom would introduce me to a banker who endured 24 meetings that week as his bank prepared to go public. Patrick introduced me to a couple who walked from their nearby home to sit at the bar and celebrate their 32nd anniversary.

Still, with a wood fire at my back, it wasn't hard to imagine a British officer pulling off his boots to warm his feet after a long ride. Glasses of beer and hard cider clink in celebration of a battlefield victory. Most assuredly, they might be saying, the

The dining room

Crown will prevail. We just slaughtered 52 of those pesky rebels, bayoneted in an open field and burned in their huts. Their treasonous compatriots are scattered. These Colonists have no spine.

Restaurant: There is still a place in this world for white tablecloths, especially striking when contrasted with rustic surroundings. Patrick doesn't believe the floors in the dining room are strictly original, but gosh, they're old. Surely, they date to the General Warren's early tavern phase, when coach drivers and passengers brushed off the dust of the road and sat to enjoy the tavern's famous hospitality. Twin fireplaces form the focal point—perhaps a sign that this sizeable room was once divided by a wall. One fireplace is functioning. The other stores firewood with esthetic grace. Step through a transomed door to the veranda known as the Front Porch. The sunny enclosed porch is lit by wrought-iron chandeliers, with the exterior wall and its shuttered windows behind you.

Admiral Vernon Room: Care to see what Admiral Vernon, the British hero who inspired this tavern's original name, looked like? Step into the Vernon Room, and there he is, in all his bewigged glory, in a portrait over the fireplace. The Vernon, with its wrought-iron chandeliers, banks of windows, and wine shelves, is one of three rooms added for banquets, gatherings, and dining. In another addition, the cheery sunroom off the tavern, overnight

Spring House Terrace

guests enjoying breakfast feel suspended in the trees canopying the terrace below.

Spring House Terrace: Pure genius. Here's the al fresco experience that 21st-century guests demand, enfolded in 18th- and 19th-century charm. Even on the unseasonable November night of my visit, tavern-goers enjoyed drinks and meals on the terrace, squeezing in a final pleasant evening before winter would force them indoors. Patrick's illusion is at work here. On the walls under the covered bar, they chipped away at the stucco to uncover the stone beneath "because this is what people like now." The spring house—no roof, but home to intimate seating—survives from the tavern's early decades, while the stone wall framing the terrace is a 21st-century creation, built in purposely rustic fashion. Honestly, I thought it was original.

Patrick's illusionist side deeply respects the history embedded in every corner of the General Warren and all the people who deliver the magical experience. As we walked through the bar on our tour, I met Tim Steen, of Artisan Construction. While Patrick stepped away to write a check, Tim warned me that he was "gonna ring Patrick's bell a little bit." He meant that in a good way.

"When I first met him, five minutes into the conversation, I knew that without him, this place wouldn't exist. Even if it did exist, it wouldn't be the same," he said. In other restaurants, it's "high turnover, high turnover, high turnover." General Warren staff are "here for life." His own workmen say the same thing, telling him, "This has the best atmosphere of any place we've worked."

From the outside: My tour of the General Warren started outside, facing the building. A road ran directly behind us, making this the perfect spot for an inn, right?

But that road wasn't there in the first days, Patrick explained. The original Lancaster Turnpike was across the field, where Old Lancaster Road makes a sharp turn into what is, today, the employee parking lot.

"People are always asking me, 'Why is this here? What's the purpose?'" he said. "I finally was able to ascertain the answer."

That answer: We stand low on the fringes of the basin known as the Great Valley. Steep hills. Ridges to climb. Heavy wagons couldn't go straight up or down. They had to navigate a series of switchbacks—exhausting and time-consuming for wagoners and horses.

"Some wagon masters would say, 'I'm gonna rest my horses before we make the climb,' or if they were coming the other way, at the bottom of a long hill, 'Let's take a break.'"

And there at the low point was a tavern, a beacon of food and drink and rest before or after that arduous stretch of road. "We're only talking 100, maybe 150 foot," Patrick said, "but when you're on a wagon full of material with a horse, a hill is a hill."

SECTION II

The history of General Warren Historic Hospitality: Treachery and defiance

William Penn, the founder of Pennsylvania, planted his first footsteps in the New World in—Delaware. He stayed a couple of days, and then he sailed the Delaware River northward, landing at a province on the other side called Upland. He asked a companion from Chester, England, to name this place. The buddy said, "Chester's a nice name." Or something to that effect. Chester County, Pennsylvania, was created.

"The land is generally good," Penn wrote, "well watered and not so thick of wood as I imagined."

Wait. What? Penn's woods weren't woodsy? Not this tract, where Native Americans had cleared out old fields. Still, Penn said the region made up in variety what it lacked in quantity. There were red and white mulberry, black and gray walnut, hickory, poplar, cedar, cypress, chestnut, ash, sassafras, gum, pine, spruce, and oak of all kinds, including the swamp oak, which had "a leaf like a willow and is most lasting."

That William Penn guy must have given up a promising career in arboreal science to pursue the family business of turning 50,000 square miles of wilderness into a haven safe from religious persecution but soon to be Ground Zero for a rebellion of earthshaking consequences.

War is embedded in the story of the General Warren.

Military rendezvous: In 1700s America, it was a truth universally acknowledged that a single woman in possession of a fortune—in this case, 350 fertile acres—must be in want of a husband.

Meet George and Esther Aston. Esther's father, Owen Thomas, owned 550 acres of Chester County land. The tract traced directly to a deed awarded to one Robert Wharton by Billy Penn himself. At some point after 1724, Owen Thomas deeded 350 acres to daughter Esther, known by now as Mrs. George Aston.

It was good land, a working farm along the Conestoga Road. Travelers carting the bounty of Lancaster County to the markets and ports of Philadelphia trundled past. On May 28, 1745, Aston—who might have had a hand in laying out this road—petitioned Chester County for a tavern license.

"That your Petitioner is Situated over the Great Road Leading from Lancaster to Philad.ª and is desirous of Keeping a Publick House Having Great Conveniancy for the Accomodating of Travellors and Petitions, as in, Duty Bound Will Ever Pray."

Actually, the handwritten petition says "*defirous,*" because we were still in "*purfuit*" of happiness back then.

No matter the spelling and the abundance of signatures from presumably upstanding supporters, the petition was disallowed. Undaunted, Aston refiled on August 27, this time with additional signers from Lancaster County.

Approved. The Admiral Vernon Tavern, one of the first taverns west of Philadelphia, was born. Its namesake was Vice

Admiral Edward Vernon, the British naval hero famous for boasting that he could take the Spanish trading post of Porto Bello, in modern-day Panama, with only six ships—and who actually succeeded in 1739. And if the name "Vernon" rings a bell, think of an elegant estate on the Potomac River, built by or for Virginia planter Lawrence Washington, who once served under the admiral. Lawrence's half-brother George eventually inherited the place called Mount Vernon. At this rustic tavern, the admiral's portrait on the signboard enticed travelers to stop for food, drink, and rest.

Those travelers might have occasionally been disappointed. Aston dropped in and out of the tavern business. Sometimes, "his private affairs interfering, put him under the necessity of laying the business of Inn Keeper aside." In other years, George Aston reapplied, "being desirous to once more operate a tavern."

Aston's "private affairs" probably involved King George's War, fought from 1744 to 1748 between Britain and France for control of the North American continent. In fact, only three years after naming his tavern after Admiral Vernon, Aston did an about-face. A British naval officer named Peter Warren had made himself a King George's War hero by capturing a French stronghold in Nova Scotia and freeing the people of New England from French raids. Aston added whiskers to Vernon's painting on the tavern sign, and *voila*—the Admiral Vernon was now the Admiral Warren.

By 1754, Aston was an experienced military hand. He was now ready to serve in a tussle we Americans call the French and Indian War, but that Europeans know as the Seven Years' War.

Call me a provincial American, but I didn't know until recently that they're the same conflict.

Whatever the name, it was a continuation of that British-French death match over control of North America and its riches. Much of the action occurred in the Ohio Valley, including what's now western Pennsylvania, but shifting loyalties played out over a shifting landscape. In Philadelphia, Benjamin Franklin led the creation of a Pennsylvania militia. Pennsylvania's governor tried to snub this populist mechanism, preferring the independent military organizations known as Associators that had fought King George's War. The Associators hung around to defend Philadelphia. Franklin's militiamen marched out to defend the wild frontier.

Which means that Aston, who straddled both conflicts, may have been more of a militia type. In the Pennsylvania frontier

The General Warren sign, revised at the urging of ghosts

region of Northampton County (today's Easton and Bethlehem), Native Americans angry over broken promises and stolen land were attacking settlements, killing Moravians, and taking captives. In 1758, while Esther Aston took over innkeeping duties, George hustled up a company, one of the first from Chester County. Captain Aston led the troop 75 miles to defend the Northampton frontier.

Chances are, the troop mustered at Aston's tavern. Under Aston's wartime leadership, from King George's to French and Indian, the Admiral Vernon/Warren began its history as a rendezvous spot for men planning or launching military movements, probably over a drink or two.

But in these fraught times, the question would become: Whose side are you on?

Skullduggery: On a day in 1777, a handsome young British officer first walked into the Admiral Warren. Any ladies present would have taken notice. Any traveler from Lancaster County might have been pleased by the officer's easy conversation in German. Any Tory would have found him a convenient depository for tips about local rebel activity.

This charismatic young man was Lt. John André. Born in London to French Protestant parents. Educated in Geneva. Cultured artist, musician, and poet. Fluent in four languages.

In short, born to be a spy. Fighting against the rebellious Colonials, André had been captured in Canada. As a prisoner of war, he was detained with a family in Lancaster, Pennsylvania. That family grew quite fond of this German-speaking charmer who gave art lessons to their son.

Housing prisoners in the heart of American communities must have seemed like a good idea at the time. André certainly appreciated it. After his release in a prisoner exchange, he gave Gen. William Howe his firsthand observations of life among the rebels. Impressed, Howe promoted him to captain and recommended that Major Gen. Charles Grey take on this cunning officer as an aide.

Soon, André found the Admiral Warren Tavern. This was not happenstance. As a paroled prisoner, he was not allowed within 20 miles of Philadelphia. The Admiral Warren stood around the 20-and-a-half-mile line. Very convenient for an exiled spy, especially in a county torn between Patriots and Tories, where rebels conspired and Loyalists happily shared what they knew.

By now, John Penn had owned the Warren since 1774—Penn, as in, basically buying back the land that his grandfather William sold in 1708. John Penn remained loyal to the crown. His innkeeper, Peter Mather, had "strong Tory inclinations" and was "said to have been working almost openly against the colonies during the revolution."

British envoys enjoyed a warm welcome at the Warren. Here, they could talk shop and glean information that high command would find valuable. John André joined in those "conferences." The natural-born artist also surreptitiously mapped the countryside, instilling British officers with strategic knowledge of the geography and landmarks of this unfamiliar land. When conventional wisdom expected the British to take Philadelphia by way of the Delaware River, it was John André who suggested that Gens. Howe and Cornwallis capture Philadelphia by circling from the Chesapeake Bay into the Great Valley.

While André and those British envoys lurked at the Warren, George Washington was doing some strategizing of his own to block the British march to Philadelphia. The Battle of Brandywine had been an annihilation, with the loss of 11 cannons and 1,100 men. Then came the wettest and most atmospherically named clash of the Revolution, the Battle of the Clouds. Washington planted his men between the Admiral Warren and a neighboring tavern, the White Horse, to prevent the British from accessing furnaces, cannon manufacturers, and the city of Reading, the Continental Army's main supply depot.

Washington's tired, overmatched troops were trapped in a triple pincer movement, and then it hit—a September nor'easter that mired horses and cannons, soaked ammunition, and made even bayonet charges impossible. Wrote a Hessian officer fighting with the British, "It came down so hard that in a few moments we were drenched and sank in mud up to our calves."

For Washington, waterlogged ammunition stored in shoddy cartridge boxes made fighting impossible. He and his troops "filed off," as one officer put it, slogging through the driving rain, teams of horses straining to pull artillery pieces uphill one at a time.

Washington left behind about 2,200 men under the command of Gen. Anthony Wayne to harass the British from the rear. Wayne thought the main Continental army would be returning. He was mistaken. Washington, thinking ahead, marched his men into place between Philadelphia and Howe's army.

Wayne was alone. But Howe was in a pickle himself, clamped between Washington and Wayne. Maybe the American cause made its stand here, wrote one Patriot soldier. "A few days will convince the World unless Providence turns against us."

Howe didn't wait for Providence. The general not known for speedy action took matters into his own hands. After all, he had excellent intelligence at his disposal.

The Paoli Massacre: "The British approached the camp from straight ahead and slightly to the left." I was reading a historical marker at Paoli Battlefield Historical Park. A shiver jolted my spine. I looked up and to the left. It couldn't be. And yet . . .

The scene feels that real. You stand in an open, sloping field ringed by trees. The only signs of a tragic yet oddly serendipitous battle are the vividly written markers and a marble monument topping a mass grave.

Warren Tavern gets its due as a key supporting player in the Battle of Paoli through a marker noting that Gen. Wayne "withdrew to this secluded spot above the Warren Tavern, screened by woods." While waiting for reinforcements that would never come, the men started campfires and built wigwams to protect their ammunition from the rain. Keep those wigwams and campfires in mind. They will matter later.

It's been said that the Battle of Paoli was planned at the Warren Tavern. Or maybe not. The British had secrets to keep, and they left behind few records of their strategy sessions. But Howe certainly had friends in this Tory stronghold. So, let's say he was supplied with detailed maps and reliable intelligence by a skilled artist and charming, canny observer such as Capt. John André, who was known to frequent the Warren.

Gen. Wayne did have one advantage. He was a native of Chester County, and so reckless in bravery that he acquired the nickname "Mad" Anthony Wayne. As darkness fell on Sept. 20, 1777, Wayne received warnings of an attack. He sent out extra pickets and horse patrols.

Somewhere in the dark, the normally cautious Howe was planning an uncharacteristically bold breakout. He wouldn't charge directly into Washington's army at the front but would smash through Wayne's guard at the rear.

This smash would be very, very quiet. Two detachments totaling about 2,000 men moved stealthily along the Chester County roads. At the head of the primary detachment, Gen. Charles Grey (Earl Grey tea? Named after the general's son) earned the lasting nickname "No-Flint" Grey for ordering flints removed from muskets. This attack would be launched with bayonets only—no musket shots to warn the rebels of their approach and signal the attackers' positions in the dark.

And, lest any Patriots try to warn Wayne, Grey rousted civilians from their beds at every home along the way, with orders to march along. One old man, at home without the protection of nephews who were serving in the rebel militia, was dragged out wearing only his nightshirt. From the exposure to the night air and the manhandling by Grey's men, it is said, the uncle soon died.

Reaching the Warren Tavern, the British column "knew nearly where the Rebel Corps lay, but nothing of the disposition of their Camp," said André. In other words, they didn't know which road to take, and the legend of Warren Tavern would earn another chapter. Troops entered the tavern and roused innkeeper Peter Mather—the loyal Tory—from bed. The other civilians gathered along the way were under guard along a row of poplar trees. Mather was tied to that mistreated elderly gent. Mather's wife

Paoli Battlefield Historical Park and Memorial

forced her way through the confusion with a pair of buckskin breeches to cover her unclad husband.

And according to legend, Mather blabbed Wayne's location. It's probably not true. More likely, the unfortunate blacksmith from the tavern's nearby forge provided what André called "forced intelligence." The rebels were close, and their pickets only a few hundred yards away.

Those pickets didn't fare well. Firing in the dark at the approaching attackers gave away their positions. Half of the 18 or so guards were killed or wounded by bayonet. By now, the surprise had been sprung. Wayne ran among his sleeping men, yelling, "Turn out, turn out, the Enemy is coming, give them (my brave Lads) Your Fire & Charge Bayonets."

Survivors would never forget the "Dreadful scene of Havock" that followed.

"The Shrieks, Groans, Shouting, imprecations, deprecations, The Clashing of Swords and bayonets &c&c&c. was more expressive of Horror than all the Thunder of the artillery &c on the Day of action," recalled British Lt. Martin Hunter.

Paoli Battlefield Historical Park

The Colonial troops—the fabled ragtag assembly of farmers, shopkeepers, frontiersmen, and craftsmen—struggled to get into formation. Wave upon wave of disciplined British troops charged, on foot and on horseback, all bayonet-forward. Six hundred Scottish Highlanders howling their Highland war yells bayoneted everyone in their paths, and then they set fire to the wigwams, because "many of the Enemy would not come out, chusing rather to suffer in the Flames than to be killed by the Bayonet."

"Chusing" death by fire? Hard to fathom, until I saw a photo of a bayonet on one of the Paoli markers. Beastly things. Plunged into the gut by huzzaing British troops, they must have caused unbearable agony. One group of "frightened Wretches," their retreat stalled by a disabled cannon, ran back to camp, only to have their positions exposed by those still-smoldering campfires. They met their ends by bayonet.

Maybe that's why the horror of that night still feels palpable in this serene setting, a labor of love owned by the Borough of Malvern, administered by the Paoli Battlefield Preservation Fund, and restored in 1999 with leadership by the fund and students at

Malvern Preparatory School, under historian Thomas McGuire. The spot is a park now. Join the afternoon's dog walkers and joggers, and it's a shock to realize that the monument-topped mound behind a low graystone wall is the actual grave of the men killed that awful night.

"We bury'd our Dead next day in the field of Battle, (52 brave fellows)," reported Colonial Col. Adam Hubley. "All kill'd by the sword and Bayonet." Lt. Hunter, the only British officer wounded in the battle, admitted that the aftermath of the Highlanders' charge, "with the cries of the wounded, formed altogether the most dreadful scene I ever beheld."

"Remember Paoli!": In the chaos of the battle, Hubley summoned American ingenuity to bluff his way out of capture by British troops. He pretended to be a British officer who "damn'd them for a parcel of Scoundrals, and ask'd them what they meant by taking one of their own Officers."

Wayne managed to retreat with most of his forces and his four artillery pieces intact. The rallying cry of "Remember Paoli!" would resonate through the revolution and into young America's continued clashes with the British in the early 19th century. Many Colonials believed that a night raid just wasn't cricket. And reports circulated that the living and the dead had been mutilated. Hubley would report seeing with his own eyes that the victors "scarcely shew the least Mercy to any."

When the two armies next met, two weeks later at the Battle of Germantown, it was another Colonial loss, but with an empowering feel. The rebels came close to upsetting the British. They rallied around a cause, and found pride in their valor, even if it meant repaying cruelty with more cruelty. Hubley confessed that "our people shew'd them No quarter," especially because it meant reminding British troops of "thier Inhumanity on that Night" in Paoli.

One final note on the General Warren's revolutionary history. The debonair Capt. André would go down in history, and meet his doom, through a little episode involving an American general by the name of Benedict Arnold. On the Battle of Paoli's second anniversary, now-Major André was in New York state, winning Arnold's promise to surrender the critical fortress at West Point. But trying to make his getaway, he was captured with secret documents concealed in his boot. On Oct. 2, 1780, John André—charm still intact—stepped up to the gallows in Tappan, New York, and was hanged as a spy.

Post-Revolution: After the revolution, Chester County Tories lost their swagger. Local militiamen drafted resolutions condemning former Tories as "unworthy the character of Free citizens" and undeserving "to remain amongst us, to participate in the blessings of that Freedom and Independence, so happily established, and which they have done all in their power to deprive us of."

Warren Tavern innkeeper Peter Mather, cleared of aiding the enemy on the night of the massacre, couldn't shake his reputation as a British collaborator. Business tumbled. Word got out that John Penn wanted to unload this unprofitable white elephant.

So in March 1786, Casper Fahnestock and two companions, including his brother Jabet, set out on foot from the German Mystic Community in Ephrata, Pennsylvania. Their sect lived simply, eschewing worldly vanities that distracted from heavenly thoughts. They dressed in rough flaxen cloaks. Fahnestock walked with a staff and carried a pair of saddlebags.

The trio stopped at the Admiral Warren. Our friend Peter Mather was still running the place. It was late, and the travelers woke him up.

"No beggars are wanted around here," Mather told the dusty wanderers.

Big mistake. Fahnestock continued to Philadelphia, where he met with John Penn—an old friend, according to one account. Fahnestock finally put down the heavy saddlebags and produced £2,000 in gold and silver coins. The Warren Tavern, and its 337 acres and side buildings, was his.

Fahnestock and his companions turned and walked the 20 miles back to the Warren. Nighttime again. A grumpy Mather roused, again. This time, they told him he could stay the night, but in the morning, he would be gone.

The suddenly homeless Mather moved to Philadelphia. For the rest of his life, he made his living by pushing a wheelbarrow. Full of what, I don't know, but it probably wasn't light or pleasant. Mather would never forget his tavern days. He couldn't, because boys would run behind him, taunting, "Remember Paoli!"

Finest establishment: Fahnestock flung open the doors to all, building a reputation for running one of the turnpike's best establishments. Travelers savored the tasty food and appreciated the clean lodgings. Lancaster's Pennsylvania German farmers carting their bounty to Philadelphia had many choices among inns, but they often opted for the Warren and the German-speaking Fahnestock's hospitality.

However, locals still held a grudge. Good food, drink, and cheer couldn't erase the stain of the Warren's Tory associations. As Patrick put it, Fahnestock "had a public relations disaster on his hands. Luckily, there was another Warren, Dr. Gen. Joseph Warren from Bunker Hill, Massachusetts."

And what a Warren he was! Renowned Harvard-educated physician and a Patriot so ardent that he might have spied on his highly placed Loyalist patients. Maybe had an affair with the wife of one, a British general, just to glean intel. In a stirring speech commemorating the Boston Massacre, he stared down hundreds of glowering British soldiers, including one flashing a palmful of musket balls.

When this Warren learned that the British were approaching Lexington to arrest John Hancock and Samuel Adams, he sent out a messenger to sound the warning to militiamen, and another as insurance that the message would arrive—guy by the name of Paul Revere. Commissioned as a major general in the Massachusetts Militia, Warren left the commanding to more experienced warriors, borrowed a musket, and dove into the fighting at Bunker Hill, paying the ultimate price through a musket ball to the head.

Brilliant. Cunning. Daring. Martyr to the Patriot cause. The perfect name for currying favor with locals boycotting the Admiral Warren. As a bonus, the thrifty Fahnestock needed only take a swipe of the paintbrush to the signboard. He changed the admiral's uniform from red to blue, and the tavern sign now welcomed guests to the General Warren.

Through the Fahnestock family's ownership until 1838, the General Warren continued burnishing its legend:

■ Casper's son Charles had the gumption to stop serving alcohol on Sundays, but he wasn't overly ideological, alcohol-wise. His cook was an African-American woman named Phillis, so renowned for her culinary skills that Charles indulged her one little quirk. When she cooked for a group, Phillis demanded a shot of liquor representing each person in the party. "When the party was small the result was good," one local historian noted, "but when the party was large, you may picture the disastrous effects yourselves."

■ Royalty on the run stayed at the Warren in 1798. Or so it's said. Three regal brothers whose father lost his head—literally—in the French Revolution (even changing his last name to

Egalité couldn't stop the tumbrel ride to the guillotine) made their way to Philadelphia. The eldest, Louis Philippe, was a legendary cheapskate, but then again, he had no money and was forced to—gasp!—earn a living in the states. Palling around with George Washington, he absorbed young America's democratic ideals, but he sloughed them off when he became king of France in 1830. His reign collapsed in 1848, amid accusations that he had been "improving every occasion for his own aggrandizement."

■ At 2 p.m. July 4, 1804, "six sharp blasts" from a bugle sent the Warren staff bustling. The turnpike's mail stage, on its inaugural run, was rounding the 20-mile marker and honoring the Warren with a stop, blatting the horn to signal the number of guests arriving for dinner.

■ In September 1831, the Warren met the fate of most taverns—a devastating fire. Immediately, rebuilding took place within "the same solid walls." Chester County's Historic Preservation Office pegged today's eastern side—yay! The bar—as the original 1745 portion.

■ How did Charles Fahnestock rebound so quickly? At the fire's discovery, he summoned five men to carry a groaningly heavy chest down the stairs. Outside, he sat calmly on that old German chest, watching the fire burn. And of course, like father, like son. The chest was stuffed with gold and silver coins, "so the house was at once rebuilt and enjoyed an even greater patronage."

■ A new signboard went up when Charles' son William took over in 1834. Six days a week, the sign read "Warren Temperance Hotel." Every Saturday at sundown, another sign took its place: "Nothing sold on the Sabbath." That's right. No alcohol, ever. Other innkeepers might have hosted "temperance inns" in name only to appease local teetotalers, but not William. The hard-core Presbyterian and strict abstainer once cut down an orchard to prevent its apples from becoming cider. He clung to his ideology and paid the price. "The new departure did not meet with favor," said one history, "and the house rapidly declined."

■ Then again, the death knell had already begun tolling for taverns up and down the Lancaster Turnpike, with construction of the Philadelphia and Columbia Railroad in 1834. The last regular stage came through in May that year. Business was plummeting, and William never had a heart for innkeeping, anyway, so he sold off the property in tracts in 1838. The General Warren closed its doors, not to be a restaurant again until 1903, and then came . . .

Born to be wild: The Warren spent various years of the 20th century as a restaurant or rest home. Then, in the 1960s—here's where Patrick Byrne shared another colorful chapter. The Warren, he learned, had been a biker bar.

Patrick learned the story on Christmas Day 1987, his first year as chef. He was thinking about investing, and he took his visiting brother, Desmond, to see the place. When the building came in sight, Desmond burst out laughing.

"We used to drive all the way here to buy quarts of Ballantine, underage, for like 35 cents!" Desmond said.

Yep, Patrick told me as we sat at the bar. "No questions asked. Put a dime and a quarter on the bar, right here, and the guy would give you a brown bag. This was where you came, and everybody knew it. Wink-wink, nudge-nudge."

And why not? Paoli marked the end of Philadelphia's Main Line (Patrick was drawing a napkin map again). The stretch from Paoli to Lancaster was "the demilitarized zone." No one bothered the Warren. Even the Pennsylvania State Police, who had jurisdiction, were 30 minutes away.

"You had this little bar on a dead-end street off the main drag with no police, no visibility, no nothing. Where would you go as a biker? This was the place to go. It was a safe haven. Unless someone was shot, everybody just did their own thing."

SECTION III

Touch history

Maybe you arrive at the General Warren in your Nissan Sentra, but walk through the door, and the smell of wood smoke instantly turns you into a coach passenger, bruised and jolted from a long, jarring ride. The best taverns greet you with the smell of wood smoke, and at the General Warren, two wood fireplaces crackle in cool weather.

Stroll the grounds and explore the inn, for the living history tableau that is the General Warren.

Bivouac: The inn faces south, absorbing the sun's light and heat. "That was inherent," Patrick said. "That was free." The sloping grounds, where burning bush plants and natural grasses frame the lush lawn, make for dreamy wedding photos. That's how they look today, but see it through Patrick's eyes, and envision stables housing horses resting from their labors. Lean-tos and tents shelter British soldiers, given safe haven in this foreign land by the Loyalist owner. "Of course," Patrick added, "the commanders were inside drinking beer and hard cider."

Peddler's village: Look past the grounds to that three-way intersection where you stopped on the way here, and the tight compound of old homes there was actually the "Warren shops," servicing the needs of travelers and armies. "There was probably a butcher, baker, and candlestick maker, and of course, the blacksmith," Patrick said, including that unfortunate fellow coerced into disclosing Gen. Wayne's location the night of the Paoli Massacre.

Turnpike days: As an innkeeper, Casper Fahnestock would collect tolls and use some of the funds to maintain his stretch of the turnpike. He would charge according to the number of passengers, size of wagons, and width of wagon wheels. The wider the wheel, the lower the toll "because you did less damage to the gravel," Patrick said.

The Lancaster Turnpike began morphing into Route 30, a.k.a. Lincoln Highway, around 1913. At this spot, the road wound under a railroad bridge, built for a freight line running behind the inn. Trains still traverse that line, carrying steel from the reborn steelworks in nearby Coatesville. But the tunnel isn't visible until you look closely at the hillside behind the employee parking lot. Suddenly, the outline emerges—a brick-arch tunnel now filled with dirt. In circa-1930 photos, the tunnel is open and the walls are painted in a checkered pattern, for visibility by passing motorists.

Our 21st-century imaginations automatically envision a walking trail through here. "I'm trying to get this open," Patrick said, "but of course, lawyers for the train company are not willing to let people in there because they can't guarantee that the roof wouldn't fall on them, or a brick or a stone wouldn't fall on them. I'm still gonna chip away at it, at some point."

"Messuage" is a word: You can't possibly read the ornate but faded script of the framed document hanging in the entrance hall, so here's a taste from a handy typed transcription: "Messuage called Admiral Warren tavern, and tract of land being the residue of 337½ A. not sold to Christian Zug, etc." This is the indenture, dated March 3, 1786, transferring the tavern and grounds from John Penn & Dame Anne to Casper Fahnestock.

The top of the parchment is ragged, and "there's a reason for that," Patrick shared. Demonstrating with a piece of paper he folded in half, he explained that a scribe would write two versions, one on each half, "and then they would take a knife and cut it unevenly. One half goes to the courthouse. One goes to the owner. You want to prove you're the owner, you went to the courthouse and matched them up."

No! Really? So, is the other half of this indenture in the county seat? "It's in the courthouse," Patrick said. My mind was officially blown. With a cellphone search, he produced other images of paired indentures, their edges torn in mirror images. "That's how they do it," Patrick said. "It worked. It's a way they were able to adapt back then to fight forgery."

19th-century Frigidaire: The stone walls of the original inn, visible at the Spring House Terrace bar, were built from German mica foraged from the property. Reading my mind, Patrick said, "It's not the mica you had in science class with the little mineral things."

Stone of a different type, transported from several miles away, tells us that the spring house was built later. Straddling a spring, "the space inside probably never goes above 60, nor does it freeze, so it's a great place for root vegetables, salted meats, things like that. It's their refrigeration system."

Sign of the times: Just as in the early days, the General Warren's sign keeps evolving. The side of the building used to read "General Warren Inne," but Patrick hated the "Inne," which he pronounces "innie." His rebranding had changed the tavern's name to General Warren Historic Hospitality, but he just didn't get around to redoing the name on that wall—until the stucco suddenly cracked, a horizontal split through the middle of "Inne."

"Of all places," Patrick said. A sign painter stacked two barstools, duct-taped them together, set a projector on top, and projected a giant "Historic General Warren" image on the wall for tracing. A ghost hunter told Patrick the cracked stucco was the work of spirits—not the kind you order at the bar—who sensed the imbalance between the tavern's old and new names. "They wanted me to change the name and were forcing me to do what I needed to do," Patrick said. "That was a $3,000 message, between my stucco guy and my painter, but I got the job done."

Any ghosts? Patrick Byrne doesn't believe in ghosts, but he has noticed that paranormal investigators draw consistent conclusions.

"Me being a nonbeliever, I'm assuming everybody here died in 1775," he said. "No. These spirits are allegedly everywhere, but they find a place of comfort and warmth and safety. They are here, they're happy with what I'm doing, so they're not creating a ruckus. We're here in harmony. They've got a place to stay. They're doing their thing. We're doing our thing."

Plus, he did move the cocktail napkins to a new storage place because—well, let's hear it from a server named Jen.

She was pulling a bottle of wine from the cellar—and this place has a true cellar, all stone walls and low ceilings and the original cooking fireplace—when a voice in her ear said, "Hey."

"I came flying up the steps," Jen said. "I took two steps at a time." Another time, a light turned itself on just when she needed it, so she knows the ghosts are simply trying to help. But with that "Hey," she drew a line in the cellar that she will not cross. Patrick obligingly moved cocktail-napkin storage to a ghost-free zone. "It's all about adapting," he said.

Beverage Manager Tom Poiesz shared a doozy. Two others were with him at the bar, near closing time. Watching the Philadelphia Phillies on TV, they said typical Phillies-fan things like, "They're not going to the postseason again," and "I don't think they'll ever get to the postseason again."

And then a fourth voice said, "I'll take that bet."

"All three of us looked at each other," Tom told me. "Did you say that?' 'Did you hear that?' And we all heard it, as plain as day."

One more story from Tom.

"Four years ago, the police show up. Every room has its own phone number. They said they got two 911 hang-up calls from the Franklin Suite. We all had to go up. We open the door. No one was in the room. No one was staying in the room. No one was in the apartment because they vacuum out the door, and you can see the footprints. There were two 911 hang-up calls from that room."

Cripes, I said. Ghosts that can dial phones. We're in trouble now.

Tom agreed. "They're high-tech now."

The food scene: Patrick summarizes the culinary scene as "American cuisine, but it's also light fare." He's proud of the adaptations made since his first days here when he arrived as a Culinary Institute of America graduate trained with European chefs (including TV pioneer Chef Tell, the one who would close his broadcasts with the catchphrase, "I see you!"). You can still show up in dress clothes for the leisurely fine dining experience with the General Warren's legendary beef Wellington or wiener schnitzel. Or, you can dash in for a light bite and shareables while waiting for the kids to finish band practice.

"Maybe one person wants a ribeye sandwich, or a vegan grinder, or maybe a shrimp poke bowl, but somebody else at that table wants a beef Wellington," Patrick said. "We can do it."

A daily special might be supplied by a local food artisan. Lettuce and herbs grown in the organic garden on the grounds wind up on the table. All are created by Executive Chef Joshua Smith.

The General Warren's renowned desserts come from a specially designed room in that cellar. Here, the stone walls were covered in modern materials to create a sanitary sanctuary for the creation and transport of brilliant pastries. Executive Pastry Chef Andy Sciarretta makes the muffins and croissants for overnight guests' breakfasts. Some of the breads for the dining rooms. Desserts ranging from flourless chocolate cake ("enrobed in chocolate granache, house-made blackberry cabernet sorbet,

One of General Warren's renowned desserts: cheesecake

blackberry coulis") to sorbet of the day to award-winning cheese-cakes. And wedding cakes—floral or polka dotted or, in one case, made to look like a tree with the happy couple's initials carved into the bark.

So much fun, I said to Andy. You get to be so creative.

"That's all I know," he said. "That's all I've known all my life."

"And that's what we do," added Patrick.

I tried: I was in a comfort-food mood, and the croque-monsieur fit the bill. French bistro ham rested on brioche bread, blanketed under a hefty mornay sauce. A mesclun salad with herb vinaigrette added a healthy note to this delightfully rich grilled ham and cheese. For dessert, the praline pecan cheesecake. Pure heaven. Creamy but textured. The candied pecan crumble wasn't sticky sweet but just barely held together. No wonder people order whole General Warren cheesecakes for their own parties.

The beverage scene: Tom Poiesz was talking about the wine, but it really applied to everything here when he said, "You'd be hard-pressed to ask for something that you like that we don't have here, or that I can't substitute."

The wine list is extensive, and every wine by the glass is custom-selected for the variety it offers in choices—say, a chardonnay that's unoaked, or a little more complex, or full-frontal toasty. Cocktails can feature locally distilled spirits. Rye has grown increasingly popular, Tom told me, and Bristol-based Dad's Hat Pennsylvania Rye Whiskey has been welcomed here since the distillery's early days recalling the roots of Pennsylvania agriculture in rye and its conversion to whiskey (plus, the name and logo are flat-out awesome).

During my visit, Tom was offering 21-day Dad's Hat Manhattans, created by aging a barrelful of Dad's Hat with a bit of sweet vermouth and French maraschino. Similar story with the 10-day Bluecoat Gin Negroni, made from Philadelphia-distilled Bluecoat (another brilliant name choice, for its remembrance of Continental soldiers). He also showed me a jar filled with a honeycomb infusing local honey into Jim Beam Bourbon.

"We always have something like this on the menu," Tom said. "It's a nice variety for people to try."

I tried: I never say no to gin. The Bluecoat Negroni arrived, a rich chestnut red. Each sip was crisp and bracing.

Lodging: As Patrick noted, the General Warren still serves its original purpose—providing food and lodging. Today's eight two-room suites each offer private baths and their own fireplaces (including the final two installed and painted while I visited). The Franklin Suite is a home away from home for business travelers, with an office area and a spectacular shower with tiled mosaic. The spacious Presidential Suite is a popular dressing room for brides and wedding parties.

Most suites were once two separate rooms, and you can see where old doors opened, and walls were broken through to create archways. Patrick showed me to my room, and I felt immediately at ease.

"If there's a word for the opposite of claustrophobia, I have it," I told him.

"You like being cozy? Then you have arrived."

This was the General Ladies. Anteroom with love seat by the fireplace. Bedroom with a separate door to a kind of in-room hallway. And what Patrick called, with only minimal exaggeration, "the world's smallest bathroom." To the warmth of a gas fireplace on a timer, I fell fast asleep under a lace canopy.

PLAN YOUR VISIT

General Warren Historic Hospitality
9 Old Lancaster Road
Malvern, PA 19355
www.generalwarren.com, (610) 296-3637

WHAT'S NEARBY

Historic Waynesborough: *"Yet the resources of this country are great & if councils will call them forth we may produce a conviction to the world that we deserve to be free — for my own part, I am such, an enthusiast for independence, that I would hesitate to enter heaven thro' the means of a secondary cause unless I had made the utmost exertions to merit it."*

Gen. "Mad" Anthony Wayne was a product of Chester County and a Patriot to the core. This is the Wayne who, surviving Paoli, demanded a court-martial to investigate his own conduct. He would conceive and execute one of the most daring successes of the Revolution, leading 500 disciplined men to scale a foreboding Hudson River bluff at nighttime. Telling Washington of the victory, he said, "Our officers and men behaved like men who are determined to be free."

See the elegant stone home that nurtured a love of liberty in young Anthony, and where seven generations of Waynes lived, with a visit to Historic Waynesborough. (www.historicwaynesborough.org)

Historic Sugartown: Take a turn off the fast lane and drop in on the 19th century. Historic Sugartown is a beautifully restored collection of buildings offering immersion in a crossroads center of commerce and socializing. In the Carriage Museum, see the massive Conestoga wagons that would have rumbled past the Warren Tavern. The General Store is stocked with bonnets and canned goods and vegetables and all the other necessities of daily life. A working bookbindery offers classes. The Society for the Prevention of Horse Thievery met here, but they didn't do much horse-thievery preventing. Mostly, they drank. (historicsugartown.org)

Historic Sugartown Conestoga wagon

Blue Bell's side exterior

Blue Bell's entrance

3.

THE BLUE BELL INN

Blue Bell, Pennsylvania

George Washington finds sanctuary

Misbehavior makes history: The Blue Bell Inn

■ A string of defeats turned George Washington into an expert at strategic retreating. After victory slipped from his grasp at the Battle of Germantown, he led his army to the safety of Whitpain and Whitemarsh townships in Montgomery County.

■ Visits to the White House Tavern (ironic, yes, but the original name of the Blue Bell) helped bolster Washington's spirits. He needed it. His troops were ill-equipped, and a cabal of officers threatened mutiny. Undeterred, he fought off threats to his leadership and honed his soldiers into a disciplined fighting force.

■ Even basketball coaches can be rebels. A longtime Blue Bell Inn manager once made himself a Philadelphia high school basketball legend, and earned a Blue Bell drink named in his honor, by daring to bench the varsity—for very good reason—before a critical game. Can the junior varsity take the team to the championship?

■ Today's scene: Select dishes and drinks from an accessible, sophisticated menu and raw bar, amid settings made contemporary while respecting history.

Built: 1743

Meet the Blue Bell Inn

The sun was coming through the window blinds on my right. Leah Kaithern Patterson, the Blue Bell Inn's general manager, jumped up and said, "Let me adjust this."

That's funny, I said. "I didn't even notice, but that's how well you do your job."

Hospitality is timeless. It spans the centuries, even if an establishment keeps pace with contemporary fashions. The Blue Bell Inn has undergone many renovations, including a major remodel in 2014, but if George Washington were to return, he could once again prop his feet by the fire. Then he'd order a Yards George Washington's Tavern Porter (naturally) and the East & West Coast oyster selections from the raw bar.

"The history piece is extremely important to us," Leah told me. "We wanted to be sensitive to that with the remodel. We want to create a really great atmosphere, have positive, gracious service, and have tasty food. We don't want it to be too fussy. We want it to be recognizable and delicious. And we want the service to be friendly but not overly familiar."

Every night, Leah talks to customers and learns that many have been coming to the Blue Bell for decades. One gentleman chose the Blue Bell for his 90th birthday party, telling Leah, "I've been coming here 75 years."

"That is incredibly moving, not only that it's a special place in his heart, but that we are continuing a tradition that people want to come back to," she said. "We do a great job with holidays, birthdays, and special occasions, but we also have a great feel where you don't have to commit to spending $80 a person. You can come in, sit at the bar, have a glass of wine and a flatbread. You can come in after golfing and have a turkey club. The accessibility is fantastic."

Co-owner Scott Dougherty worked at the Blue Bell in the 1990s, when there was little competition for fine dining, and 800 people a night was not unusual. Now, he "remembers everyone," Leah said. Staffers of today might have eaten here as kids. Baby showers and bridal showers host four generations of women who had their own showers here. One mother had her baby shower at the Blue Bell, and her son is now busing tables.

They were here in the womb, I said.

Leah nodded. "I think that's saying something about what this is to people, and what it is today."

As if to prove the point, she spotted a familiar family being seated across the room. One woman was carting a baby seat.

"They had the baby!" Leah said, adding that "they had their rehearsal dinner here." She thinks the new mom's parents did the same.

The days are gone when the Blue Bell was one of the few choices around for a night out. Today, "there are a lot of awesome restaurants," Leah said. "We are extremely appreciative of every single person who walks in that door, whether they're spending $2.50 on a soda, or whether they're spending $325 on a bottle of wine. Anybody who walks in that door, we appreciate it."

A Blue Bell Inn tour

The Blue Bell Inn has been altered and added to "over the years, over the years, over the years," said Leah. "Every single area is different."

Choose from cozy tables and distinctive bars indoors and out. Go casual on the patio or dressy in the Founders' Room. See and be seen at the raw-bar bar, or snuggle into a quiet corner.

Call for a reservation, and you might be asked whether you're celebrating an occasion or just looking for a fun night out. Whatever your mood, all those spaces mean that "we're ahead of the game," Leah said. "There aren't a lot of places like this where you can really, really make everyone happy."

Main Bar and Café: Open, airy, and bright with contemporary cheer, but textured and grounded in history. The Blue Bell Inn's high-ceilinged central space manages a delicate high-wire act. Step through the front door and onto the white oak floors, and see history unfolding from the 19th century to our time. The raw bar and adjoining cherry-wood bar with leathered granite top keep you in the 21st century. Rustic wood shelving displays vintage bottles from the 19th and 20th centuries, in varied sizes and colors, some found during excavations on site.

Terrace, Patio Bar, and Patio: Situated at busy intersections of well-traveled roads, many taverns added gas stations in the automobile age. The Blue Bell Inn pays homage to its gas station days with garage doors along a long hallway called the Terrace, and in the intimate bar that opens to the patio. When diners are relaxing and enjoying the evening, the Terrace "gets a nice buzz," Leah said. The brick-walled Patio Bar, with exposed beams along the ceiling, expresses whatever mood suits the moment. "Maybe the Flyers or Eagles game is on, and people are hooting and hollering and having a great time," Leah said. "On Thursday nights, it's really intimate. It's date night back there. It's lovely, and it's quiet, and it's perfect." The Patio is its own little outdoor world, the place for live music three nights a week, amid the waterfall, fire pit, and flowers in bloom.

The back bar: Sometimes, you just want to belly up to a dark bar with an ornate, mirrored back. Amid the Blue Bell Inn's friendly, modern bars, the owners had the wisdom to keep this telling piece of the past. The inn's original bar and a cozy lounge nestle beside the raw bar, for a quieter spot with dim lighting that contrasts with the brighter Main Bar.

And if it could talk—oh, the stories it could tell. "I can never get it clean of all the nicotine built up over the years," Leah said.

Renovations moved the bar from its spot in the original building to this central area. "We wanted to stay true to history," said Leah.

The Porch: In vintage photos of the Blue Bell hanging here and there, you can see a long porch spanning the building. Today, fully enclosed, this is the Porch, a bright, intimate room that's popular for showers.

Oak Room: The main dining room of the Blue Bell "is very celebratory," said Leah. Upholstered booths line the wall. Conical pendant lighting fixtures dangle between exposed beams. Put your hand on that rear stone wall, and you're touching the original inn's exterior wall.

Founders' Room: "This is the original," Leah said as we stepped into the Founders Room. It's the Blue Bell's anniversary or hot-date spot, intimate and just dark enough to cast an air of mystery around conversations whispered over black-clothed tables.

Clearly, the room didn't look like this in George Washington's day, but I imagine he'd appreciate the serene tone. Dark wood gleams on the fireplace surround. An enormous beam seems to hold up the ceiling by sheer will. Elegant brass studs dot the textured wallpaper.

SECTION II

The history of the Blue Bell Inn:
A rebel army's growing pains

In this part of Pennsylvania in the fall of 1777, George Washington made a specialty of losing battles on the way to winning a war.

Brandywine, September 11—a loss but Washington proclaimed himself "happy to find the troops in good spirits."

Main bar and café

The Raw Bar

The back bar

Founders' Room

The Oak Room

Paoli, September 22—a murderous rout, but it stirred patriotic fervor. Germantown, October 4—didn't go as planned, but the Continental Army's heroic stand convinced the French court that these upstart Americans could be worth supporting.

After Germantown, Washington retreated here, to Whitpain and Whitemarsh townships. With time to regroup and resupply, he prepared his troops for what would be a harsh but pivotal winter in Valley Forge.

"A bloody day" in Germantown: The British wore crisp red coats. The Highland Scots dazzled in kilts and feather bonnets. The Hessian infantry topped their heads in brass-fronted miter caps.

"The Americans dressed as best they could." That's how a website called British Battles put it. By the time of the Battle of Germantown, the Continental Army was approaching uniformity with blue and brown coats. The militia dressed in rough homespuns.

No matter. Even in defeat, Continental soldiers and militiamen were gaining the confidence to stare down their splendidly uniformed foe, and George Washington hungered for a win. The British had marched into Philadelphia on September 26.

British commander Gen. William Howe chose encampment in Germantown, north of the city, to hold off any attack.

Washington saw his chance when Howe dispatched two regiments to attack a Delaware River fort. The Continental commander planned a four-pronged surprise attack, to be launched, "precisely at 5 o'clock with charged bayonets and without firing." After all, it worked in Trenton, and a win would boost morale before fighting ceased for the winter.

But creeping up on the British camp this foggy morning, one of the Continental divisions encountered a picket ("piquet," in the parlance of the time). Shots were fired. Dogs barked. Alarm cannons boomed. The surprise was spoiled.

The British pickets fell back to Cliveden, the impressive estate of Pennsylvania Chief Justice Benjamin Chew where their regiment was camped. Chew didn't happen to be at home, seeing as the somewhat suspect Tory-sympathizing jurist was held by Colonials under house arrest in New Jersey. British troops ordered into Cliveden's imposing stone mansion rushed to barricade the doors and close the first-floor shutters. At the upper windows, marksmen took their posts. As if made to order, they now had a fortress.

American troops trapped between Cliveden and the British line put up a fight. In the confusion of fog and cannon fire and darkness caused by fields of buckwheat set afire by British troops, two American units fired at each other.

While other Patriot divisions pushed the British back, Washington heeded one general's advice that an army never advanced with a fortified castle to the rear. Three regiments, backed by cannon fire, couldn't destroy the hardy stone structure. In the delay, Howe regrouped and British reinforcements started arriving. Even as the Americans ran low on ammunition, Washington stayed in the thick of things, conspicuous on his white horse, the half-Arabian named Blueskin.

At fighting's end, the bodies of American soldiers who penetrated Cliveden's interior left the grand home looking "like a slaughterhouse." The survivors retreated as they arrived—up Skippack Pike, toward the village about 15 miles from Philadelphia then known as Pigeontown. The dying stumbled about, seeking refuge. Women and children ran to meet the retreating soldiers, imploring news of their fathers and brothers and uncles.

At the tavern then known as the White House, the one that would later become the Blue Bell, pursuing British cavalry caught up with the Colonial militia. The charge of thundering horses, ridden with cool precision by sword-wielding professionals, sent the ill-trained volunteers into a panic. "Consternation" was on their faces, wrote one account. "Sadness," too, which I thought an interesting choice of words, but certainly men who leave their homes during harvest to fight for liberty, suddenly confronting the reality that battlefield victory requires more than spunk, should be allowed to feel sad, even as a one-ton horse topped by a trained assassin bears down. In this skirmish, American officers rode to the front line—what was left of it—and drew their swords and threatened or pleaded, trying to get these sad men to turn about. No use. They didn't want or couldn't take another brutal battle. In a confused and desperate scramble, they knocked over fences to escape danger.

And yet, in the aftermath of Germantown, Washington's troops remained in surprisingly good spirits. Washington was to call it "a bloody day," but potential allies took notice of American gumption.

"Although the attempt was unsuccessful," wrote American Commissioner to France John Adams, "the military gentlemen in Europe considered it as the most decisive proof that America would finally succeed."

A soldier's life: Joseph Plumb Martin never ran any farther than he had to. Other soldiers in retreat would run as far and as fast as they could but, said Martin, "I never wanted to run, if I was forced to run, further than to be beyond the reach of the enemy's shot, after which I had no more fear of their overtaking me than I should have of an army of lobsters doing it."

Martin knew how to turn a phrase. He would have been great company around a tavern fireplace, sharing tales of his soldiering days. His stories of service in Germantown and beyond, written in his 1830 memoir, "A Narrative of Some of the Adventures, Dangers, and Sufferings of a Revolutionary Soldier," brought the life of foot soldiers into vivid relief. The Connecticut-born private in the Continental Army fought in Germantown, ordered not to fire "till we could see the buttons upon their clothes," but the coy foe hid their jackets "before we had either time or leisure to examine their buttons."

At battle's end, Martin "had now to travel the rest of the day, after marching all the day and night before and fighting all the morning." For weeks, in the area around the White House Tavern, "we were kept marching and countermarching, starving and freezing." When the temperature turned pleasantly warm, the still air couldn't dispel the smoke from campfires, and Martin's "eyes were so affected by it that I was not able to open them for hours together." The ground remained so sloppy that "any hogsty was preferable to our tents to sleep in."

To "cap the climax of our misery," there was nothing to eat. Martin found a spot where "sometime before" some cattle had been slaughtered. He gorged himself on an ox milt—possibly the spleen—and considered himself lucky, for a time.

"I had not had it long in my stomach before it began to make strong remonstrances and to manifest a great inclination to be set at liberty again. I was very willing to listen to its requests, and with eyes overflowing with tears, at parting with what I had thought to be a friend, I gave it a discharge. But the very thoughts of it, would for sometime after, almost make me think that I had another milt in my stomach."

Let that be a lesson. Avoid ox milt, especially if the ox in question was slaughtered on some distant past day during an October warm spell.

And yet, despite the hunger and cold and thirst, foraging turnips and walnuts to eat, suffering either smoke from campfires or the lack of fires for a bit of warmth because they couldn't give away their positions, or freezing from marching through creeks or sleeping in mud, or arriving at Valley Forge with troops who were "not only shirtless and barefoot, but destitute of all other clothing, especially blankets"—Martin stayed. He fought when compelled. He marched when ordered. And he revered his commander.

"The General well knew what he was about; he was not deficient in either courage or conduct, and that was well-known to all the Revolutionary Army."

George Washington in Whitpain and Whitemarsh: Valley Forge has gone down in history for its frigid cold and its bloody footprints in the snow, but the weeks leading up to it were no picnic, as Private Martin attested. Washington had to keep his troops away from the clutches of the British, but close enough to Philadelphia to strike if the opportunity arose.

Montgomery County, about 15 miles from Philadelphia, became one big autumn headquarters for an army estimated at 10,000 to 13,000 men. They denuded the land of trees for fires and huts. They commandeered livestock and foraged crops. The people of Whitpain Township and surrounding areas "shared the trials and conflicts of that dark period along with the other districts of the county." Field hospitals treated men for frostbite, pneumonia, and rat bites. Those who died were sometimes buried in churchyards, or sometimes in farm fields, under plain stones marking graves of the nameless.

From October 20 to November 2, 1777, Washington made the Whitpain Township estate known as Dawesfield his headquarters, with occasional visits to the White House Tavern. Washington's host at Dawesfield was James Morris, a man you might call a lapsed Quaker, once censured by his meeting for "acting in a military way" as an officer of the Pennsylvania Regiment of Artillery. After the Battle of Germantown, Morris levied fines on local Quakers who missed militia maneuvers. As captain of the Montgomery County Light Troop, he would help quell the Whiskey Rebellion in 1794. A very un-Quaker Quaker, but according to a Morris family history, other relatives were also disowned by their societies for Whiskey Rebellion service, so military service was in his blood.

While at Dawesfield, Washington convened a Council of War. His most trusted aides were there, plus at least one foisted on him by congressional promotion. They included:

■ Gen. Marquis de Lafayette, who still couldn't get his leg, wounded at Brandywine in September, into a boot. He had been recovering in Bethlehem but was so itchy to get back in the fight that he insisted on being moved to Montgomery County.

■ Gen. Anthony Wayne, so mortified by rumors that his negligence caused the Paoli Massacre that he insisted on a court-martial. That trial was underway at Dawesfield and then suspended while Washington convened the Council of War. Before the trial began, Wayne possibly stopped by the White House Tavern for a shot of liquid courage. Wayne was acquitted "with the highest honor," the court declaring that he did every duty "that could be expected from an active, brave and vigilant officer."

■ Maj. Gen. Adam Stephen, a Scottish immigrant, physician, and French and Indian War veteran whose relationship with Washington could be called testy. He considered Washington a "weak man." Washington once reprimanded him for inflating casualty numbers. And now, even as he sat in on the Council of War, he was on the verge of being booted from the army. Seems that as the Battle of Germantown was ending, Stephen was discovered drunk as a skunk. He was found guilty and cashiered from the army for "unofficerlike behavior, in the retreat from Germantown, owing to inattention, or want of judgement; and that he has been frequently intoxicated since in the service."

The Council of War would decide against an attack on the British in Philadelphia. As the daring Nathanael Greene, one of Washington's most trusted generals, put it, "An attack upon the city of Philadelphia appears to me like forming a crisis for American liberty which if unsuccessful I fear will prove her grave."

Even without battle plans to prepare in these weeks after Germantown, as the days grew colder and Washington sometimes popped into the White House Tavern for refreshment, the army was not inactive. This was a time for regrouping the units and pestering British outposts.

They could do all this unmolested by the British because Howe just wasn't driving a stake in the heart of the rebel army. He moved into Philadelphia—and stayed. Why? Maybe his heart wasn't in the job. On October 22, 1777, he sent a resignation letter, seeking release from "this very painful service." He might have even harbored thoughts of negotiating peace with the Colonials, instead of bringing them to heel.

So, on a frosty morning in early November, Washington could march the troops a few miles from Whitpain Township, to Whitemarsh Township. The cold and hungry men were to meet the British again, in early December. Warned of an attack, American cavalrymen charged into the advancing British. The next day, Howe tried to attack the Colonials again, but his men "found all their cannons mounted and the troops prepared to receive us," Capt. John André recorded in his journal. "We have marched back like a parcel of fools."

Valley Forge lay just ahead. But after a year of battlefield hardening, this motley collection of soldiers was losing the "ragtag" and becoming "army."

The Conway Cabal: If ever a man needed a drink in a cozy tavern, this would be it. George Washington was seething. Licking his wounds from one defeat after another was bad enough, but while here in Whitpain and Whitemarsh, Washington was forced to face down backstabbers, malcontents, and mutineers.

It started with the Continental Army's northern department and its October 17 victory in Saratoga, New York. Gen. Horatio Gates, department commander and a rival for overall command, had led the victory but was letting word seep out quietly. Maybe

Gates feared that his generous terms of surrender would tarnish the feat. Whatever the reason, Washington fumed. The sly Gates was letting whispers of victory float to Continental Congress while Washington was forced to share news of defeats.

One night, a drunken Gates aide told an aide of a Washington ally about a letter from Brig. Gen. Thomas Conway, a Frenchman, to Gates. The letter listed 13 reasons why the Americans lost at Brandywine. The indiscreet drunk reached into memory to quote one juicy sedition: "Heaven has been determined to save your country, or a weak general and bad counselors would have ruined it."

Washington didn't confront Conway directly. He simply penned a note repeating the scurrilous phrase and coyly masking the fact that he hadn't seen the original letter. "I am, sir, your humble servant, George Washington," he concluded. Washington would have been an excellent middle school teacher, quietly alerting troublemakers that he knew what they were up to.

The pro-Gates faction in Congress didn't dare come out publicly against the revered Washington, but they tried to box him in. They created a Board of War to reshape the army, with Gates as president and Conway as inspector general, but it turned out to be politically unworkable. Casting around for the man to do the job, they realized that George Washington and his talented staff had been tireless on the task. Washington floated above the fray, and the Conway Cabal petered out. Gates, admitting defeat, insisted to Washington that he had been "of no faction" seeking an overthrow. Washington agreed to "burying" their differences, "in silence, and as far as future events will permit, oblivion."

Jack Friel defies a maddened crowd: "We want the varsity! We want the varsity!" The crowd chanted in time to stomping feet. It's 1968 now, almost two centuries after George Washington's visits to the White House Tavern, but it's nice to know that his rebellious spirit lived on in a longtime manager of what was now the Blue Bell Inn.

Before getting in the restaurant business, Jack Friel was the basketball coach for North Catholic High School, in the basketball-crazy Catholic League, in the basketball-crazy city of Philadelphia. His city champs were scheduled for a playoff contest against Wyncote's Bishop McDevitt High School, in the hallowed hall of the University of Pennsylvania's Palestra arena.

"We want Hank!" the North Catholic fans were chanting before the game. "We want Hank!" They were shouting for Hank Siemiontkowski, their 6-foot-7 superstar.

Friel would not appease the crowd. Hank and his varsity teammates would not take the court. That morning, they had gone to a special Mass and then got permission to go to breakfast. Be back by 9:15 for second period, they were told.

By 10:30, Friel went looking around the neighborhood. He found his players walking toward the school.

"On your way back," he told them, "think about not playing tonight."

Around noon, one of the junior varsity players heard a rumor that the varsity had been benched, but he figured his teammates were joking. Everyone knew that the JV players wouldn't get their chance for Palestra glory for another year or two. Just before the final bell rang, they were told to report to Coach Friel. From 2:45 p.m. until 3:30 p.m., they waited. Then Friel appeared.

"Fellows," he said, "you're going down to the Palestra a year early."

What happened that night, as one Philly sportswriter put it, "was the stuff dreams are made of." Bishop McDevitt scored the first basket, but that was its only lead of the night. The North Central JV, which had lost earlier that season to McDevitt's JV, dominated on defense and offense. The crowd adopted a new chant.

"JVs to the cham-peen-ship!" they shouted. "JVs to the cham-peen-ship!"

Near the end, McDevitt narrowed the gap to six points. But North Catholic kept pressing. The buzzer went off, and North Catholic had the win, 77-60.

Jack Friel hugged his players and dabbed at his eyes. "Gee whiz," he kept saying. "Gee whiz. JV players, coming into the Palestra, winning. You can't imagine how much this means. You can't imagine."

He had thought about the critics and the certain vitriol before he made his decision, but there was "no question" in his mind about what to do.

"They're good boys but they very frankly put athletics ahead of academics, and they were wrong," he explained later. "We're concerned about the future. What we teach now is going to affect these boys five years from now."

Coach Friel drink

After the win, Friel did hear from people flooding his home and office with letters and calls, but the critics had been silenced.

"Our boys were stunned when they heard the news of your disciplinary action, and just never could play their normal game," wrote one admirer. "Perhaps we will learn a lesson from this game. Best of luck." It was signed by the father of a star McDevitt player.

Around 1974, Jack Friel came to work at the Blue Bell Inn. Before long, he was general manager. I imagine he often had to tell the story to rapt diners, eager to hear how he took the Palestra floor as boos rained down from a crowd out for blood. His choice of drink was Seagram's V.O. Canadian whiskey. He also drank coffee, "coffee until it came out of his ears," longtime server Ronnie Scherf told me. "And sugar. He loved desserts."

He was also "lovely with children," she said. If mom and dad were trying to have a nice dinner, he would divert the kids with a walk around the restaurant and an offer of ice cream. As newspaper reporters often noted, he was a small man, 5-foot-5 and gaunt. One reporter noted his "very tired eyes," but then again, that was mere days after the shocking decision that made him an instant legend.

"He was of small stature, but he wielded a big stick," Ronnie said.

Jack Friel died of a heart attack in July 2006, only 74 years old. On the menu of the Blue Bell Inn, there is always a brown-liquor drink called the Coach Friel. It might be the rich combo of Basil Hayden's bourbon, Grand Marnier, Averna, and bitters that I sampled during my visit. I happened to look up the origin of the name "Friel" and found that it comes from Firghil, a descendant of the most prolific warrior in Irish history, whose name combines the words for "man" and "valor." So when you stop at the Blue Bell, raise a Coach Friel, and toast "Sláinte" to the valorous man who took a stand for education over winning—and won, anyway.

SECTION III

Touch history

History peeks out here and there at the Blue Bell Inn.

Memories by the platter: Look high over the bar at the display of Blue Willow-style ware hanging on the wall. Boxes of the dishes were found in the basement, left over from the days before they were replaced by plain white plates. Leah rescued the blue ware from captivity and reintroduced color to the Blue Bell tables.

Election-night countdowns: Stand at the back bar, the Blue Bell's original bar, and imagine the huddled sidebar conversations that took place here while local politicos waited out election-night returns. The Blue Bell Inn was a longtime hangout for the Montgomery County Republican Party. On election nights, they would march in as a group, "camping out, waiting for the ballots to come in," said Ronnie Scherf.

Peeking-into rooms: I just made up that term, but I can get very nosy in old inns. The Blue Bell is made for meandering, and the must-see spaces include several that are typically used for board meetings or other small gatherings. So, assuming that they're not booked for some Fortune 500 confab, don't miss the Board Room, with its spectacular stained-glass wall insets showing grape hyacinth—a.k.a. "bluebells," underscoring the level of detail that went into renovations—or the vintage-charming Blue Room, paneled in wall coverings of ducks and birds. The original inn's upstairs rooms include the spectacular Hunt Room, featuring a jaw-dropping wallpaper mural depicting the historic "Pigeontown Hunt" that originally attracted 18th-century gentry to this spot.

Pigeontown Hunt mural in the Hunt Room

The food scene: The Blue Bell Inn menu is American, said Leah. "It is approachable. Well-executed. Consistent. Tastes great."

It is all "food you've seen before," but done really well, she added. Everything except the bread is made in-house. The raw bar is irresistible. From the bar menu, try the Margherita flatbread, or the cheesesteak-bending steak sandwich toast of prime beef carpaccio with horseradish aioli, caramelized onions, and Blue Bell "Wiz" (that's Philly talk for Cheez Whiz, or here, the Blue Bell version). The dinner menu's braised short rib, beef Bourguignon-style, is "beautiful," and the juice goes into the "fantastic" short rib tater tots. The lobster roll is "fabulous." The shrimp cocktail is made with the highest-grade shrimp, "massive like baby lobster—huge, and it's delicious." The "beautiful" bronzino (I had to look it up; it's a fish) is stuffed with crab and scallop rousse, "sautéed and served with beautiful greens and sundried tomatoes."

For dessert, try a "super light" tiramisu, or the crème brulee, or the "really fun play on carrot cake, a carrot cake bread pudding."

"It's fun," Leah said. "Ultimately, if your staff is happy, your food is happy."

I asked about her favorite dish. She didn't hesitate. It's the ahi tuna tartar—sushi grade tuna, ginger soy ponzu, served over sliced and fanned cucumbers, with a little sriracha aioli, "and it is perfect. Perfect. I eat it almost every night. I love it. I love it. I really love it."

The beverage scene: Whether casual imbiber or connoisseur, you will find what you want at the Blue Bell. The wines, a passion of co-owner Scott Dougherty, come from top wineries around the globe, categorized on the menu by U.S., "The Old World" of France, Germany, Italy, and Spain, and "Southern Hemisphere" of Africa, Argentina, Chile, and New Zealand. With Blue Bell Inn's purchasing power, it can buy reserve wines—Leah called them "super-boutique"—covering most of the allotment designated for Pennsylvania, such as Spottswoode Estate from Napa Valley.

Beers range the gamut. Raise a Budweiser and toast "Dilly, dilly" to the Philadelphia Eagles. Or sip a local brew, which showcases "so much going on in the community," Leah said. Conshohocken Brewing Company Puddlers Row ESB is brewed just down the road, an English style ale that would probably taste familiar to the Founding Fathers. The Yards George Washington Tavern Porter is available year-round "because George used to hang here," said Leah, gesturing with fingers crossed. "George and I, just like that."

The spirits menu also spotlights locals along with the nationally known, like the BBI Frosted Martini on Tap, a pour of chilled Grey Goose Vodka garnished with bleu cheese-stuffed olives. Vodka lovers can try Philly-based Stateside, or Boardroom, from Lansdale. If, like me, you're partial to gin, try the Philadelphia-based Bluecoat or the Revitalist, also made in Lansdale and awesome in the Summertime Cucumber Cooler.

The Blue Bell Inn's spirit of community infuses the food and drink menus. Choose from the "Drink Pink" rosé selections, and $1 from every glass, or $5 from every bottle, goes toward sponsoring #TeamBBI at the Susan G. Komen three-day walk for breast cancer research in Atlanta. It's inspired by a BBI employee whose mother died from breast cancer. Try the luscious Butternut Squash & Lobster Bisque, and $1 goes toward Toys for Tots, also supported by BBI as a donation site.

"Being a community landmark, it's so important to give back to the community," said Leah. "It's important to give back when so many people are giving to you."

The author in Blue Bell's opulent restroom

Any ghosts? The spirit world seems satisfied to leave the Blue Bell Inn alone. Ronnie Scherf has worked here since 1994, diving into every public room and cellar corner, "and I've never had anything happen." Coworkers might claim that doors closing on their own are courtesy of a ghost. "No," says Ronnie. "It's the uneven floors."

PLAN YOUR VISIT

The Blue Bell Inn
601 Skippack Pike
Blue Bell, PA
www.bluebellinn.com, (215) 515-5792

WHAT'S NEARBY

Cliveden: It's the same house where British troops found shelter during the Battle of Germantown. George Washington and his troops tried to level the Benjamin Chew home, but its sturdy stone refused to crumble.

Bad for George Washington, but good for us. Today's Cliveden is a vibrant living museum, open to tours from early April to late December (and the arboreally rich grounds are open largely year-round). See how the Chew family lived for 200 years, delve into the fascinating view of history through the lens of kitchens (yes, kitchens!), and explore the impact of slavery, yesterday and today, based on meticulous research into the Chew family papers.

In October, there's the Revolutionary Germantown Festival, called Philadelphia's largest one-day festival, and featuring a re-enactment of the battle that sent George Washington into a serious rethink of his strategy. (www.cliveden.org)

The soldiers' burial ground at Boehm's United Church of Christ: Not all rebels wear uniforms. Some wear clerical garb.

America of the 18th century was a sort of Protestant Wild West. Sects squabbled over doctrine. Congregations splintered over devotion to church or directly to God. Old World clashes over baptismal practices were still stirring up New World rumbles.

The frontier pastor needed a thick skin, and John Philip Boehm was born combative. Once ordered dismissed from a post in his native Germany—something about rye bread used for communion—he told a deacon trying to stop him from reading at a service, "I am here at my place, which God and the church have entrusted to me, and I ask you to be quiet, so that I can fulfill my duty."

In the colonies, Boehm founded the German Reformed Church and protected it like a bulldog. By the 1740s, Boehm planted his church in opposition to efforts by Count Nicolaus Von Zinzendorf, founder of Bethlehem, PA, to unite the Moravian, Lutheran, and Reformed churches. Boehm said his congregants "recognize no one as a member, much less as a minister of our church, who contaminates himself with the Moravian soul destructive doctrine, until his total repentance of his serious lapse and return to our doctrine and Church, based upon God's Word."

"Soul destructive doctrine." There's refreshing honesty. Plus, Boehm might have once invested in a pub.

That endearing factoid came to me from the friendly Rev. Bill Middleton, at Boehm's UCC, just up the street from the Blue Bell Inn. I discovered this historic country church on the autumn day of my Blue Bell Inn visit, stopping for a graveyard stroll to clear my head. There on Penllyn-Blue Bell Pike, it's the last of John Philip Boehm's 12 churches, since rebuilt but founded as a small stone building "with remarkably heavy walls and a very long, steep roof."

Germantown soldiers' graves at Boehms UCC

Just like the inn then known as the White House Tavern, this church would find the war at its doorstep. Pressed into service as a hospital for the Battle of Germantown's wounded, it was a place for healing and death.

The dead share a mass grave in the churchyard. Their names are lost, but their sacrifices are remembered. Step into the graveyard, along the church's east wall, and read the marker erected in 1967 by the Daughters of the American Revolution, Valley Forge chapter.

"Under this stone and the area immediately around it are buried unknown soldiers of the American Revolution who died in this church after the Battle of Germantown, 1777."

Beside the stone, a 13-star American flag flutters in the wind. (boehmschurch.com)

4.

McCOOLE'S AT THE HISTORIC RED LION INN

Quakertown, Pennsylvania

Rumbling for tax revolt

Misbehavior makes history:
McCoole's at the Historic Red Lion Inn

■ Drunken mobs. Hostages. Marches and rescues. Will the ringleader of this revolt hang for his crimes? This is the home of Fries Rebellion, a tax revolt we didn't learn about in history class, but it was a doozy.

■ Extortion! Tavernkeeper Walter McCoole risked Quaker censure for selling alcohol "in a base & scandalous manner."

■ In the heart of a Quaker Underground Railroad network, the Red Lion Inn could have been a stopover.

■ Drunk again. President Ulysses S. Grant canceled his appearance at the Centennial Exposition of 1876 after a stay at the Red Lion Inn. Or so legend has it. The 186,000 expo-goers who saw Grant there would probably beg to differ.

■ Lassie ate here. At least, Lassie's real-life inspiration ate raw steaks right off the floor. Lassie's creator, a Red Lion Inn regular, was quite the dashing daredevil who met his end on a World War II spy mission.

■ Today's scene: "Upscale atmosphere for the Working Person's Wallet," says the McCoole's slogan. Come for the flame-grilled burgers, and oh, that crab cake. Wash it down with a selection from McCoole's Red Lion Brewery.

Built: 1740s

Front entrance to McCoole's

Meet the owner

In the dining room of McCoole's at the Historic Red Lion Inn, all stone and wood, it feels as if another rebellion could break out at any moment. Owner Jan Hench might have something to do with that, starting with the day just before settlement on her purchase of the dilapidated inn. A petite woman with short blond hair, she tells the story in her slightly gravelly voice.

The year was 2002. She had the idea of reviving this historic inn. Just before settlement, she saw moving men loading the tavern's Red Lion Inn sign into the truck.

Oh, wait. Did I hear the server say there's French onion soup? Yum. Anyway, where were we?

Right, so Jan saw moving men taking the sign away. It wasn't an original, but the Colonial-style replica had its own, long history. It was hanging on the dining room wall when Jan first saw it. Now, she made a declaration.

"You take that sign, and the settlement is off." Was she serious? Hell, yeah. "It's part of this building. It needs to stay."

An hour later, the sellers called. The sign needed to stay, they concurred. They were taking it to an area that had nothing to do with Red Lion Inn. Best that it would stay.

I looked at the sign, hanging where Jan first saw it, behind a table of women catching up on their travels and families. McCoole's is the kind of place where lunch hour stretches into the afternoon. At least it did on this Friday. Nobody seemed in a hurry to leave.

After Jan took ownership of the building, she discovered why the sign hung in that place of honor. Behind it was a black drape, and behind the black drape were three giant holes in the wall.

You buy a 254-year-old tavern, you get what you pay for. Besides, Jan is one of those crazy old-building people who knows that the only thing to expect is the unexpected.

"The fireplaces weren't working," she said. "The stone wasn't pointed. The ceiling was horrible, absolutely horrible. None of this wood was here. It was all covered in drywall and stained with watermarks and painted this burgundy color that was dreadful, and the drywall was stuccoed with this lumpy stucco to cover marks and cracks. Me, I don't care. I live with cracks every day of my life. I live in a house that's over 100 years old. I couldn't care less about cracks."

When it came up for sale, the building was a sort of boarding-house, but dining had been dormant for at least nine years. Jan already owned a building across the street and thought that saving the inn would help stabilize the corner she calls "the gateway" into Quakertown. She decided to take a look "because I remember what it had looked like, at least the barroom."

When she visited this time, that barroom "was nothing but a big, giant storeroom. The bar was completely gone. There were holes in the floor." Over the years, "little by little," owners had sold off fixtures and features. Though the building remained structurally sound and the floors were salvageable, overall, "it was a big mess."

"I just bought the building because I wanted to save it," she said. "I had to start from scratch and recreate everything."

On the décor front, recreating the tavern appeal demanded "a lot of collecting." Some things came from Jan's house. Others came from friends saying, "You want this? This'll look good in the store."

As a result, furnishings are a pleasant mishmash of new and old, wood and metal. My table in a cozy corner, next to cubbyhole shelving stocked with copper tea kettles and pitchers, appeared to be repurposed from who knows what, with metal strips hammered along each end, and nail holes visible in the trim.

The Red Lion signboard

"When I was a kid, I watched 'Gunsmoke' all the time," Jan said. "When I started to work on the interior, after we got the core, the body, the roots renovated and started working on interior design, I started watching a lot of old cowboy movies to get ideas."

Before McCoole's, Jan had never run a restaurant and had no intention of starting. But when her first restaurateur didn't work out, she thought, "If I have to eat somebody else's nonsense, I might as well just open this myself."

On a tour of the building, Jan introduced me to an electrician named Bill, at work in the basement. I'm writing a book about rabble-rousing taverns, I told him.

"Well, this is the place to be," Bill said.

Jan concurred. "We're still making our own rabble-rousing here."

A McCoole's Tour

Ask to see Jan Hench's album of restoration photos, and the transformation is mind-boggling. A tour tells the story of holes patched, wood features recreated, and stone uncovered.

"This building," said Jan, "is something else."

The dining room: The majestic lion of that Red Lion Inn sign stands guard over the inn's original section. Stone walls radiate coolness and character. Two fireplaces anchor the back wall, including one with a single, massive stone serving as a lintel. Be sure to look up at the ceiling beams. All woodwork was milled on site because the building's dimensions were too irregular to shop out the job. "You can't just order six 6-by-8 ceiling beams when one is 20 feet and three-quarter inches, and its neighbor is 19 feet and one-half inches," Jan said.

The barroom: The graceful, intimate bar was built from scratch by a father-son team, with curving ends, carved corbels, and copper top hand-hammered—on site, of course. The ghost of tavernkeeper McCoole—Jan calls him Walter—must have been supervising for historical accuracy because one old-timer who had lived at the inn for nearly 20 years insisted that this new bar had been there all along. "He argued with me that he thought it was the original bar," Jan said.

Tin incorporated into the bar ceiling was sprayed with copper paint. "We actually had a paint booth that was set up here," Jan said. "We couldn't take it out and bring it back because the copper paint ran like a mo-fo." Yes, she said "mo-fo." I'm adding that one to my vocabulary.

Martini Lounge: Jan personally restored the red, gray, and white penny tile floor in the Martini Lounge. This section was the building's first addition, a cozy space facing the street. The booth is defined by repurposed stair rails. The funky feel is embellished with mosaic tables, wing chairs, brass lighting, and an ornately carved upright piano originally from a nearby elementary school.

Porches: The McCoole's exterior brims with color, porch posts and rails and windows trimmed in burgundy, gold, and green. This is the place to remember that old buildings have a habit of getting older every year. Restoration is never once-and-done. In 2016, pulling down the stucco to fix an exterior leak ballooned into repointing the stone behind it, then rebuilding the upper and lower porches, and finally recreating every second-floor window from the outside in, reworking from stone to brick to glass. The next winter, channeling running water away from the building required stonemason Mike Fichter to close a window hole, but today, "you can't even tell a window was there," Jan said. "He put stone in, and it looks just like the 300-year-old stone on the outside of the building. He is amazing."

The dining room

The bar

Dining room corner

Dining room fireplace

Piano in McCoole's

Funky mosaic tabletop

SECTION II

The history of McCoole's at the Historic Red Lion Inn: Crossroads of insurrection

Some taverns seemed made for ruffians the second the last stone was mortared into place.

Quakers rumble: Maybe it was the unsavory reputation of the calloused clientele. Maybe it was the unbridled revelry or the danger that a fiddle tune would inspire vigorous dancing. Maybe it was the practice of making toasts, which tiptoed near blasphemy. Maybe it was the political leanings of the pub-going rabble, undermining Quaker control of Pennsylvania.

Whatever the reason, Quakers did not like taverns. They once tolerated drinking, but attitudes started shifting early in the 18th century. Taverns attracted a disreputable crowd, and taverns sold liquor. Therefore, liquor was sinful. By mid-18th, many Quakers were clamoring for abstinence.

So, a Quaker named Walter McCoole opens a tavern in the 1740s in a village called Quakertown. One can imagine. His congregation was unamused. Selling liquor, they determined, amounted to extortion of the unfortunate souls in thrall to intoxicating spirits. The congregation sent McCoole a stern letter, declaring him guilty of "great Injustice & of Oppression in extorting Money from many ignorant persons in a base & scandalous manner." He faced expulsion from the congregation unless he would "oblige himself to make Restitution to the persons injur'd by him."

Fat chance. McCoole kept the doors open. I don't know if he was officially expelled. I suspect he didn't care.

Fries Rebellion, Part I: The three prisoners probably rued the day they took posts as tax assessors. A cushy government job wasn't supposed to end in captivity by a rowdy, armed, and drunken mob.

But there they were in early spring 1799, held prisoner in Enoch Roberts' tavern, the old McCoole's. Pennsylvania German farmers had been meeting at this inn and others, agitating against a new tax. Here at Enoch's, the simmering discontent was boiling over.

Pennsylvania had stirred up another tax rebellion challenging the authority of the federal government. The Keystone State was famous, or infamous, for tax revolts, and an auctioneer named John Fries brought his to Enoch's Tavern.

John Fries was a native Pennsylvanian who started life as a cooper, making barrels. He fought for the Continental Army in the Revolution. As a member of the State Guard, he helped stamp out the Whiskey Rebellion in 1794. He even acquired a dog on those excursions, naming it "Whiskey." Five years later, after his own rebellion had fizzled, that little dog would cause him trouble.

Back home in eastern Pennsylvania, Fries (pronounced "freez") bought 13 acres and turned to auctioneering for a living. He traveled about, and he was comfortable speaking to crowds. Fluent in German and English, he became well-known. Neighbors listened when he talked politics. And by 1798, politics was all anyone talked about.

The U.S. was in a quasi-war with France, racing to beef up its army and navy and defend against invasion. Defense costs money, and the U.S. Congress, from the capital in Philadelphia, imposed its first-ever "house tax," charging Pennsylvania with raising $237,000 toward the $2 million cost.

Pennsylvania German farmers were not amused. First of all, President John Adams blundered by hiring pacifist Quakers and ex-Tories to collect the levies from the patriotic veterans who had fought for the Revolution. Any assessor lurking around homes to count windows—by some accounts, the basis of the tax—had to watch his head, because housewives were known to send dousings of hot water pouring from those upstairs windows.

Second, the new Alien and Sedition Acts criminalized any words deemed "false, scandalous, or malicious" against the United States government, the president, and any member of Congress. Opposition to national laws by way of riot or insurrection was also banned. The "alien" part of the acts gave the president powers to arrest, imprison or deport any alien considered dangerous or treasonable.

So, that would be Pennsylvania Germans—"aliens"—who stood up to oppose an unfair tax on their homes? Hadn't these men just fought for the colonies in an uprising against unjust taxes and for liberty?

They met in taverns. They got liquored up. Government officials might have regretted convening at least one meeting to explain the tax, which devolved into a rally by protestors wearing their Continental Army uniforms, waving liberty flags, and brandishing guns.

The rebels took their insurgency straight to the assessors. They harangued, bullied, and threatened. Fries started leading 60 men on intimidation raids, sending assessors skedaddling out of town.

On March 5, 1799, Fries told an assessor he would assemble 700 men in the morning. Seven hundred might have been a stretch, but the next day, Fries rallied about 100 men and marched them to Quakertown. There, the mob captured three hapless assessors and held them prisoner at a place the insurgents knew well, a place where they had met before—Enoch's Tavern.

Inside the tavern, Fries' men manhandled the assessors. They called their prisoners "stamplers"—an insult slung at government supporters, but especially Quakers who hadn't fought for the liberty these men cherished in their very bones. The government wanted to make them all slaves, the protestors insisted. They said George Washington was coming to fight for their side. They'd been drinking at an earlier meeting. They were drinking here, too. They were flat-out drunk.

Fries had been out of the room. When he entered, he seemed surprised to discover the abuse underway. He gave one assessor a drink and took all three into another room. He asked for their papers, the ones showing the results of their assessments. Naturally, they obliged. Fries walked away, and back came the men, armed with clubs, staves, guns, and swords, and threatening to use them all. A man named William Thomas finally told them to knock it off, because he knew one of the assessors. The insurgents stopped and, like chastened children, apologized.

Fries, who had been conveniently absent for both rounds of abuse, stepped back into the room and gave the assessors their papers. Leave, he told them, and don't do any more assessing or you'll be shot. Oh, and tell the government that I have 1,000 men who will not submit to this law and are ready to fight.

The government had not been idle during all this. Word arrived that U.S. Marshal William Nichols had arrested 19 fellow insurgents and was holding them in a tavern-turned-jail of his own, the Sun Inn in Bethlehem.

From Enoch's, Fries led the enraged conspirators to yet another tavern. There, the mob vowed that Nichols could not hold their friends. Even when told to stand down because a sympathetic

local guard troop was on its way to free the prisoners, Fries resisted. Don't go home, he told the men. March with me to Bethlehem.

What happened next? For Part II, turn to the chapter on the
Sun Inn, Bethlehem.

Fries Rebellion, Part III: Fries Rebellion sent shudders
through the Federalist establishment, the wing of government
advocating consistent federal power over states. President Adams
called first for the insurgents to retire. They were doing that when
he suddenly authorized his secretary of war to muster 1,200—
1,200!—members of the Pennsylvania Militia. Fond of drink and
women, the militiamen turned the hunt for rebels into one big
carouse across the countryside.

"Conceive your house entered at dead of night by a body of
armed men and yourself dragged from your wife and screaming
children," wrote a Philadelphia newspaper editor. That editor and
another who dared to question the militia's bullying tactics were,
themselves, dragged from their offices. One was beaten. The other
was publicly whipped.

Fries didn't hide. He was in a village near Quakertown, con-
ducting an auction when cavalry members closed in, weapons
drawn. Fries ran, and so did the townspeople. The marauders
chased the crowd, nearly killing two men with gun and sword.
While Fries hid in a briar patch, his little black dog, Whiskey,
went looking for him. The cavalry commander found the dog first
and let it lead the way, and so, the dog named after one rebellion led authorities to the hiding place of the head of another
rebellion.

At Fries' trial with three others, prosecutors trotted out an
old definition of treason, conflating organizing to resist federal
law with waging war against the U.S. government. The judge pre-
siding over Fries' first trial—there would be a mistrial and a repeat—told the jury "if you suffer this government to be destroyed,
what chance have you for any other? A scene of the most dreadful
confusion must ensure. Anarchy will ride triumphant, and all lovers of order, decency, truth, and justice be trampled under foot."

Both times, John Fries was found guilty and sentenced to
hang. While Fries awaited his fate after the first trial, Secretary of
State Timothy Pickering delivered this cold-blooded calculation to
Adams: "Painful as is the idea of taking the life of a man, I feel a
calm and solid satisfaction that an opportunity is now present, in
executing the just sentence of the law, to crush that spirit which

if not overthrown and destroyed, may proceed in its career, and overturn the Government."

John Adams couldn't do it. Though the conspirators had mounted a "wicked and treasonable insurrection against the just authority of the United States," they were guilty of nothing more than "high-handed riot and rescue, attended with circumstances hot, rash, violent, and dangerous." The uprising was "speedily suppressed without any of the calamities usually attending rebellion." The "ignorant, misguided, and misinformed" insurrectionists had resumed a "proper sense of their duty."

All were pardoned.

Too late for two Fries Rebellion members who died from yellow fever in a Philadelphia prison. That pardon, though, contributed to a death sentence on Adams' presidency. In the 1800 election, a Pennsylvania win would have returned Adams to office, but Pennsylvania Germans, seething over their mistreatment, turned out for Thomas Jefferson Republicans. Adams was ousted.

Fries died in 1818, living on borrowed money in the years after escaping the hangman. His body lies in the old Reformed Church in Trumbauersville. Historians today call him a scapegoat for Americans who demanded from the government the same liberty they had fought for in the Revolution.

And by the way, when you raise a drink in honor of John Fries at McCoole's, you can thank him for one lasting difference. Congress has imposed many additional taxes since 1798, but our homes have never again been taxed by the federal government.

President Grant regrets: The Centennial Exposition at Philadelphia attracted 10 million people, enticed by their first look at such wonders of the modern age as the telephone and the "typographic machine."

President Ulysses S. Grant himself was to attend. He had announced the exposition in 1873, eager to show the world American progress and ingenuity. But after a stop at the Red Lion Inn on his way to Philadelphia, Grant sent his regrets. A sudden illness, he said.

Or an epic hangover? "It's widely believed that he drank to excess at the Red Lion and was unable to travel to Philadelphia the next day," a local history buff told the Allentown *Morning Call* as Jan Hench was reopening the refurbished inn.

Great story, except for one problem. Grant opened the fair on May 10, 1876, with 186,672 people in attendance. America, he proclaimed, was now surpassing the Old World in law, medicine, theology, science, literature, philosophy, and the fine arts.

Actually, "proclaiming" might not be the word. Grant spoke so softly that a reporter just 20 feet away couldn't hear a word. Maybe that was the taciturn Grant's usual speaking voice—hard to believe for a general who commanded an army.

So, back to that stay in Quakertown. Perhaps there's a kernel of truth in tales that Grant enjoyed the Red Lion's hospitality over-much. U.S. Grant avoided alcohol during his presidency, at least in public. But away from the prying eyes and wagging tongues of official Washington, could he have surrendered to the alcoholism that bedeviled his entire adult life? It's a mystery of history, but let's allow "Unconditional Surrender" Grant a few hours of release from the pressures of running a country, here in the shelter of a cozy tavern.

Toots, the collie better known as ... : If Jan Hench had known the story behind the rotted floorboards in the dining-room corner, she wouldn't have replaced them. "I probably would have put a little fence around it with a sign that said, 'Lassie Ate Here.'"

Yes, that Lassie, and even better, the author who shaped her into a literary sensation could stake his own claims as spy, adventurer, and iconoclast.

To the beginning. Eric Knight was born in Yorkshire, England, to a wealthy bounder who walked out on the family and left them destitute. While Knight's mother worked as governess for a Russian royal family in St. Petersburg, the boy lived with aunts and uncles in England. One uncle regaled Eric with tales of the American West, so around age 15, he sailed to America, worked in a Philadelphia lumber yard, and won a scholarship to Yale. When war broke out in Europe in 1914, he joined the Canadian Light Infantry, fighting for the United Kingdom alongside another future literary legend, hardboiled mystery writer Raymond Chandler.

After the war, back in the states, Knight wrote newspaper film criticisms so biting and on point that Samuel Goldwyn offered him a screenwriting job. He was good, too, writing scripts for A-listers. Director Frank Capra admitted to swooning at first sight of the "red-mustached American captain with a British accent; a Yorkshireman whose unruly shock of red hair seemed as full of mischief as his sharp ferretlike eyes... He had all the talents that could be compressed into a single writer: wit, compassion, sensitiveness, an intriguing style; and a great, great love for human beings."

As for that American captain thing, Knight had been turned down for British service in World War II—too old at 42—but accepted by the U.S. and assigned to the Office of Strategic Services.

The OSS was the predecessor to America's CIA. So, Knight was a spy. And he was bicoastal, regularly traveling to Hollywood and Washington from his Bucks County home called Springhouse Farm, circa 1808. In Hollywood, he bought a collie for his wife, Jere. This puppy, so small she fit in Knight's pocket, was named Toots, after a popular song of the time, "Oh, Toots."

"She was the most warm, the most loyal, the most loving, devoted dog. We had her from babyhood on, until she died of old age, at 14," recalled Jere Knight.

Eric Knight boasted that Toots knew multiple languages, but some believe she was simply responding to slyly delivered hand signals. Sometimes, Toots traveled with Knight. Sometimes, she stayed home in Bucks County, waiting patiently for him by the front gate.

And sometimes, starting in 1939, she joined Knight for dinner at the Red Lion Inn. The canine character she inspired, Lassie, made her debut in 1940, with Knight's novel, "Lassie Come-Home." The author's literary reputation blossomed along with Lassie's fame. Their dinners were a celebration of their bond. While Knight ate his dinner from a plate on the table, Toots ate a raw steak thrown on the floor (hence, the rotted floorboards).

In 1943, Knight was in his OSS role, flying over Dutch Guiana, en route to Africa, when the plane went down. All on board were killed. Amid the wreckage were large amounts of cash. What were Knight and the OSS up to? To this day, the crash remains a mystery.

Even amid wartime intrigue, Knight's thoughts turned to Toots. In one of his last letters, he fretted that she was getting feeble. "I sorrow about her, and she sorrows for us away in the war," he wrote. "She's a big chunk of my life and history, with all the thousands of miles she's traveled with us, and she can't understand these war-time absences."

Toots outlived Knight by two years. She is buried on Springhouse Farm, the place where she waited for him to come home.

SECTION III

Touch History

A little bit rebellious, a little bit artsy—McCoole's at the Historic Red Lion Inn serves up a flavor that's all Bucks County.

Underground Railroad hideout: In the basement of McCoole's, Jan showed me a room where, it's said, freedom seekers hid on the perilous journey through the Underground Railroad. A guard might have kept sentry—not to keep others from getting in, but to keep the fugitives from getting out.

"If the slaves would go out in the town and people found out where they were hiding, they would torch and burn the house where they came from," Jan said. "It was very important that the slaves couldn't leave because of something happening to the business itself."

McCoole's claim as a hideout could be bolstered by the region's active Underground Railroad network and the known station nearby, at 401 South Main Street. There, ardent abolitionist and devout Quaker Richard Moore, with his wife, Sarah Foulke Moore, provided a stop for freedom seekers on the stretch from Philadelphia to northern New York and Canada. Moore used his redware pottery business as a ruse, sometimes concealing freedom seekers under the straw bedding that cushioned pottery being carted to market.

A state historical marker approved in 2018 notes the 600 escapees believed to have been aided by Moore. Did Moore send some of those 600 to safety in the basement of McCoole's? I like the thought, although Moore was also so ardent a temperance man that workers built his home without help from "spiritous liquors." Maybe his revulsion over slavery trumped his disapproval of the demon rum. Even if not, the region teemed with fervent abolitionists and Underground Railroad conductors, many of them Quakers, who could have welcomed the option of a haven safe from slave catchers in the basement of a sturdy tavern.

Penny pitching: The gentleman who insisted that the recrafted bar was the original told Jan a great story. Customers would sit at the bar and pitch coins onto the top of the bar back. Once a month, the bartender or owner would climb up, retrieve those pennies, nickels, dimes, and quarters, and buy everybody beers. Sounds like a tradition worth reviving.

Art works: "All art is subversive," said Pablo Picasso.

Lion mural on the exterior wall guarding the parking lot

I couldn't find any references to Picasso ever visiting Bucks County, but he had the right idea. Great art upends conventions. Maybe that explains the allure of Bucks County for creative types. The first artists flowed here in the late 19th century, lured by fresh air, verdant scenery, and the cheap realty (in those days) of abandoned mills and picturesque farmhouses. Writers, composers, architects, and actors followed, breaking the shackles of the corporate machine and recharging the soul.

From the lion mural on the exterior wall guarding the parking lot to the artwork hanging on the walls, McCoole's at the Historic Red Lion Inn projects the Bucks County arts vibe:

■ Jeri Lee Nichols painted the front ladies' room to feel like the inside of a birdcage. With Janet Bishop, she also produced a large painting on the wall between the two bathrooms.

■ In the back bathroom, Jim Lukens, owner of a studio across the street from McCoole's, painted scenes of the Burgess Foulke House and Liberty Hall, historic buildings in sight of the tavern.

■ The stained-glass window in the Martini Lounge, Art Nouveau-style in swirls and geometrics of yellow, green, red, and lavender, was made from glass salvaged from the building's doors and upstairs bathrooms. Jan said she worked with Allentown-based glass design firm Neff-Chattoe Co. to "pick a somewhat period design" for the window, installed in a former doorway.

■ The Red Lion Inn signboard that almost killed the sale was made in scenic Bedminster Township, Bucks County. Today, a string of lights gives the stern lion a playful aura. The sign always stayed indoors because, as Hench tells it, the owner who commissioned it in the 1970s "ran into too much red tape trying to hang it outside, so he said, 'To hell with it,' and shoved it in a room upstairs, where it stayed for years."

■ Paintings of trees in the barroom were done by Quakertown High School art students.

■ Works for sale from local artists hang on the walls and stand on mantels.

I asked, Why local art?

"Why not?" said Jan. "It's part of Bucks County. I thought it was a really important part of renovating this space, to make things interesting. When you have all this art in here, people look at it and have conversations."

She has noticed, in other restaurants, the stifling effect of cell phones, "but that doesn't happen as much here because all this stuff is homey and opens people up. They talk and they have conversations and have a good time."

The food scene: Jan calls the culinary scene "eclectic," with a healthy dose of farm to table. There are steaks, creole fare, seafood, and pasta.

I tried: They were out of the coconut crab cake when I visited, but just the aroma of the twin boiled crab cakes arriving at my table made my heart jump for joy. It was exactly as a crab cake should be, perfectly crispy-broiled, with the barest filler holding together the lump crab.

The beverage scene: No specialty mixed drink here, but always a drink of the week, plus a selection of whiskeys, cordials, after-dinner martinis, and specialty coffees.

Try pairing your entrée with an ale, IPA, or another sampling from McCoole's Red Lion Brewery. It's brewed in small batches right next door, in the McCoole's Arts and Events Building, so you know it's fresh. I tried the Red Lion Brewery Stout—nice and tangy, with an almost citrusy element.

McCoole's annual Beer Fest, scheduled every year in late April or early May, benefits Tales of Valor, Paws of Honor. The nonprofit pairs veterans who have mental or physical disabilities with companion and service dogs trained to meet each vet's specific needs.

Any ghosts? There may be ghosts, but they don't bother anyone. They move things—really move things like a piece of glassware, in ways that the rumble of a passing truck won't do.

Customers sometimes tell Jan, "You know, there's a woman in the restroom," when they have no idea about the woman who occasionally appears there and likes shiny things. Jan typically doesn't experience anything, but she believes that Walter McCoole is "still here, for sure. I am not a ghost person, but there are too many things that happen in here that you just can't explain."

She keeps paranormals at bay, "because the spirits get riled up." However, one psychic did tell Jan that they like her. "They like what I've done to the place. They like that I leave them alone, and they're pretty much allowed to do whatever they want, and they have no intention of doing any harm to anyone."

PLAN YOUR VISIT

McCoole's at the Historic Red Lion Inn
4 South Main Street
Quakertown, PA 18951
www.mccoolesredlioninn.com, (215) 538-1776

WHAT'S NEARBY

McCoole's Arts & Events Place: Every Colonial tavern had a stable for the hardworking horses that carried people there, but in most cases, those wooden structures lacked staying power. The stable at McCoole's not only survives but is integral to the Quakertown pub and arts scene. In the 1990s, the building was converted into a professional theater. When it went up for auction in 2007, Jan thought, "What are the chances?"

So, she acquired it and created a banquet and meeting space. "I was just trying to keep my head above water in the restaurant, let alone get into catering, but there was a need for it," Jan said.

Before long, the arts came calling. Students from the Upper Bucks Alliance for Creative Expression rehearse and perform here, because "there are children that don't want anything to do with sports," Jan said. "We try to get them involved in other avenues." Since 2015, the center has been home to Star of the Day Event Productions, presenting live theater, comedy, and events such as a Gatsby-themed Valentine's Day extravaganza.

The Liberty Bell slept here: Philadelphia was defenseless. Redcoats had a clear path to the capital city. The one-ton bell hanging in the Pennsylvania State House steeple could be melted down and recast as cannonballs and musket rounds—30,000 pieces of ammunition aimed at Colonials fighting for freedom.

A few things of earthshattering importance happened under and around that bell since 1753. Inscribed "Proclaim LIBERTY Throughout All the Land Unto All the Inhabitants thereof," the bell would ring to convene citizens to protest the latest British outrage, or cheer the reading of "the unanimous Declaration of the thirteen United States of America," the one that began, "When in the Course of human events," and concluded with, "we mutually pledge to each other our Lives, our Fortunes, and our sacred Honor."

On July 4, 1777, the bell rang to commemorate the Declaration of Independence's first anniversary, but by September, the approach of British troops cast a pall over the city. Col. Benjamin Flower received the order to remove the State House Bell and 10 church bells from their towers and "convey them to safety."

Sure. Easy as pie for this ambitious hatmaker-turned-supply officer. All you need are carpenters to unhitch the bells, carts each sturdy enough to support a one-ton load, horses strong enough to haul them, and secrecy to evade enemy capture.

On that secrecy thing, Flower had an idea. Military carts would draw attention. Lehigh Valley farmers, on the other hand, constantly trundled into the city and then out for the journey home. The bells were destined for Allentown, so why not hitch a ride?

Around this time, a German farmer and distiller named Frederick Loeser rolled into town with a wagonload of grain and applejack brandy. Applejack was a lucrative line, no doubt, and Loeser proudly drove a fine, new Conestoga wagon pulled by four strong, black horses. He stopped overnight at an inn and came down the next morning to find that the army had commandeered cart and horses to carry the State House Bell. No problem, Loeser said. Let me be of service. So the officers restored his team and cart and recruited him to help spirit the State House Bell into the countryside.

That's one story. Others claim that John Jacob Mickley—farmer, battle veteran, and ardent Patriot—drove the State House Bell's cart, his 11-year-old son at his side and sometimes taking the reins.

Whatever the truth, the caravan left Philadelphia in mid-September. Camouflaged by hay and manure—no one ever said the fight for liberty was pretty—the bells began the 60-mile journey to Allentown. The caravan would grow into a 700-wagon train smuggling valuables out of Philadelphia, escorted by 200 North Carolina and Virginia cavalrymen (so much for secrecy).

At a juncture known as the Great Swamp, and possibly nick-named Quakertown as a slur on its Quaker residents, the train halted for the night. Philadelphia was to their backs, to the south. Allentown was 15 miles north.

The tavern called Enoch's stood at this crossroads. Abel Roberts, co-owner with his brother Enoch, extended the tavern's hospitality to men and horses. I like to picture the cavalry officers and farmers, weary but reinvigorated by the thought of mission's end approaching, gathering here for rum punch and locally sourced applejack. Soldiers bivouacked in the fields. Horses were fed and watered, maybe some sheltered in the inn's stables.

And at least one cart, the sturdy one carrying the State House Bell, was steered to the rear of a squat stone house across the intersection. While troopers and horses slept, the bell was tucked away from sight.

On September 23, 1777, the State House Bell and its companions reached Allentown. There, they were hidden under the floorboards of Zion's Reformed Church until the British left Philadelphia in June 1778.

From your seat at a window of McCoole's, the tavern where soldiers and farmers found respite, you can see that squat stone

Liberty Hall

house, now known as Liberty Hall. The compact stone home built in 1772 was destined to harbor a bell rushed out of Philadelphia for very practical reasons. The journey would ultimately preserve a treasured symbol of freedom that would come to be known as the Liberty Bell.

TAVERN AT THE SUN INN

Bethlehem, Pennsylvania

Crossroads of the Revolution

Misbehavior makes history: Tavern at the Sun Inn

■ A fine inn at a central location—and outside of British control—provided a safe harbor for all manner of revolutionaries. Name a Founding Father or fighting general, and he was here—John Adams, George Washington, Marquis de Lafayette, Alexander Hamilton, Ethan Allen, generals Steuben, Greene, and Pulaski.

■ War came through the front door, in all its stench and death and deprivation, when Bethlehem was pressed into service as a hospital town.

■ Suites! Running water! The technologically innovative Moravians built their tavern with unheard-of luxuries.

■ Fries Rebellion, Part II: If you value your head, don't peek out the window.

■ Stopping the wrecking ball demands a rebellious spirit, even if it wears the guise of a sweet, white-haired lady.

■ Today's scene: Food and drink that fit the space—a tavern feel updated for today's palates, with locally distilled spirits inspired by Christmas City itself. It's all offered through a unique partnership between hospitality and historic preservation.

Built: 1758

Meet the owners

We were discussing renovations made to Tavern at the Sun Inn. Brett Biggs pointed to the Dutch door separating the bar from the dining room.

Co-owner of Tavern at the Sun Inn Brett Biggs

"That door alone took us almost two and a half months," he said.

Good grief. Why?

"Because when you have an old inn and start breaking down walls, you run into a pile of hell," he said.

Old inn owners know all about piles of hell. Brett and his tavern co-owners have drilled through concrete to install piping. They disentangled three years' worth of red tape to get a distillery license. Success in this business demands a hard head for butting through obstacles.

First, a word on the unique nature of this establishment. The building's owner and rescuer from demolition is the Sun Inn Preservation Association, created in 1972. Tour the association's brilliant work in the first-floor tavern rooms, restored in exacting detail.

On the floors above and below, your food and drink are provided by a separate entity, Tavern at the Sun Inn, co-owned by a group of Bethlehem-native friends. Chef Billy Gruenewald, also a Bethlehem native, oversees the cuisine.

Got it? Let's start with Tavern at the Sun Inn.

In the Sun Inn's long history, January 10, 2015, is a milestone date. Brett Biggs is a financial planner by trade, so he can pull random dates like that from his brain. On that day, he was approached by two Sun Inn Preservation Association officials, then-president Seth Cornish and board member Mike Santanaso, Brett's friend since they were 5-year-olds playing soccer.

"Hey, do you want to start a distillery at the Sun Inn?" they asked.

These three, plus another soccer-days best friend, Colin Anderson, would become the tavern's co-owners.

"They love Bethlehem," Brett said. "They love the history of Bethlehem. It was a good match."

But did you notice that the original pitch was about starting a distillery? The Sun Inn has hosted many restaurants over the years, but the kitchen ranges had been cold since around 2000. When Pennsylvania opened small-distillery licensing in 2012, a distillery in the old inn seemed a good fit. King George II himself licensed the original Sun Inn as a house of entertainment. A distillery would generate revenue for the preservation association. History would come full circle.

But King George proved less stodgy than 21st-century bureaucrats. Distilling spirits close to tavern diners, not to mention schools and churches? No go. Not in the inn. It took three years, but the Christmas City Spirits distillery found a spot outside of town, working toward a fall 2018 opening, with a tasting room in Tavern at the Sun Inn's basement Rathskeller.

While the initial distillery plans stalled, the holidays were approaching. You know. Christmas. Bethlehem. They kind of go together around here. On Christmas Eve in 1741, Moravian missionaries gathered in this new place for a service. In the adjoining stable, sheep bleated and cattle lowed. They named their sanctuary community Bethlehem. Today, the holidays are a time for breathtaking light displays and Bach Choir concerts, Christkindlmart shopping and Moravian nativity scenes.

A restaurant at the Sun Inn was always part of the distillery's growth plan. With prime tourist season on the horizon, the plans were flipped. Restaurant first, distillery and tasting room second.

"We kind of flung the doors open," Brett said. "That is how it happened, and we're still plugging along."

Brett and his partners all appreciated food and beverage, but "we weren't stupid enough to think we ate in a restaurant once, so we know how to run one," he said. They reached out to Chef Billy Gruenewald, who also owns and operates the popular People's Kitchen, serving such delights as breakfast mac & cheese, and croissant French toast. He'd be at the top of my list for a chef, too.

"He does simple food really, really well," said Brett. "It's perfect for this location. We wanted to maintain a taverny menu."

Many beverages either tell a local story or have roots in history—but adapted to modern tastes. The shrub is a concoction of fruit preserved in vinegar, and sometimes added to rum, "which they called 'rattleskull' because it was disgusting."

"We're taking elements from the past and trying to be as accurate as possible while still creating a marketable product because nobody wants to come in and drink crappy rum with vinegar in it," Brett said.

Clever warnings against serving to underage or visibly intoxicated guests set the tone. Says one: "We shall take no part in furthering the corruption of intoxicated patrons or individuals who have become blatantly drunken through copious previous imbibing of hardened alcohol beverage. They shall be refused service forthwith."

The message: History is real, and it's fun. Brett is a big fan of "The Simpsons," with its "amazing network of things going on, but it's entertaining. We kind of take the same approach. The historic experience is rewarding if you want to pay attention to it. If you just want to come in and eat, you can come in and eat."

Deep Bethlehem roots tie the owners to this project. In the Sun Inn's attic is a 1984 certificate of appreciation for Sun Inn Preservation Association founder Hughetta Bender, signed by Mayor Paul Marcincin—who was Brett's great-uncle. It's safe to say that, genetically, Brett is the history of American settlement wrapped in one person. One branch of the family tree is 100 percent Slovak, with a first-generation grandfather who came to work in the Bethlehem Steel mills, because "that's where everybody's grandfather worked." On his paternal grandmother's side, his lineage traces to the Mayflower.

Bethlehem has transformed "incredibly" since Brett's youth, those ghost-town days of steel's demise. Now, just look around. Fegley's Brew Works, the Apollo Grill, the Hotel Bethlehem shined up to its former glory, Bethlehem Musikfest attracting 1 million people every summer. Bethlehem is back.

I asked Brett if he looks around Tavern at the Sun Inn and wonders what the heck he's done.

"Initially, it was a lot of that," he said. "Now, it's figuring out how to make it better."

The partners share a common desire with the original inn-keepers, hosts of the bright lights of the Revolution and countless other weary travelers.

"We want, first and foremost, for guests to have a good meal and enjoy themselves and feel comfortable here," Brett said. "That's the main purpose, and that's the root of what this building was. We're not here to change that. We've started the journey of doing that, and we're getting there."

A tour of Tavern at the Sun Inn

In most of the taverns on my Pennsylvania pub crawl, you can almost hear the echoes of fists smashing and chairs cracking over heads.

The echoes are fainter at the Sun Inn. Catering to the upper crust meant upholding certain standards. Guests expected relief from the dust and jouncing of the road. They demanded the comforts of home—and many came from very comfortable homes.

Besides, revolutions aren't sustained on passion alone. A refined inn provided a quiet place for reflection, strategizing, and plotting the next steps that get an insurgent one of two things—a new nation, or a date with the hangman.

1758 Moravian Sun Inn: Step into the first floor, and experience Moravian hospitality, circa 1760. The Moravians, I'm told, were friendly folk but reclusive. After Bethlehem's founding in 1741, everyone labored for the good of all in a self-contained, self-sustaining "general economy." But within about 10 years, neighbors started demanding Moravian goods, while even the industrious Moravians found it necessary to deal with these "strangers" for necessities they couldn't produce themselves—iron, gunpowder, glass, salt.

Recognizing that traders and merchants needed lodging, the Moravians built an inn at the far end of town, convenient for guests but apart from their enclave. Moravian elders required innkeepers and traders to hand over their profits for community use, but in time, a few hundred yards of distance between inn and compound couldn't diminish the irresistible whiff of capitalism. Opening the gates to outsiders would fundamentally change the

Moravian lifestyle, as tradesmen and craftspeople shrugged off church restrictions and set up their own profit-making ventures.

Or as John Adams put it in a letter to Abigail, "Christian Love is their professed Object, but it is said they love Money and make their public Institutions subservient to the Gratification of that Passion."

Before long, modern amenities and excellent port wine and Madeira made the Sun Inn a favored halfway stopping point for Colonial-era elite traveling from Philadelphia to New York. They knew where they'd find chocolate and coffee, butter to slather on their bread, and the likelihood of fresh eggs and meat for any meal.

Bar and dining rooms: Climb the stairs to the second floor, and you're about to break bread and enjoy a cocktail or beer in the same rooms where early travelers gathered to eat. The only space they wouldn't recognize, even though they'd feel perfectly comfortable, is the newly designed bar and lounge. The tavern partners, with help from an architect, adopted a clean, contemporary approach, nodding to history without dunking us in the past. Small tables furnished with Early American-reproduction Windsor chairs sit under the windows with impossibly deep,

Bar windowsill

gracefully arching windowsills. Walls are painted in historically accurate milky whites and grays.

Brett Biggs has learned a few things about running a restaurant, like "the psychology of sitting at a bar," he told me. "If you don't have a footrest, you're going to lose 20 percent of your sales because people aren't comfortable, and they move. Ladies love purse hooks, so we got Colonial purse hooks. They're wrought iron."

I looked under the bar. Yep. Wrought-iron purse hooks. "I installed those myself," Brett said. All the renovations, he added, were "a group effort."

Bar

So, belly up to the bar, plant your toes on the footrest, and hang up your purse. The sleek bar top of ambrosia maple was

Dining room

made by local craftsman Stephen Metz of Highpoint Woodworks, from a tree that grew in nearby Hellertown. The striations and tiny holes in the wood were made by voracious emerald ash borers—bad for Pennsylvania's tree canopy, good for adding character to bar tops.

And if you find yourself humming Jason Mraz's "I'm Yours" or Toto's "Africa," it's because you caught a phrase from the uniquely arranged music piped in through smart speakers.

"We tried classical music, and it was too stuffy," said Brett. "You can't put modern music in here, because that completely destroys the atmosphere." Someone on staff suggested the winner—"modern music played for classical guitar, and it just kind of works. If you're younger, you know the songs, and if you're older, it's not displeasing to the ear."

Rathskeller Colonial Cellar: "The old inn brilliant with lights shining from every casement with the rich familiar music of the famous trombone band pouring its sweet, almost human notes upon the summer air wrought such a change that one lost sight and sense of time and generation."

Willy Wonka wasn't the first hero of hallucinogenic literature. In 1914, the Sun Inn's cellar inspired a writer named James B. Laux to write "Brother Albrecht's Secret Chamber." Synopsis: A tipsy monk stumbles from the Sun Inn's basement into a long-lost cave. There, George and Martha Washington, Ben Franklin, the Marquis de Lafayette, and the inn's other distinguished guests are resurrected and rekindling old friendships—or tweaking old rivalries, such as gossipy Ben Franklin reminding John Adams of his deflated welcome in Paris when the disappointed French realized that John wasn't his dashing cousin, Samuel Adams.

Today's Rathskeller doesn't lead to a secret time-travel chamber. Bummer. But it is the ideal spot for following Brother Albrecht's example and sampling a brew, wine, or spirit. It's where we encounter another spectacular, hand-crafted bar, made by local woodworker Pete Connor.

"Pete's a salt-of-the-earth guy," Brett said. "He just loves milling wood." Brett put his hand on the bar with smooth top and rough edges. "Pete fell out of this tree. Broke his hip."

The Sun Inn folks also bought some wood from Pete and turned it over to a woodworker named Evan, who created the beautifully rustic barstools. Brett showed me a picture of Evan, happily up to

The Rathskeller Colonial cellar

his ankles in sawdust while using a "schnitzelbank," an ancient German bench that uses foot power to clamp a piece of wood in place for carving.

"He just loves wood," Brett said. "He doesn't shortcut anything."

Behind the bar, a mini-history of the weaponry of war is on display. In Bethlehem's tight-knit world of craftspeople and history buffs, it seems that the Sun Inn's cider maker also recreates historic weapons for TV and film. Did you happen to see the "Turn" episode when the world's first combat submarine—a sort of fat-bellied barrel decked out in cranks and gadgets—tried to blow up a British ship in New York Harbor? That submarine actually existed, and Damian Siekonic recreated it for the AMC series.

Damian's handiwork—minus the submersible—hangs on the wall and sits on shelves. There's a blunderbuss, crossed swords, and a couple of Brown Besses, the muskets fired at American revolutionaries by British soldiers. Brett pointed toward a firearm with an oddly blunted end.

"That's actually a grenade launcher," he said.

SECTION II

The history of Tavern at the Sun Inn:
A rogues' gallery of rebels

Before the Revolutionary War, the Sun Inn occupied a convenient halfway point for travelers journeying from Philadelphia to New York. While revolution raged, the British might occupy one city or the other, but Bethlehem stayed out of English hands.

Stop at the Sun Inn, and you never knew who might be imbibing from the punch bowl at the next table. The guest registry was a veritable rogues' gallery of rebels.

John Adams: The first time John Adams stayed at the Sun Inn, George Washington had recently scored victories at Trenton and Princeton, but that didn't make travel around the colonies any less treacherous. To avoid British-controlled roads on his way to Baltimore in January 1777, Adams zigzagged around Massachusetts, New York, New Jersey, and Pennsylvania before reaching his destination.

Crossing the Delaware River from New Jersey on this trip brought Adams to Bethlehem. He discovered a "curious and remarkable town," with well-tended fields and savvy agricultural planning that meant full bellies year-round. With their waterworks pumping fresh water into town, the Moravians had "carried the mechanical Arts to greater Perfection here than in any Place which I have seen," Adams marveled.

For rooms, Adams was directed to the public house of Mr. Johnson, "which I think was the best Inn, I ever saw." Here at the Sun Inn, "you might find every Accommodation that you could wish for yourself, your servants and Horses, and at no extravagant Rates neither."

Nine months later, Adams returned to the Sun Inn, but in a sour mood. Continental Congress was fleeing Philadelphia for Lancaster, heading west by way of Bethlehem to the north. Delegates convened at that "best Inn," assembling in the great room on the second floor—today's Sun Inn dining room.

With Philadelphia about to fall, Adams spent his time in Bethlehem despairing the lack of "one great soul" to salvage the revolutionary cause. George Washington had missed his chance to "cut to pieces Howe's army" outside of Philadelphia. On the

Hudson River, Gen. Horatio Gates was "playing the same timorous defensive part, which has involved us in so many disasters."

"We have as good a cause as ever was fought for; we have great resources; the people are well tempered; one active, masterly capacity, would bring order out of this confusion, and save this country," he lamented to his journal—and probably to anyone within earshot, from what we know of the obnoxious and disliked Mr. Adams.

While in Bethlehem and the Sun Inn this second time, with the weight of the world on his shoulders, Adams attended church with the Moravians. Men sat with men and women sat with women. He confided to his journal that the women, dressed alike and wearing bonnets, "resembled a garden of white cabbage heads." I like to think of him at the service, shielding his face with a hymnal to conceal a secret smile when the image popped into his worried mind.

Ethan Allen, "abandoned wretch": Brett Biggs likes to note that some of our revolutionary heroes could be jerks (except he didn't use the word "jerk." I'm going with the G-rated version.)

Case in point: Ethan Allen. Patriot. Check. Mistreated prisoner of war. Check. Land speculator and founder of Vermont. Check. Turncoat. Quite possibly.

Ethan Allen started the war in true rabble-rouser fashion. His Green Mountain Boys were already terrorizing the Vermont countryside to defend their land rights, even after a court gave dibs to New Yorkers granted the same territory. Diving into the revolution, Capt. Ethan Allen and his Green Mountain Boys won an early, morale-boosting victory by pounding on the gate at Fort Ticonderoga and announcing to the sleepy commander that they were taking the fort. Then his men got totally drunked up on British rum. But at least they had the fort's cannons.

Taken prisoner in a rash attack on Montreal in 1775, Allen was shipped back to England for execution, but the British kept him alive, fearing reprisal executions of British prisoners in the colonies.

Swapped in a prisoner exchange, he arrived back in America on May 6, 1778. One week later, he was in Bethlehem, stopping at the Sun Inn with Gen. and Mrs. Horatio Gates (that's John Adams' "timorous defensive" general). They were on their way to Peekskill, New York, a strategic Hudson River depot.

Through it all, Vermont was always on Allen's mind. When Continental Congress declined to recognize Vermont as a state, due to still-simmering territorial disputes, Allen looked northward. He and others started negotiating to make Vermont part of Canada, potentially putting the Green Mountain State in the British empire he was warring against.

"I am assured by all that no dependence can be had in him—his character is well-known, and his Followers, or dependents, are a collection of the most abandoned wretches that ever lived, to be found by no Laws or Ties." The writer? The governor of Canada with whom Allen was negotiating.

The negotiations would fail, but Allen did manage to free more than 200 fellow Vermonters from British captivity. His beloved Vermont would act as its own republic until 1791 when Congress finally conferred statehood. Ethan Allen, who died in 1789, would not live to see that day.

Nathanael Greene: South Carolina and Georgia were in dire straits, thoroughly under the British thumb. Going over George Washington's head, Congress sent Gen. Horatio "timorous defensive" Gates to drive out the British. Bad move. When Congress finally asked Washington for help, Washington knew whom to send—his friend Gen. Nathanael Greene, a man defining "competence" in its highest and best meaning.

A Quaker fascinated by military history, Greene worked his way up from private to trusted Washington confidante. In the South, outgunned, outnumbered, outmanned (yes, I just paraphrased "Hamilton"), he moved his forces like chess pieces, needling British Gen. Cornwallis at every turn, only fighting when he could force a confrontation on his terms. Each step drove Cornwallis farther north, on the path leading to Yorktown, Virginia.

Bethlehem must have made an impression on Greene and his wife when they stayed at the Sun Inn in 1778. After the war, two of their daughters were schooled at the Bethlehem Female Seminary, a groundbreaking institution devoted to the Moravian belief that women had minds to cultivate. Greene wouldn't live to see his daughters' schooling. Retiring to a Savannah River farm, after a springtime when he declared "the weather is mild and the vegetable world progressing to perfection," Nathanael Greene died suddenly in June 1786, only three years after his tenacity and making-something-from-nothing strategy helped win freedom from Great Britain.

Three immigrants walk into a bar . . . : America was a melting pot even before the United States of America came into existence. When 13 little colonies had the nerve to stand up to the British empire, adventure seekers and freedom lovers worldwide joined the fun. Some would find their way to the Sun Inn.

With Friedrich Wilhelm August Heinrich Ferdinand Steuben— better known to history as Baron von Steuben—at hand, George Washington could fight fire with fire. If the British Army could march its highly disciplined men into danger, it was time for the Continental Army to do the same. Steuben grew up the son of a military engineer, was a Prussian officer by age 17, and served in Frederick the Great's headquarters in Russia. Out of the army and in need of a job, he put himself in the path of Benjamin Franklin in Paris, who arranged an introduction to George Washington.

At Valley Forge, Steuben had the job of training soldiers. Wearing full dress uniform, he would prowl the lines of ragged soldiers, swearing in French and German. When that didn't work, he hired a translator to swear in English. Steuben implemented a sort of boot camp, training soldiers before they were placed with their units. While the winter of 1777-78 would go down in history for its bitter cold at Valley Forge, Steuben would enjoy a January evening at the Sun Inn.

Casimir Pulaski, exiled from Poland for fighting against Russian rule, found a perfect fit for his insurgent instincts and his military genius in the American rebellion. The trusted aide to George Washington transformed the cavalry into a fighting force. He came to the Sun Inn after the Battle of Brandywine, visiting his convalescing comrade Marquis de Lafayette. Staying again while recruiting cavalry in 1778, he valiantly protected Moravian women from the lascivious desires of rowdy troops, and in gratitude, the women embroidered a silk banner for him.

At least, that's the legend. It could be more along the lines of Pulaski seeing examples of the women's superb design and craftsmanship and ordering a banner for his corps. Although, it's also said that he did place guards at the Single Sisters' House while troops were passing through, which certainly makes sense. In any case, Pulaski was carrying that banner into a fierce charge in Savannah, attempting to rally fleeing French troops, when he was mortally wounded. He would die in this foreign land because America, he once told George Washington, is "where freedom is being defended."

When Marquis de Lafayette was recovering at the home of Bethlehem's farmer-general, people noticed sparks flying between the charming, married convalescent and the prominent farmer's pretty daughter, Liesel Boeckel. But any speculation about Lafayette and his pretty nurse is just that—speculation. Historians only know that Marquis de Lafayette spent two days at the Sun Inn nursing a leg wounded at the Battle of Brandywine in September 1777. He rented the entire top floor—the second-wealthiest man in France could do things like rent one-fourth of a hotel—but by now, much of the town was a hospital for the wounded. Lafayette found the bustling inn, crammed with stinking, sickly, moaning, dying men, a bit distasteful.

He moved down the street to the home of Frederick Boeckel and Boeckel's wife, Barbara, and daughter, Liesel (or Elisabeth. Accounts vary.) Lafayette would read books, claiming interest in an account of Moravian missionaries in Greenland. He would write letters. "Messieurs the English paid me the compliment of wounding me slightly in the leg." He was "in the solitude of Bethlehem," where "the fraternity lead a very agreeable and tranquil life." In the midst of the "typical disputes and discussions found in all armies," he said he was "always even-tempered and easygoing and am happy to be liked by everyone, foreigner or American. I like them all."

But military affairs were never far from his mind. He could hardly walk, but he would fight the detested British by letter. From Bethlehem, he urged French authorities to attack India and the British West Indies. Lafayette, said one correspondent, would happily sell all the furniture in Versailles to support "his American cause."

After four weeks, "agreeable and tranquil" Bethlehem could no longer contain him. Washington was in Montgomery County, rebounding from the loss at Germantown. Lafayette's swollen foot still couldn't fit in a boot, but he mounted a horse and pointed south. Time to get back in the action. The residents of Bethlehem declared him to be "a very intelligent and pleasing young man." As for the Moravian women, "the Marquis could not have failed impressing the sisterhood." Pretty Liesel Boeckel spent the rest of her life as a nurse, dying a spinster around 1831.

Alexander Hamilton: When war broke out in the colonies, a young immigrant from the British West Indies sought military glory, serving as an aide to George Washington and commanding three battalions fighting with French troops to help win at Yorktown. After the war, he put his fertile brain to work on a financial system that opponents argued gave too much power to the federal government. In 1804, he died in a duel, after a derisive comment made its way, via dinner party, to the vice president of the United States.

The eventful life of Alexander Hamilton would wind its way to the Sun Inn in 1791. Hamilton was apparently on a countryside vacation in the midst of fending off claims that he was founding the First Bank of the United States to line his own pockets. "Col. Hamilton has taken a trip to Bethlehem," quipped Thomas Jefferson, the hyperkinetic Hamilton's arch-nemesis, to President Washington. "I think to avail myself also of the present interval of quiet to get rid of a headach which is very troublesome, by giving more exercise to the body & less to the mind."

George Washington: The industrious Moravians of Bethlehem and its sister community in Lititz, Pennsylvania, had big buildings. Gen. George Washington needed them for hospitals. He politely declined requests to put the hospitals elsewhere. "It is ever my wish and aim that the public good be affected with as little sacrifice as possible of individual interests—and I would by no means sanction the imposing any burthens . . . which the public service does not require."

Washington's hospitals brought pestilence, stench, and death to Bethlehem, but apparently, Bethlehem held no grudge. On July 25, 1780, the music-loving town greeted George Washington with the sound of its famous trombone choir. Touring the Single Brethren's House—once commandeered for a hospital but now back to a residence—the general and his party enjoyed refreshments of cake and wine in the chapel while Brother Jacob Van Vleck played the organ. More music in the evening, vocal and instrumental, in sacred selections.

In this summer, Washington was managing a war in the North and the South, but the French had finally presented the Continental Army with 5,000 troops. On this July evening, he retired to the Sun Inn, for a night of rest before resuming his war duties.

"Gen. Washington left for Easton early this morning," wrote a Bethlehem citizen, "and before starting expressed himself as much pleased with the attentions shown him."

In less than 15 months, Gen. Charles Cornwallis would fly the white flag at Yorktown. Six months later, in April 1783,

Washington announced the "Cessation of Hostilities Between the United States of America and the King of Great Britain."

In 1791, President Washington would show that he had taken notice of the gifts that the Moravians of Bethlehem and their other mission towns could offer this young country. "From a society whose governing principles are industry and the love of order much may be expected towards the improvement & prosperity of the country in which their settlements are formed, & experience authorizes the belief that much will be obtained."

Wartime worries: The mood in Bethlehem was grim. Troops camped in fields around the town, destroying fences and trampling the Moravians' carefully tended crops ("22 acres Buckwheat, entirely ruined," read one account). "Low women and thieves" followed in their wake. The director general of Continental Army hospitals, expressing apologies for these "dreadful times," appropriated some of the Moravians' buildings—lodgings for communal living by gender or marital status—as hospitals for the Brandywine wounded.

The Moravians differed among themselves on pacifism versus taking up arms for the revolution, but they united in this time of caring for soldiers. The Single Brethren's House and the Sun Inn would shelter wounded men. Moravian men stayed at the sides of the sick and wounded. Women prepared bandages. Carpenters made coffins and dug graves. Hundreds of soldiers died from typhoid, to be buried along the Monocacy Creek. Many townspeople also perished.

To relieve the overcrowding, army doctors began eying other large buildings, including the Single Sisters' House and the Widows' House. Here, the Moravians blanched. With Continental Congress in town, Moravian administrator the Rev. Mr. John Ettwein saw his chance. He gave a tour of the communal homes to Adams, President of the Congress Henry Laurens, and other delegates. Residents sang and played the organ. These women, Ettwein pleaded, would be bereft and distressed if ejected from their homes.

Back at the Sun Inn, Laurens directed Richard Henry Lee to issue a proclamation. Adams, John Hancock, and the other congressional delegates in Bethlehem concurred. The attention given the sick and wounded by the Moravian Brethren had been "diligent," and the desire to provide relief "benevolent," they decreed.

Therefore, "We desire that all Continental officers may refrain from disturbing the persons or property of the Moravians in

Bethlehem; and particularly, that they do not disturb or molest the houses where the women are assembled."

Fries Rebellion, Part II: When we last left the anti-tax Fries Rebellion, it was 1798, and farmers fueled by rage and alcohol were holding tax assessors hostage in the Quakertown tavern known as Enoch's, now McCoole's at the Historic Red Lion Inn. Adjourning to another tavern, they learned that 19 of their compatriots were being held at the Sun Inn in Bethlehem. The mob marched—or more likely by now, staggered—the 15 miles to Bethlehem.

Some accounts say there were 150 men total. Others say 400. In either case, they way outnumbered the guard of 13 or 14 men under U.S. Marshal William Nichols at the Sun Inn. While Nichols prepared for the onslaught, he set a few prisoners free on bail and told them to report to Philadelphia.

Then he sent a delegation to meet the insurgents at the Bethlehem toll bridge, hoping to talk them into turning back. Fries stood fast. He would leave this town only with the freed prisoners. So he paid the toll, crossed the bridge, and led his men to the Sun Inn.

Let me repeat that. He paid the toll. In the middle of an insurgency. Over taxes. But this whole fight was over the justness of some laws and the unjustness of others. Tolls made sense. They financed the upkeep of the roads and bridges that farmers and merchants and artisans used to transport their goods to market and, apparently, mount occasional raids on federal jails.

At the Sun Inn, the unarmed Fries went inside after telling his men to hold off on any attack unless he was killed. Negotiations dragged on. The atmosphere grew tense. Three especially detested tax and court officials named Stephen Balliett, Jacob Eyerly, and William Henry hardly dared look out a window. Every time they tried, they would see insurgent guns aimed at their heads.

Inside, Fries told Nichols to relinquish the prisoners.

"I cannot give them up willingly, but if you take them by force, I cannot help it," Nichols responded.

Fries got the picture. He told his men to force their way in, firing only if the marshal's men fired first, and then just to blind their foe with smoke. While they barged in, Fries mentioned to Nichols that he couldn't guarantee the safety of Balliett, Eyerly, and Henry.

That was what Nichols needed to hear. He gave up the prisoners to protect the safety of his men, without seeming to cave in to a rebel's demands.

What happened to the insurgents? Did they go back to their homes? Did they hang? Turn back to McCoole's for Part III, when Fries' own dog nearly spells his doom, and John Adams must decide whether the conspirators go free or go to the gallows.

Hughetta Bender: She was a white-haired woman wearing spectator pumps, but she had the rebellious heart of a bewigged Colonial.

In 1971, the outlines of the Sun Inn weren't visible from the street. Years of additions had encased the original structure, nesting doll-like, behind "modernized" exteriors.

"The Sun Inn was really like a beautiful woman who had gained a lot of weight," said Hughetta Bender. "She really was underneath all this stuff, but people didn't recognize her."

The rundown building's owner planned demolition, to make way for shops. The city declined to buy the property. Hughetta Bender heard about the inn's history. She also learned of restoration feasibility studies, long collecting dust. "It's now time for action," she said. So she gathered a gang and created the Sun Inn Preservation Association, which bought the building for $140,000. That was 1971.

"Restoration of the inn," she said the next year, "would make a marvelous Bicentennial birthday present for the city."

She rallied preservationists, the mayor, redevelopment officials, building owners, and business leaders. SIPA raised $2 million, earning the Pennsylvania Historical and Museum Commission director's praise as the state's most aggressive single-purpose preservation group.

They missed the Bicentennial target date, but in 1982, the revived Sun Inn, restoration based on plans still in Moravian archives, was unveiled.

Today, Hughetta's vision seems prophetic—a restaurant where local farmers contributed to Colonial-inspired dishes, and the Sun Inn as "the focal point" along a street filled with specialty shops. "Anyway," she said, "that's my dream."

She had long been involved in community projects, a woman of her time—college-educated and married to a Bethlehem Steel Corp. official, closed out from careers but channeling her talents into paid and unpaid posts. Church leader, Girl Scouts commissioner, director of the county Children's Aid Society. She studied horticulture and once worked as a laboratory technician. During World War II, she headed local Red Cross volunteers.

She knew grief, too. Her first husband died only a year after they married, leaving her with a small daughter. Her second husband died after 35 years of marriage, 10 years before she and the Sun Inn found each other.

As initial contributions for restoration started pouring in, she seemed confident. "It certainly looks as if we're well on our way," she said. When the job was done, Bethlehem thanked her with plaques and certificates and putting her in the lead car as grand marshal of the Halloween parade.

"You can be sure of this," opined the Allentown *Morning Call* after Hughetta's death in 1995 at age 89. "If Hughetta Bender had not come to Bethlehem, the Sun Inn—the 1758 stagecoach stop that is a centerpiece of the city's charm today—would be gone." Her legacy "serves as proof that an ordinary, dedicated citizen can mobilize a community and make a difference." She made people care, and she "raised money, lots of money" to restore the inn. "Along the way, she built bridges between groups who were not accustomed to working together. She navigated among Bethlehem's egos and personalities and made them her supporters, even got them to open their pocketbooks, and always did it with a smile."

SECTION III

Touch history

The Sun Inn's unique composition of first-floor historic site and second-floor dining rooms offers a rare glimpse into 18th-century tavern life, untrammeled by the 21st century.

The tavern experience: Step into the main hallway, and the innkeeper greets you from his desk. To the left, a fire beckons in the "*gast-stube*," or gathering place. Someone might be playing the harpsichord. The grandfather clock chiming the hour was made here in Bethlehem.

You follow the tempting aromas to the kitchen down the hall, for a

Gast-stube Lafayette recuperating chair

The walk-in fireplace in the kitchen

Suite at the Sun Inn

peek at what's on the menu. The innkeeper's wife, careful to keep her skirt from going up in flames, is tending several dishes cooking over small coal fires in the walk-in fireplace. Toward the rear of the room, a butcher might be cleaning wild game or fish, for a true catch-of-the-day special. You might marvel at the innovation of an inn with running water, pumped from the Monocacy Creek to a holding tank and gravity-fed here through hollowed logs.

After your meal and presumably a punch or rattleskull concoction, you find your sleeping space. If your budget is tight, you sleep on the top floor. Four beds each in four rooms, four people per bed, sleeping head-foot-head-foot. Top occupancy, that's 54 men, probably quite smelly and packed like sardines.

If you're more high-toned, you get one of the Sun Inn's four suites, and what a revelation this is. No other inn in the colonies, not even in Williamsburg, offers such luxury. A living room with fireplace connects to two bedrooms. A servant assigned by the innkeeper keeps the fire burning, brings your food, and empties the "necessary chair" pot. Life among the Colonial elite certainly has its privileges.

Sun Inn "bar and grill": When an original guest of the Sun Inn enjoyed a drink, it might have been served from the bar in the great room. Which means that Continental Congress met in a room with a bar. Handy.

This bar tucks into a corner, just like City Tavern's. It features a drop-down grill, to keep liquor safe from theft and riot, just like City Tavern's. Coincidence? Actually, Brett Biggs told me, City Tavern's rebuilders modeled their bar after this one, here in the prestigious Bethlehem inn that predated the original City Tavern by 17 years.

Any ghosts? Old buildings creak and moan, Brett believes. He has never had any ghostly encounters. Unless. . . There was the time he lost a pair of prescription sunglasses. Looked everywhere. Waited a month before finally ordering a new pair. He went to pick them up and then drove straight to the Sun Inn.

"I walk in the front door, and they're sitting on the innkeeper's desk," he said. "I asked everyone. Nobody saw them. Nobody put them there."

Ghost hunters say a little girl named Sarah hangs out in the attic. One paranormal team claims to have snapped a photo of a white-haired woman, just like preservationist Hughetta Bender, wearing a white apron, just like Hughetta. Spooky. Then again,

Bar and grill

a debunking ghost hunter insisted the image of the woman in a window was "simply a distorted reflection of a fireplace which sticks out from the wall."

The food scene: In the Sun Inn's earliest days, visitors "showed up and ate what they had, which might have been the stew of the night, or somebody shot a deer, and they had roasted venison," said Brett Biggs. Essentially, it was farm to table out of necessity, not choice.

Today, Tavern at the Sun Inn offers the best of both worlds. Choose from about nine small plates, and four or five entrees. A "small plate" can be as simple as the Goundie Soup of white cheddar, muenster, and Sun Inn Ale, or as substantial as the Rebel Burger of certified Angus beef, white cheddar, arugula red onion, smoked ketchup, and house spicy pickles. Pass around the Innkeeper Meal of homemade bread, pickle jar, grainy mustard, dried fruit, and cheese. Craving a classic pork chop, filet mignon, or Atlantic salmon? Those are the large plates, along with Gruenewald's mac and cheese making its way here as Jefferson's Mac of parmesan béchamel and seasonal vegetables, with optional chicken or shrimp.

The Lafayette

In short, you won't go hungry. More than that. You will leave filled up on excellent food. The selection isn't 30 pages of sports-bar wings and wraps, but each choice is tempting. Mix and match, or go the traditional route with salad and entree.

I tried: The Lafayette. My bartender, Pat Quinn, recommended it, and it was the right call. Maybe it was the Gruyere horserad-ish cream. Maybe it was the tarragon butter. Maybe it was the perfectly cooked sliced roasted beef, all served on a crispy-chewy roll. Every bite was a delight. Tangy. Tender. Soul-satisfying.

The beverage scene: The drinks here "fit the space," said Brett. Try a Lost Colony wine or a Moravian Mule, a lighter take on the Moscow version. Ales of the Revolution are so popular that Tavern at the Sun Inn might be the second-biggest purveyor of the Yards' special brews honoring the Founding Fathers, behind only City Tavern.

Not that a mere name is enough to win shelf space. Selections are carefully curated. The handful of Pennsylvania wines on the menu made the cut from about 80 sampled. The cocktails are mod-ern takes on Colonial recipes or themes. The Fish House Punch was inspired by a 1732 recipe from Philadelphia's Schuylkill

The bartender, Pat Quinn, serving a General Galvez drink

Fishing Club, also known as "the Fish House," blending dark rum, cognac, peach brandy, lemon juice, and freshly brewed tea.

"It's quite good," said Brett. "The original version is powerful. We do tone it down a little bit, because otherwise, it's like drinking straight liquor with a little bit of tea in it. It'll do some damage if it's not served properly."

The dry ciders were produced nearby at Blackledge Winery, a research winery producing small batches of wines, ciders, and meads using documented traditional methods. Eliza's 1728 cider is based on a recipe from "The Compleat Housewife," published by Eliza Smith, "who was kind of the Betty Crocker of the day," in Brett's description. The Blackledge Winery proprietor is Damian Siekonic, the reproduction-weapons maker. At the time of my visit, a Sun Inn cider was finishing in a barrel in the basement of Damian's early-1700s stone farmhouse.

"He does not produce for the sake of production, and we happen to be a benefactor," Brett said.

I tried: The General Galvez, a concoction of Bluecoat Gin, St. Germain, lemon and lime juice, and shaved Fresno chili. The garnish comprised two of the tiniest chili slices I've ever seen. If chilis can be adorable, these did it. As for the drink—crisp, spicy, lively but smooth. If I weren't driving, I'd have had two.

PLAN YOUR VISIT

Tavern at the Sun Inn
564 Main Street
Bethlehem, PA 18018
www.suninnbethlehem.org/tavern, (610) 419-8600

WHAT'S NEARBY

Historic Bethlehem: Downtown Bethlehem is a history lover's walkable paradise. Every aspect of Moravian life is here, spotlighting a self-contained commune where men and women shared equal rights and were equally educated, everyone received health care, and different races and ethnicities lived in harmony. At the Colonial Industrial Quarter, still-standing buildings like the tannery and mill combine with ruins of the pottery and butchery houses to provide vivid images of a thriving commercial corridor. The Moravian Museum of Bethlehem was the Gemeinhaus, or community house, where the original 80 members lived, worshipped, and learned under one roof. At the Goundie House, pay homage to Moravian town brewer and businessman John Sebastian Goundie, and to the two indomitable women, Mrs. Ivor Sims and Mrs. Edmund Martin, who sat on the front stoop on a day in the 1970s and stopped the wrecking ball from its dirty job. (www.historicbethlehem.org)

Stay the night: From simple and cheery to grandiose and breathtaking, the rooms of the Sayre Mansion fit every taste. Built in the heart of town by a railroad executive, the spectacular mansion's showcase room is the glass-roofed conservatory (www.sayremansion.com). For that grand hotel experience, stay at the beautifully restored Hotel Bethlehem, a lavish testament to the towering power of 20th-century steel. (www.hotelbethlehem.com)

6.

THE JEAN BONNET TAVERN

Bedford, Pennsylvania

Hotbed of the Whiskey Rebellion

Misbehavior makes history: The Jean Bonnet Tavern

■ In the hardscrabble world of western Pennsylvania, whiskey ruled daily life—a comfort to the soul, and legal currency in all sorts of trading. At the Jean Bonnet Tavern, Scots-Irish farmers plotted to defy an unconscionable tax on their livelihood.

■ Pirates! No, not plundering the Juniata River. But original tavernkeeper Jean Bonnet just might have had pirates of the Caribbean blood in him, via an uncle hanged by Blackbeard.

■ Speaking of hanging, the Bonnet Tavern's stairwells, ceiling beams, and porch rails were handy for dispensing swift frontier justice to spies, highway robbers, and horse thieves.

■ The stone home was built by trader, George Washington scout, and all-around scalawag Robert Callender.

■ Today's scene: A popular hangout for locals and a haven for time-traveling motorists craving good food and friendly service amid rustic style.

Built: Circa 1762

Meet the owner

It was a Saturday night. Busy, as usual. Brandon Callihan was then-manager of the Jean Bonnet Tavern. He and co-owner Shannon Jacobs were working the bar when Shannon asked a casual question.

"Why don't you just buy this place so I don't have to do this anymore?"

Jean Bonnet exterior

Brandon swears that he had never given it much thought. "Maybe in the back of my mind," he admitted, "but it was too big of a venture."

That question set a process in motion, and on June 8, 2017, Brandon Callihan took ownership of the Jean Bonnet Tavern. Veer off the Pennsylvania Turnpike, and you'll find one of Pennsylvania's most famous establishments.

The morning I arrived, stools were still upturned on the bar and high-top tables. Steph Brumbaugh was behind the bar, getting ready for the day. Before she went to hunt down Brandon in this sprawling complex of bar, dining room, patio, porches, inn, and gift shop, she offered me a cup of coffee. I was a weary traveler from the Turnpike, myself. That offer made her an angel from heaven.

Brandon arrived, a bearded young man with red hair and an open countenance. His story is one I've heard before but never ceases to amaze me—the local who trains at the highest levels, works at bigtime places, and realizes that there's no place like home to park his talents.

He worked at the Jean Bonnet (French pronunciation, please— Zhawn Boh-*nay*) before leaving for college. Graduated from the

Owner of the Jean Bonnet Tavern Brandon Callihan

Culinary Institute of America in 2007. Worked in a big resort but "didn't care for it." Came back here to work the kitchen before rising to manager, a role he held for many years. "We always laugh that people work here three or four times and keep coming back," Brandon told me as we sat in a booth. "I worked here three times before I ended up buying the place. I think it has a draw."

It's easy to see why. The staff is cheerful, appreciative, and helpful to each other. The atmosphere is efficient but not pressured. The place has calmed down a bit since rebels defied the federal government's authority to tax their whiskey, and the days when a man was hanged in the stairwell, but the stone walls still seem to aspirate the tumultuous history they witnessed.

As we talked, Steph and a maintenance man walked past, laughing.

"Those two are probably picking on me," Brandon said.

"No!" Steph insisted. "Never!"

I took her side. After all, she gave me coffee. "Steph? Never!"

So when Brandon bought the place, the paperwork part he thought would take six months actually took one year, but time was on his side. The Jean Bonnet had already been restored in the 1980s by owner Mark Baer and then polished up by Shannon Jacobs and his wife Melissa in the 2000s. Brandon didn't have the months or years of renovations that other tavern buyers endure. When he came in as the owner, "we didn't change anything."

"Nothing," he said. "Everything stayed exactly the same. We kept all the same crew. All the same managers. The only thing that changed was the name on the top of the paychecks."

One year later, some regulars still didn't know about the ownership change. Brandon is happier to put the restaurant front and center than himself. When the local Chamber of Commerce wanted to make a big splash about the change, Brandon answered in two words.

"Absolutely not. You change ownership, everybody thinks, 'We better not go. We better be leery.' I'm not the kind of person who cares. We kept it quiet. Now most people know, but we kind of proved it by not changing anything."

The Jean Bonnet is "a bigger business than most people think," Brandon said. Changing ownership hands meant transferring the books on 92 employees, about half of them full-time. "It's deceiving. On a busy Saturday night in the summertime, there's probably 50 working at one time, when you add all your servers, your bartenders, your hostess, your busers, your cooks, your dishwashers, the Cabin Shoppe employees, the managers."

That corps can feed a multitude. With 300 guests possible to be seated at once, on the porches and patio, and upstairs and downstairs dining rooms, it's "kind of common for us to do 700, 800 people on a Saturday in the summertime," Brandon said. "Then it gets fun."

If that's your idea of fun. For Brandon, it really is. He has appreciated the "old-restaurant business" since he was young. Likes to eat, too, and here in Bedford, Pennsylvania, the dining choices have skyrocketed. Local pubs and restaurants "find they can be busy and serve good food."

Best of all, they don't fight. There's no "city atmosphere" here.

"We all work together, as a small town. There's no competition," Brandon said. "There are more people wanting to eat in Bedford than there are restaurants, so there's no sense being harsh about it. We all work together. Another restaurant ran out of printer paper. They grabbed a couple rolls from us. A couple days later, their order came in, and they brought it back. We could have said, 'No way, you're on your own,' but we said, 'We got a whole boxful. Come on in.'"

You would think, I said, with the pie being smaller in this area, that the opposite would be true, as if restaurants and inns would be fighting each other.

Nope, Brandon said. "There's plenty of business in the area, so we all work together."

A tour of the Jean Bonnet Tavern

Rugged, remote, and beautiful. Bedford County, Pennsylvania, marked the frontier of 18th century America. In 1758, British military engineers carved a road through the wilderness under the direction of Gen. John Forbes—the only road connecting Eastern Pennsylvania to the Ohio River and the riches of the vast western lands. The road, called "the turnpike" by locals, intersected with a slightly earlier road built along Native American trails.

That juncture was a good spot for Native Americans to establish a trading post, selling goods to the pioneers and drovers surging westward. Around 1762, an Indian trader named Robert Callender built more than a home here. He built a statement— four stories in stone, with 10 fireplaces, the entire house framed in chestnut timbers the same massive size from basement to roof.

The building today, tucked in a hollow at the intersection of Routes 30 and 31, probably looks much like it did in 1780 when a new owner named John Bonnet saw the site's potential and petitioned for a tavern license. He signed his name in the form of his native French—Jean Bonnet.

The tavern: A wide porch leads to the front door, with its farmhouse door handle. To the left, a cozy room with a fireplace offers a spot for quiet, even furtive, conversations. You are drawn, though, to the right, to the tavern. A long bar anchors the interior wall. Tall-backed booths line the walls. Pub tables fill the space between the bar and two fireplaces in brick and stone.

The Bonnet's early guests had to be hardy folks. Drovers herding sheep and cattle stopped here, drinking and fighting and robbing. For the more genteel "carriage trade," the first stagecoach from Philadelphia to Pittsburgh in 1804 took seven grueling days. Coach drivers passing on the turnpike, one pointing west and one pointing east, greeted each other by sounding their horns.

Outside porch of the Jean Bonnet Tavern

Approaching the Bonnet Tavern, as it was called in Jean's day, all those travelers on horseback, foot, or coach had to forge the Juniata River. No bridges or ferries existed to carry them across, so some arrived wet and ready for a drink by the fire.

While standing by the fireplaces, look upward to find the beam carved with a carefully arranged slot and hole. Just right for looping a rope through. You know—the kind that ended around a man's neck. Or so they say.

"The rumor is that the tavern was one of the only public structures around, so if they thought you were guilty of something, they pulled you in here and had a trial," said Brandon. "You were guilty, and that was it. You were hung. There was no waiting, no process, no appeal. They used to do it outside if it was nice, out off the porches, and inside if it wasn't nice."

Tavern fireplaces

How Jean Bonnet felt about the rough justice delivered here isn't known, but he was no stranger to hardship and the necessity of survival. His descendants told Brandon that the voyage to the colonies was so harsh that four Bonnet siblings died. Only Jean and a sister remained.

Another tale says that Bonnet's uncle was a Caribbean sugarcane farmer who "basically couldn't stand his wife. Drove him nuts." Compounding his misery, his ships carrying sugarcane to Europe were repeatedly plundered of their lucrative treasure.

"So he bought a ship and became a pirate and was hung by Blackbeard," Brandon said. "Supposedly. The family told me the story that his uncle became a pirate."

The hanging in the stairwell: When you pass the stairway in the main hall, take time to pause and reflect on the fragility of life.

"Don't hang me," says a voice. "I'm not ready."

Well, ghost hunters say they hear that repeated plea. The legend of the stairwell hanging is one of the Jean Bonnet's most persistent, although the details differ from one telling to the next:

■ Gen. Forbes, building his road in 1758, discovered a spy in his midst. The man was quickly tried, found guilty, and hanged.

Hmmm. It's not known exactly when this home was built, but 1758 was a full four years before it's known that a building was here.

■ Highway robbery was a real and pervasive threat. One robber caught by the townspeople was brought here since taverns often doubled as courthouses. Trial. Guilty. Hanged in the stairwell.

■ And my favorite told to me by my husband's cousin, a native of the area. A white man burst into the inn. "I'm being chased by Indians!" he yelled. The patrons provided shelter, but when the pursuing Native Americans arrived, they said they were giving chase because the man stole their horses. Trial. Guilty. Hanged in the stairwell.

The stairs stop at the first floor, and you don't see them winding their way above, so you might wonder about the efficacy of hanging a man here, but consider two renovations. Somewhere in the mists of time, someone walled in the stairs on the upper floors. It was once one open stairway all the way to the top. Plus, the stairs originally descended into the basement, home of today's dining room. Tie a rope around an upper stair rail, slip a noose around a man's neck, give him a push, and justice is served, perhaps.

The basement, and its body: Enter from outside or down the curving stairs from the tavern, and step into an atmospheric sanctuary in stone and brick and tile. This is the Jean Bonnet basement dining room, a cozy haven that invites conversation, laughter, and maybe a chill up the spine.

I happen to be a connoisseur of fine chairs, and I noticed that the chairs down here are in the distinctive Bedford County style of hickory slats shaped into seating. Since my husband's family comes from this area, we have a hickory rocker that's remarkably comfortable for an all-wood chair.

"They've been here for a long time," Brandon agreed. "They take a beating, and they're always fine. Once in a while, I have to tighten up a nail. The chairs upstairs, they're breaking all the time. But these are tough."

Let's hear it for craftsmanship. The day I visited was also the debut of the dining room foyer's winter decorations. Décor here is a family affair, led by Brandon's mother, Christine Callihan, who adorns the rooms with a natural, elegant touch. The tavern Christmas tree was trimmed in early American fashion of oranges spiked with fragrant cloves. The foyer features a stand of tree branches cut from the property, strung with lights, and adorned according to the season—evergreen needles, pine cones, and ornamental snowy owls for winter.

Brandon and I stepped into the back area of the dining room, where the hangman's stairs once came down. Those chestnut beams are so close here that you can see the hacks made by each swing of an ax. Brandon pointed out that they "look wet all the time, but if you touch them, they're bone dry."

Eww. He was right, though. They glisten but are dry to the touch.

The floor we're standing on was once dirt. In the 1950s or so, an owner dug down to create more headroom. Three guesses what they found.

"They found a skeleton down here, and he had a bullet hole in his head," Brandon told me. "There wasn't much left of him."

The buckles from the clothing seemed to indicate that the body was quite old, but a buried body with a hole in the head got the coroner's attention. An investigation was done, just in case of modern-day foul play, "but nothing came of it. He just got shot in the head and was buried inside."

The mystery of his identity lingers. "Who?" wondered one old history. "White man or Indian, outlaw or farmer." Outside the tavern, that same history notes, farmers plowing the fields occasionally unearthed skeletons bearing signs of broken necks.

When you think about it, the Jean Bonnet can get rather gruesome.

Porches and patio and goats: The mountains are in full greenery. Flowers are blooming, and the air is fresh. The lure is irresistible. Warm weather brings visitors flocking to the Jean Bonnet for alfresco dining on porch and patio. A February warm spell puts people in a Jean Bonnet mood, and even snow "doesn't bother us," Brandon told me. "Bring on a snowstorm, and we're real busy."

Heck, yes. Nothing better than a tavern on a snowy day.

The Jean Bonnet grounds remain welcoming to locals and travelers seeking respite. Outside, find a bench and take a breather from the grind of the road. Walk around and explore the herb garden, or stop to pet the goats. They're in a pen beside the parking lot. Kids love them. They eat vegetable scraps from the kitchen and pretty much anything else visitors want to share.

"One guy stops at midnight every night on his way home from work and gives them his banana peels," Brandon said. "They love it. People love them, for some reason."

Jean Bonnet goats

About that "for some reason." On my visits, the three resident goats included a large 15-year-old—quite elderly for a goat, I'm told—who's a real sweetheart when you're on your side of the fence. But those who step through the gate, into his turf, get a dose of ornery.

"It's deceiving," Brandon said. "For as old as he is, he's quite agile."

The other two, gentler souls were once exhibited at fairs. They came here because their owner's daughter couldn't bear to see them go to a butcher. She is among those who regularly stop to visit.

SECTION II

The history of the Jean Bonnet Tavern:
Rebels and rogues welcome

Hold a mirror to the Jean Bonnet Tavern, and the reflection shows the perilous, cutthroat life of America's first western frontier.

Robert Callender, patriotic scoundrel: March 1765. Eighty-one horses set out from a tavern in what is now Greencastle, Pennsylvania, bound for Illinois. Some horses carried shirts—innocuous items for sale and trade in the vast frontier. Others concealed deadlier goods. Selling tomahawks, gunpowder, and scalping knives to Indians was illegal, for fear that white settlers would find themselves on the receiving end, but contraband meant big money for unscrupulous traders.

Britain's Deputy Superintendent of Indian Affairs George Croghan headed this scheme. Croghan bought the goods, including barrels of illicit rum, and sold them back to his employer, the British Indian Department, at inflated prices. He and three partners, including Pennsylvania Regiment Lt. Robert Callender, would each skim 25 percent shares.

The pack train wound through Pennsylvania's mountainous frontier, where Scots-Irish settlers, living on land stolen from Native Americans, were under attack. The prospect of slaughter and kidnapping was so real that many taverns were built, not with stairs, but with ladders that could be hoisted through weighted trap doors, turning upper levels into escape rooms.

At present-day McConnellsburg, about 38 miles from Callender's stone manse in Bedford, 50 angry frontiersmen demanded that Croghan's caravan yield its murderous goods. The charismatic Callender, with full military bearing, chastised the rebels. Look for yourselves, he said, directing them to the 2,200 shirts concealing the contraband. Most of the attackers were appeased until a cask of scalping knives fell and shattered open.

The next day, as the pack train neared Sideling Hill, shots rang out. Four horses were killed. The drivers scattered. The armed rebels who would come to be known as the Black Boys, for blacking their faces to elude identification, torched 63 loads of contraband, including the knives and such, but not the rum, which they kept for themselves.

This was the opening of Smith's Rebellion, an outburst considered the first armed uprising by Colonials against the British. Callender sought reimbursement for his losses—pretty cheeky, given that the excursion was illegal—and frustrated superiors with his ever-changing story about the Sideling Hill affair.

The Irish-born, well-connected Callender had a habit of seeking outsized compensation for losses. He once claimed that Indian theft of his goods cost him £8,100—a mere $932,650 to us. Decent society frowned on his deftness at getting permission to peddle rum to Native Americans, but they were happy to earn money from his commissions to make, say, 150 liquor kegs.

For two decades, the wily Callender constantly reinvented himself along the political, ethnic, and religious fault lines driving frontier turbulence. From fur trader, to Indian fighter, to Forbes' wagon master general, and back to trader, he remained open to the idea of a profitable scheme.

In a letter dated 20 October 1755, Callender read, "Mr Gist being appointed Captain of a Company of Scouts, and informing me that you had a mind to engage in our Service—I thought it expedient to acquaint you, that if you can assist him in Recruiting some likely young Fellows, acquainted with the woods, that you will meet with proper Encouragement for so doing; either by receiving a post among us, or full Satisfaction for your trouble. I am &c. G:W.

G:W. was George Washington, commander of the seething western campaign as British, French, and Native Americans vied for control of the Ohio Valley. Callender supplied victuals for the troops, operated mills, and may have acted as a scout for Washington.

The "full Satisfaction" for his troubles? Transfer of 690 acres in Bedford County, originally deeded from William Penn through— surprise!—land agent George Croghan. Then as now, cronyism had its rewards.

Let's simply think of Callender as colorful and charismatic, a natural-born leader who saw no conflict in turning a healthy profit for his troubles. He was a founder of Pennsylvania's Carlisle Borough, a Patriot who saw Revolutionary War service before his death in 1776, and member of a Committee of Observation, one of the local bodies that wrested oversight of the colonies from the British government.

Hollywood would immortalize his scoundrel side as villainous Indian trader Ralph Callendar in 1939's "Allegheny Uprising," pitted against our hero John Wayne, playing the Smith's Rebellion leader who fought to keep guns from the hands of Native Americans.

One person, at least, pined for the real Robert Callender. At his stone home in Bedford County—one of several Callender dwellings—legend has it that his mistress waited, expecting he would return and marry her. It's said that she still wanders the Jean Bonnet Tavern, yearning through eternity for her charming, charlatan lover.

The Whiskey Rebellion: Imagine living in one of the most beautiful but rugged places known. Your family subsists on cornmeal, hominy, pork, a few vegetables, and the deer or squirrel you hunted yesterday.

The mountains and valleys outside your home are abundant with grain and meat. Just swing an ax for lumber. But there's no money to be made because you can't justify the cost of moving heavy commodities over the mountains to eastern markets.

Unless . . .

Maybe that grain can be distilled into something more portable, and—shall we say?—potable. "A horse could carry but four bushels," wrote an insightful Colonial, "but he could take the produce of 24 bushels in the shape of alcohol."

In the barely accessible mountains of western Pennsylvania, whiskey was a beverage, and it was legal tender. Constables, jurors, and ministers were paid in whiskey. When an innkeeper—at the Bonnet Tavern, let's say—heard the horn announcing the stagecoach, he would set 'em up, 3 cents a shot.

By 1790, the U.S. government needed mounds of money to pay off war debts. Excise taxes on liquor had failed before for lack of compliance, but western Pennsylvania, where every fifth or sixth farm housed a liquor still, offered fertile revenue grounds.

For two years, the law was basically ignored, but grievances mounted. Treasury Secretary Alexander Hamilton devised the taxing scheme, and wasn't he profiteering in bonds to pay off the very debts the tax was supposed to relieve? Why didn't the government tax land, so that speculators, as well as farmers, paid their fair shares? Where was the liberty these veterans of the Revolution had fought to win?

"Why," one canny petitioner asked, "should we be made subject to a duty for drinking our grain more than eating it(?)"

Grievances turned to action around 1793. The hardboiled chief of excise collections, Gen. John Neville, was burned in effigy. Armed gangs broke into the homes of tax collectors, terrorizing women and children. One collector was tarred and feathered, made to promise never to collect the tax again, and tied to a tree, naked. And the rebels tore down part of his house. Witnesses against the insurgents found their barns burned. So did distillers who dared to comply with the law.

The rebellion erupted on July 14, 1794, when Neville and a U.S. marshal appeared at the door of a distant Neville relative named William Miller. Refusing to pay the levy, Miller felt his blood boil at the prospect of going all the way to Philadelphia to defend himself in federal court.

Another 30 or 40 other drunken men, also boiling mad, arrived waving pitchforks and muskets. A rumor spread to a nearby militia that Neville was taking prisoners to Philadelphia. The militia set siege to Neville's home, quickly growing to 500 insurgents—many of them military veterans—fighting a small force of soldiers summoned from Pittsburgh. Inside, women lying on the floor loaded weapons. Neville's slaves were said to join in the firing against the attackers.

The skirmish gave the frenzied insurgents a martyr—beloved militia leader James McFarlane, shot and killed in the fighting.

Two weeks later, 500 angry men descended on the Bonnet Tavern. George Washington, they heard, was calling up soldiers. Maybe it was the liquor, but the prospect of their 500 against Washington's 13,000 didn't put the fear of God in them. Washington's "Watermelon Army" of mostly New Jersey soldiers couldn't frighten these "Whiskey Boys."

The Whiskey Boys erected a liberty pole at the Bonnet. "Liberty and No Excise," proclaimed a banner. In this rebellion, liberty poles sent the same message they sent before the American Revolution: We will no longer be governed by this government.

Plus, this pole sent another message to Philadelphia. Tavernkeeper Jean Bonnet was not only a Whiskey Rebellion supporter. He was French. In post-Revolutionary America, some fondly remembered France's help defeating the British and pined for all things French, including the blood-drenched revolution still slicing through France. The Federalist establishment was aghast, believing that French officials were manufacturing a rebellion—such as one over, say, taxes on whiskey—to replace the unfavorable U.S. government with one friendlier to the French revolutionaries.

A few days later, the 500 poor farmers grew to 7,000 insurrectionists. Taking the lead was a bombastic figure named David Bradford. "Some thought him a second-rate lawyer," wrote one historian. "Others disagreed. They said he was third-rate."

The rebels marched into Pittsburgh but didn't deliver on their threat to burn the city. They burned only one home, having been calmed by more moderate leaders than Bradford, who "thought it safest to give good words and good drink, rather than balls and powder."

President Washington and his allies believed the validity of the U.S. Constitution was at stake. If the republic were to stand, a minority could not simply refuse to comply with a duly-passed law. As a Pittsburgh judge put it, "If one law is repealed at the call of armed men, government is destroyed; no law will have any force."

Liberty poles were rising in Pennsylvania and Maryland. In the Bedford town square, about 300 men—half the number of men ages 18 to 53 from surrounding townships—erected a liberty pole, while the local sheriff conveniently ignored the rowdiness.

Of course, the sheriff happened to be a tall, strong man named Jacob Bonnet, son of Jean. Love of *liberté* ran in the family.

From Philadelphia, Washington did something that no president in U.S. history would ever do again—lead troops into the field (unless you count Bill Pullman in "Independence Day"). David Bradford, fond of riding a white horse and wearing gaudy military trappings, scoffed. "We will defeat the first army that comes over the mountains and take their arms and baggage," he said.

But as historian Leland Baldwin wrote, "had there been a competent leader to take the helm it is within the realm of possibility that the current of American history would have been changed." The "children of the backwoods" harbored "vast potentialities of destruction," but they were rudderless. They knew they had no chance against a fully equipped army that stretched a full mile on the march.

Plus, the sight of Washington's army occupying the ground where it all started, camping around the Bonnet Tavern, must have been disheartening. The Whiskey Rebellion fizzled. Washington left Bedford on October 21, 1794, assigning the task of rounding up the rebels to none other than the despised Alexander Hamilton.

Dragoons galloped through the countryside, injudicious in their hunt for liberty pole erectors. In Carlisle, a sick boy was shot and killed. In Myerstown, a drunk in a tavern blurted to a group of soldiers, "Huzzah for the Whiskey Boys!" Resisting as he was hauled away, he was stabbed by a bayonet. With his last breath, he gasped, "Success to the Whiskey Boys."

Prisoners were marched to Philadelphia, so wretched-looking by arrival that even the chief of excise collection's son "could not help being sorry for them." I don't know if Jean Bonnet was among them, but I doubt it. He was a prominent man, with a sheriff for a son. Their less fortunate compatriots were paraded through the streets of Philadelphia before a cheering throng, past a pleased-looking Washington, while the bells of Christ Church pealed.

The rebels languished in jail for six months or so. All but two were acquitted.

Dan Morgan, a "big-chested and bull-necked" ally of George Washington had, before the Revolution, withstood 499 lashes for striking a British officer. As a major general of the Virginia militia, he rallied the troops for a crucial victory at Saratoga. For the Whiskey Rebellion, he joined his commander for one last campaign, probably missing the irony of the onetime rebels stamping out a rebellion. Even though he didn't mean it as a compliment, he gave the Whiskey Rebellion its epitaph.

"Patriotism is ever in their mouths," he said of Whiskey Boys, "while the spirit of the incendiary actuates their hearts."

SECTION III

Touch history

If the Jean Bonnet Tavern walls could talk, the tales they could tell would be blood-curdling.

Twin fireplaces: In the tavern, two distinct fireplaces hunker side by side on the back wall. No one knows why, especially since the larger of the two doesn't share a chimney or flue with the fireplace below, which was against common practice and would have made it pretty costly to build. One fireplace is what you'd expect in a 250-year-old tavern, a low, humble collection of bricks and stone.

Next to it, like a showy neighbor, is the taller fireplace with brick lintel and, inexplicably, an asymmetrical arch of stones laid vertically into the wall above.

"That wouldn't have been an original fireplace," said Brandon. "It would never have been that high." The arch, the only one known in the building, was probably the stonemason's signature.

The mysterious arrangement put Brandon into a quandary for his first Christmas as owner. Where do they put the Christmas tree?

"Do we put it in the middle of the wall, or in the middle of the arch?" he said. "Or in the middle of the fireplace? It's going to drive me nuts because one way or the other, it's not going to be centered." He settled on a corner by the stairs to the basement.

Basement hearth: The basement focal point is its fireplace. Now this, you think, is a colonial hearth. Almost tall enough to

Basement fireplace

Basement dining room

stand in. Real logs burn on the brick base. An iron hanging rod holds a lidded pot.

"Back in the day, this was the tavern kitchen, with the big cooking fireplace," said Brandon. He marvels at a neat warm-weather trick it does. The chimney goes straight to the roof—no upper floor fireplaces to break the line. On summer days around 11 a.m., sunlight streams straight down from overhead and puddles on the brick hearth.

"It's like Stonehenge!" I said.

"It's perfectly over the chimney, and it's a straight shot down through," Brandon confirmed.

Heavy stones and curved ceilings: "I'll show you something neat," Brandon said. "I just noticed it the other day when we were putting up Christmas decorations."

Constant discovery is one of the joys of old buildings, compensating for the crooked stairs and cranky plumbing and crazy extension-cord configurations. Brandon and I stepped onto the second-floor porch. There over the door, stretched amid the fieldstone, was a lintel in one, long piece of stone.

"The way this building is built just blows my mind," said Brandon. "Look how big that stone is. That's one stone across the top. That's like six feet long." Same story at every door along the porch, these sweet balconies going with every room.

Someone hoisted these up here, I marveled.

"If you look at the whole building, it's the same all the way up to the top," he said. "The feat to build this building is just amazing."

This is also the place to see the Jean Bonnet's famous curved porch ceilings. Why they were built that way is yet another mystery, but the effect is otherworldly. Step onto the balcony with your morning coffee in hand, and the ceiling arching overhead wraps you in a protective cocoon.

Washington slept here? In the two-room Suite 4, Brandon said there's no way to prove it, "but we think Washington could have stayed in this room while his troops were here."

"The theory is that the front room was like an office area for him. When his troops camped on the property, he would have been inside. He was on the property, so it made sense that he would have stayed inside."

Certainly not implausible. Whenever an inn was convenient, that was where Washington slept. Plus, Brandon said, "it was a bar, and he loved beer. He made his own beer. This would have been his suite. This would have been more his taste."

The Cabin Shoppe: The Cabin Shoppe gift shop, managed by Brandon's sister, Shana Kauffman, is an experience in it-self—an 18th-century, two-story (note the compact stairs in the corner), log farmhouse transported here from Fayette County, Pennsylvania, in 2006. A fire burns under a stone mantel carved in rough fashion, "R.C. 62." The irresistible selection of tasteful, carefully curated merchandise includes kaleidoscopes, pottery, pewter and ceramic dishware, jewelry, soaps and scrubs, books on local history, and Jean Bonnet Tavern coffee mugs and pint glasses.

Any ghosts? Without being asked, Brandon said he doesn't "particularly believe" in ghosts.

"And I try not to," he added as we stood in the dining room, "but a lot of things happened that I can't explain."

So, a brief tour of the Jean Bonnet Tavern ether-verse:

■ The guest in Suite 4—the maybe-Washington's room—who woke on Halloween morning to the smell of oranges. "There are no oranges in my room," she wrote in the guestbook.

■ A new staffer approaching Brandon suddenly did a double-take that he knows well. Did she see a gray, hazy thing moving across the floor? Well, yes. "Oh, yeah," Brandon said. "You just saw your first ghost."

■ A buddy of Brandon's helped with an overnight floor scrub-bing in the basement. In this stone-walled space, rugs undulated. The friend heard his name spoken in his ear. The "gray, hazy thing" drifted across the floor and up the stairs, followed by foot-steps in the tavern. They checked. No one was there. The exasper-ated friend asked, "Are we done yet?"

■ That photo, taken by a server of two friends in the dining room. Brandon called it up on his cell phone. See the guy between them? Shoulders, face, nose, eyes. I was thinking, well, if you say so, but suddenly, I gasped. There it was—the distinct outline of a man. On the Jean Bonnet Facebook page, one commenter said he could see it, too, "but unfortunately I also see all the point source light sources that could be causing some kind of refraction and a reflection in the lens elements. Nonetheless, it is pretty cool!" That could be, but it's worth checking out the see-through man with the forlorn face.

■ Brandon walked out of his office one night and nodded at the man standing in the corner. The man nodded back. Halfway through the tavern, Brandon stopped. "We're empty," he thought. The restaurant had closed. The staff had left. There were no B&B guests. He turned back around, and the man was gone.

■ The Jean Bonnet's ghost cat is partial to Room 1. "He messes with people," Brandon said. "Lays on them." But the cat's evening rambles take him elsewhere, too. Dining room guests will say, "I can't believe you have a cat walking around here." Brandon will say, "We don't have a cat." They say, "I just saw a cat walking around." Yeah, Brandon responds. "We have a ghost cat."

The food scene: "We really stress homemade," Brandon said. "We make it here. We bring in minimal ready-to-go ingredients." The marinara sauce is purchased, because variances in tomatoes make consistency impossible, but "pretty much everything else, we make from scratch." Soup and stocks— from scratch. Meats— cut in-house.

Are you kidding me?

"We do all that in-house," Brandon assured me, "and I think it really shows for quality." Herbs used in the dishes are grown

Jean Bonnet's ghost cat in a mural

on the grounds, "basil, thyme, rosemary, parsley, cilantro—pretty much all of them." Even in winter, your pesto was made fresh from the summertime harvest and frozen for year-round enjoyment.

Of course, homemade can even mean changes in the taste from one day to the next, because "maybe the onions were a little hotter or the celery a little sweeter this time. It gives that little variation that's homemade, the little things that give it a unique twist."

I tried: When it came time to order, the Jean Bonnet French dip was tempting, or the tavern crab cake sandwich, "broiled to perfection." Locally raised bison burger spotlights the Jean Bonnet's commitment to local foods. Lemon ricotta chicken? Awesome way to liven up poultry.

With all these choices, I didn't hesitate. Lobster mac 'n cheese, please. Hot, creamy, and flavorful, it was the perfect pairing to the fire crackling behind me in the dining room. I regret not topping the meal off with the Jean Bonnet's famous hot oatmeal pie, but there's only so much a person can consume. It's a treat that dates back to the Civil War, when pecans were scarce, requiring the invention of a mock version. I thought I would try it on my next visit, but I didn't. My husband and I celebrated our anniversary with an overnight stay, and after my delectable entrée of scallops in basil pesto over asparagus—a combination that has my name all over it—I couldn't pass up the lemon cheesecake with blackberry sauce. Sheer heaven. Creamy and tangy. Now I know why everyone talks about the Jean Bonnet cheesecakes.

The beverage scene: Welcome to a showcase for local microbrews. The ever-changing taps offer whatever's new and seasonal from Pennsylvania breweries. The Jean Bonnet gets one or two kegs at a time, and when they're empty, "that'll be it, and we'll get another one," Brandon said. "Our tap list changes probably twice a week."

I tried: A favorite I've often had there is the Sly Fox's O'Reilly Stout, rich but light, not too sweet, the perfect accompaniment to that lobster mac 'n cheese and, I suspect, many other items on the menu.

Lodging: Each of the Jean Bonnet's four rooms or suites has a unique flavor and feel. Room 1, with its canopy bed, is the coziest. The unique straight-back chair handmade by an Amish craftsman, with a desk extension and clawfoot arms, is surprisingly comfortable. In suite 3, Brandon thinks the anteroom might

Sly Fox's O'Reilly Stout

Suite at the Jean Bonnet Tavern

have been a nursery, "because a lot of people hear a baby crying at night when there's no baby."

The bright, spacious Room 2, with its gas fireplace, is "everybody's favorite room," and I can say from experience that it's homey and comfy and ideal for a restful night after a memorable dinner. The large Suite 4 beckons with two queen beds in connecting rooms.

All are cleaned to spotless perfection by a sweet lady named Janet Kinsey, who takes pride in her 26 years here. The rooms have been quietly upgraded over the years. New flooring, replacing old floors that were crumbling to sawdust, included sound-proofing to muffle the sounds of the tavern below. Keeping up to date with the demands of contemporary travelers, each room has a private bath.

"Everybody wants the historic rooms, but not a 200-year-old bathroom, which to be accurate, would be an outhouse outside," Brandon said. "Nobody would do that."

PLAN YOUR VISIT

The Jean Bonnet Tavern
6048 Lincoln Highway
Bedford, PA 15522
www.jeanbonnettavern.com, (814) 623-2250

WHAT'S NEARBY

Omni Bedford Springs Resort: President James Buchanan was in the lobby of the Bedford Springs Resort when he received the first-ever transatlantic cable. One of the first indoor pools in America was here, fed by the mineral springs that had long attracted visitors. One of America's first golf courses was built here. Rescued from oblivion through a $120 million restoration in 2007, the dazzling Omni Bedford Springs Resort offers trails, pools, golfing, spa days, and dining amid historic elegance. (www.omnihotels.com/hotels/bedfordsprings)

Fort Bedford Museum and Old Bedford Village: Explore the wild frontier at an interpretive site where it all happened. Fort Bedford Museum, at the recreated garrison where soldiers mustered to fight the French and Indian War, is newly refurbished with dynamic galleries and displays. Watch for events, from French and Indian War seminars, to Colonial Christmas cookie-making, to beer tastings. At Old Bedford Village, let a 21st-century app guide you through 18th- and 19th-century life. Come for special events to meet Civil War generals, see living history demonstrations, and enjoy a candlelit Christmas. (Both close for the winter. Visit www.fortbedfordmuseum.org and www.oldbedfordvillage. com for details.)

Flight 93 National Memorial, Shanksville: The Flight 93 Memorial is an evolving remembrance of the 40 people who gave their lives to thwart a 9/11 attack on the U.S. Capitol. What started as a fence adorned with handmade tributes has blossomed into a visitors' center and memorial, open year-round. The Tower of Voices dedicated in 2018 was designed to ring with 40 chimes sounding in both dissonance, recalling the tragedy of the site, and consonance, honoring the joint sacrifice of the 40. (www. nps.gov/flni/index.htm)

7.

THE BLACK BASS HOTEL
Lumberville, Pennsylvania

Life and much death on the canal

Misbehavior makes history: The Black Bass Hotel

■ George Washington did not sleep here. When he arrived looking for shelter, the Tory proprietor turned him away.

■ Come dine where rowdy Irish canal diggers, mistreated by contractors and snubbed by townspeople, lived, fought, and died—and were autopsied. Enjoy a meal at the autopsy table.

■ Or have a drink at the spot where a drunken canal man murdered the owner.

■ A bridge marks the spot, telling the tale of past spans and offering the rare chance to walk a Roebling bridge without any traffic hazards.

■ "Don't be good!" Herbie Ward would say as a farewell. The spunky, legendary past owner of the Black Bass sued the Commonwealth of Pennsylvania to keep his treasured inn from sliding into the canal.

■ Today's scene: Refined country getaway, well worth the trip far off the beaten path.

Built: 1740s

Meet the proprietor

"My impression of the Black Bass is that it started life as a brothel."

No! I scrambled to turn on my recorder. Say that again, please, I asked Grant Ross.

"I think they all started life as brothels." He punctuated with a growl, a cross between a pirate's "Arrrr" and a birr of his native

The Black Bass Hotel

Scotland. Then he continued. The typical 18th-century fur trapper could be "pretty lonely. You spend a lot of time on your own, and when you are meeting with other people, do you want to be meeting with other trappers and adventurers? Maybe."

That makes this establishment "no different than any other. It's part and parcel of the frontiersman's lifestyle."

The Black Bass Hotel sits on the very edge of Pennsylvania, looking across the Delaware River to New Jersey. Grant Ross has been the general manager since 2008 when the Black Bass underwent a top-to-bottom restoration. He keeps all the pieces afloat in this self-contained world of tavern, lodging, and general store.

Grant has a gift for the sly practical joke. In the building's original section, he told me about the night George Washington knocked on the Black Bass door and was turned away by the Tory owner. He pointed to the door.

"If you look very carefully," he said, "you can see George Washington's handprint."

Yes. I looked. Gullible me.

Grant can also tee up a factoid for shock effect. We were sitting in a small dining room, part of the original building, as he shared the history of the Irish canal workers who essentially came to Pennsylvania to die. They were dropping in such large numbers that Bucks County commandeered the Black Bass as a morgue.

Every two weeks, the coroner would come by and conduct the autopsies.

"Now, the coroner needs an autopsy table," Grant said casually. He tipped his head toward the room's long center table. "There it is."

I looked at the table to my left. I'm sure my eyes grew wide. I'll fill you in on the table's provenance later. This just shows the kind of fun Grant likes to have with the quirks of this aged inn. So, for instance, he says that water puddling where a 19th-century owner was murdered signals that a ghost is about to manifest—except that it's actually leakage from the dishwasher.

At one point, I asked Grant if there had been much whiskey-making in this region.

"Not to my knowledge," he said. "Give me half an hour, and I'll make you a story up."

In one of the rooms, Grant proudly showed me an intricately carved bed with unique side pieces framing the mattress.

"This is an antique," he said. "I should say it was an antique."

Was? Seems the bed was once appraised at $28,000 for insurance purposes. However, its standard double size—adequate for

Proprietor Grant Ross standing at the autopsy table

Victorian-era sleepers—was too cramped for today's queen-sized dreamers.

"So we ripped it up and put it back together again, bigger," Grant said. "Now it's got no . . ."

"No value whatsoever," I finished.

"The value," Grant said, "is that it's super cool."

I asked what kind of guests the inn attracts. Immediately, he said, "Lovely, lovely people." Some come for weddings. Some do the B&B circuit, escaping New York or Philadelphia to breathe in the Bucks County history and scenery.

"You go to a hotel in New York, you know what you're getting," he said. "You come to a bed and breakfast in a sleepy-hollow town, then you're coming for something else."

His journey to sleepy hollow took twists and turns worthy of the Bucks County backroads. He has worked in corporate hotels in London. He owned a 400-year-old hotel in his native Scotland. He married an American woman. They had kids. He leased out the Scottish hotel and came to the U.S. He spent a year stalking the Black Bass, trying to buy it. This was the mid-2000s, pre-financial crash, and banks queued up to lend him "a bizarre amount of money."

A friend who's a contractor told him that one of two things would happen. "You're going to run out of money, and I'm not going to get paid," said the friend. "Or I'm going to get paid, and then you're going to run out of money. But you're going to run out of money."

When the building finally went to auction, bidding crept beyond Grant's limit. He walked away, "all pissed off," when his real estate agent came running.

"I know the fellow who's bought it," the agent said. "He has no idea what he's going to do with it."

"Two days later, I'm having a meeting with Jack in his office, and this is how it all manifests itself," Grant told me as we stood in the hallway amid the lodging rooms.

Jack is Jack Thompson, prominent area businessman. He and his family were longtime patrons who bought the Black Bass and restored it to its current splendor. Admire a painting, such as the brilliantly executed depiction of men lingering in an Old World square, and it could be a work by Jack's wife, the supremely talented Loraine Thompson.

"Probably the reason Jack bought this place was to have someplace to hang his wife's artwork—which we say to them," Grant said. "They are the most humble, nicest people you ever want to meet."

Every business has to deliver returns, but "back in the day, and you can quote me on this, Jack was never worried about making a profit." During the restoration, he told Grant to "do it properly."

"Doylestown and this area have been so good to me for so many years," Mr. Thompson told Grant. "If I can offer something back and do something of a philanthropic nature here, I'm quite happy to do that."

A stay at a country inn comprises 50 transactions, Grant tells staff. For the customer, each transaction must go well.

"It starts with being able to find your phone number. Then it's the person who answers the phone, and then getting directions here." He pronounced "directions" as the Scottish *DIE*-rections. "Then the valet parking your car properly. Then the hostess (host-*ESS*) greeting you properly. Then your table being nice and tidy and clean and your menu being presented properly."

Too many screw-ups and the claws are sharpened for the Yelp review. Get each transaction right, and guests have gotten the experience they craved.

"Places come and go," Grant said. "Managers and owners come and go, and places fall into a state of disrepair, and then they get built up again. That's the nature of this business. When a place has been here for 270 years, and people have been coming to eat here for 270 years, there's no reason to suspect they will stop tomorrow because you are not here. But you have to be consistent with what you're offering them. You still have to have a nice product."

Tour the Black Bass Hotel

"Rustic elegance" is hard to get right. The Black Bass Hotel nails it.

Canal Pub: It's easy to imagine. The canaller or riverman steps into the dark, low-ceilinged stone tavern. He stops to thaw his hands at the hearth, his wet clothes steaming as they dry. Then he steps to the bar and asks for the winter warmer known up and down the river—"a strong compound of hot ale, apple-pulp, sugar, cinnamon, and cloves served in steaming mugs."

The Canal Pub

Sigh. Even then, there was no escaping pumpkin spice drinks.

At today's Black Bass, the original back is the front, and vice versa. The main entrance opens into the second floor. Walk up the hall and turn left down the basement stairs, and you see the original stone exterior wall and the front door that faced the old main road, the one that ran by the river until the canal moved in.

The Canal Pub used to be long and narrow before the current owners carved off a section for the restrooms. Now, it's a cozy square, with treadle sewing machine tables along one wall, small round tables in the middle, and a banquette accented by comfy pillows in a niche beside the fireplace.

Except for the addition of a bar back, the well-worn bar hasn't changed much since the Thompsons bought the Black Bass. Instead of barstools, seating is a series of flat wood benches for two—maybe three, if you don't mind snuggling with a stranger. The footrest of wood carved with hearts was once a fireplace mantel, but "we don't have a history or provenance on it," Grant said. The bar is a small affair, the kind where conversations start easily, although you might have to reposition your line of sight around the post blocking the view of your new companions.

The restaurant, and lobster ravioli: For years, my sister told me about a stunning experience, stopping for lunch one day on a covered-bridge tour with her husband. This old country inn had a long dining room, where a wall of windows overlooked a river spanned by a walking bridge. There, she ate a lobster ravioli that she still tastes in her dreams.

Nearing the Black Bass on the day of my visit, I crossed a covered bridge. When I walked into the dining room, I saw diners enjoying lunch at tables stretching along a wall of windows. They were looking out toward a walking bridge spanning the Delaware River.

Some places just never leave you. In this remote town that has brought time to a halt, I had stumbled upon my sister's unforgettable getaway. This room is a Black Bass fixture, the place for anniversaries, dates, friend get-togethers, and—while I was there—a birthday party.

I don't know if canallers and boatmen ever stood on the Black Bass Hotel's second floor just to admire the river and the verdant island on the other side. They wouldn't have had a miniature suspension bridge to give the vista an exclamation point, but I like to think that a bird's-eye view renewed their appreciation for the river that shaped their daily lives.

The tavern dining room and bar: Two eras, connected rooms. The stone-walled dining room, with fireplace, original artwork, and a massive coat of arms dominating the chimney, belonged to the original tavern. Cozy red chairs invite diners to settle in for a leisurely meal with the feel of an early American feast.

Step through the arch into the next room, and it's now the Gilded Age at the turn of the 20th century. This intimate bar was once a wraparound porch. In 1890, the porch was enclosed, "which makes this bad boy here"—Grant rested his palm against a post smack-dab in the middle of the room—"a real pain in the neck." There's no moving the charming little feature. It's structural.

But pain-in-the-neck posts aside, this room invites you to slow down and sip a cocktail or two. It's the showcase of former owner Herbert Ward's love of all things English. He especially revered the Royal Family—appropriate, since the Black Bass was a Tory bar during the American Revolution. Glass cabinets, built to the ceiling, overflow with Windsor memorabilia. Cigar boxes, plates, tea cups, pepper mills, a champagne bottle celebrating the royal wedding that was sure to be happily ever after, the one

Vintage sign behind the bar

Dining room

where Prince Charles married the charming Lady Diana Spencer. Regulars still bring mementos from their travels across the pond, and Black Bass staff find room for them.

Behind the bar is a tin tableau—more than 100 miniature lead soldiers and horses, parading in royal procession for Queen Victoria's coronation coach. "I'm told there's only three or four in existence," Grant said.

SECTION II

The history of the Black Bass Hotel: Slumberville

The river flows, but time has stopped in this sprawling inn and the town of Lumberville, nicknamed "Slumberville."

Frontier accommodations: In 1746, a lumberman and his sidekick guided a raft loaded with timber down the perilous, 200-mile Delaware River journey from Cochecton, New York, to eager markets in Philadelphia. It was the first time anyone had accomplished the feat, and they sparked a sensation in Philadelphia. Until then, lumbermen sent logs down the swollen springtime river and hoped their lucrative commodity didn't snag on sandbars or rocks. For his exploit, the daring lumberman earned the lifelong title "Lord High Admiral of the Delaware," probably bestowed in a well-lubricated pub ceremony, with punch bowl for a crown and fireplace poker as sword tapping each shoulder.

Maybe he stopped at the cozy new inn called the Temple Bar, the one catering to lumbermen and trappers. For all the rafters who followed, this would become a halfway point. Some hauled their rafts out of the river here, for an overland trip to avoid the falls just downriver. Others simply needed the break, after long days on rafts left unsheltered from the need for a 360-degree view of river hazards. A raft snared on the rocks meant jumping into the frigid water, freeing the craft, jumping back on, and spending the next hours in wet clothes. The warm-up of hot rum and butter at the tavern in the town then known as Wall's Mills would have been a welcome treat.

George Washington didn't sleep here: Funny thing, history. A door opens to George Washington's knock, and the house becomes part of a national park—or at least gains a selling point for generations of real estate agents.

Slam the door in his face, and the house becomes a footnote in history. Unless you're the Black Bass, and you embrace your contrariness. That's when sending the Father of Our Country out into the winter night becomes a tale to share for centuries.

As war general and as president, George Washington traveled. In battle, he occupied a tent to show solidarity with his soldiers. Otherwise, he sought accommodations in the finest homes around. In December and January 1776, Washington spent 10 crucial days in this region, in the days around his Delaware River crossing to surprise British and Hessian troops in Trenton.

The Black Bass—maybe the Temple Bar then, or Wall's Landing—could have been quite suitable. Room for his entourage. Private space for strategizing. A comfortable bed for sleeping away the cares of the day.

Then again, you have to wonder about the strength of his military intelligence if he sought shelter from a Tory. Was he misinformed? Was he gambling that a knock on a random door might reveal a Patriot harbor in a Tory region? Did he think he could muscle his way in?

When his presidency ended, George Washington finally returned to his beloved Mount Vernon and rested his head on his own pillow. The Black Bass had its chance to claim that "George Washington slept here." But his head never rested on a Black Bass pillow.

"Drunken, dirty, indolent and riotous": Building a canal was easy, the saying went. All you needed was a pick, a shovel, a wheelbarrow, and an Irishman.

Starting with the construction of the Erie Canal in 1815, states were locked in a race to dig canals and ship their wealth of coal and lumber and grain to the wide, wild West. Canal laborers were the foot soldiers of this arms race. As more and more native-born Americans said "heck, no" to the backbreaking work, more and more Irish—plus immigrants from Germany and elsewhere—flocked to pick up the pickaxes.

On the canal worksites, they went to work at sunup. At sundown, they put down their tools. Pay could be maybe 50 cents or even one dollar a day—not bad by Irish standards, but the contractors in charge weren't known for paying on time. A jigger of whiskey might be offered, too, a single-shot fortification for facing the same trials the next day.

Naturally, a lot more whiskey flowed than that daily jigger. Townspeople tsk-tsk'd. "Inebriates," they called the men. "Dens of iniquity," they called their camps. One critic sniffed that the filthy women and children "required only a little industry to preserve both in a state of cleanliness, for water was abundant in the river close at hand, and soap abundant and cheaper than in England." Of course, wages were often paid in scrip that soap merchants wouldn't accept, but that didn't matter to this critic, who seemed to equate workers and their families with cockroaches—"drunken, dirty, indolent and riotous, so as to be objects of dislike and fear to all those in whose neighborhood they congregate in large numbers."

Add to this toxic stew the diseases unknown to immune systems from Great Britain. In the sodden, riverside trenches, feasting mosquitoes transmitted malaria. Raw sewage spread cholera. The nameless dead were buried in mass, unmarked graves, including one on Bull's Island, across the river from Lumberville.

The workers at the Delaware Canal, running in front of the Black Bass, were not spared. The men were dying, but not their wives and children, who didn't venture to the dig sites. It was an early 19th-century medical mystery, and the people of Bucks County wanted to solve it. The county coroner scheduled visits to perform autopsies every two weeks. That raised the issue of interim storage in summer weather when the ravages hit their peaks.

Here was a tavern built into the riverbank on a stone foundation. Cool year-round, and ideal for keeping things that spoil—onions, carrots, potatoes, corpses.

The birth of a canal: The first canal moving coal from the Pocono Mountains was a hybrid "slackwater" canal in 1829. Boats would traverse the open Lehigh River until reaching rapids or falls, where locks would lift them to the next placid stretch of water. The problem: It linked to a New Jersey canal that funneled coal to the New York marketplace. From Harrisburg, state lawmakers hungrily imagined an Easton-to-Philadelphia extension that would keep coal, and its profits, in Pennsylvania. But another, cost-efficient slackwater canal on the Delaware River would have required ceding some control to the state of New Jersey.

Well, harrumph to that. The inland, Pennsylvania-exclusive Delaware Canal would pass the Black Bass Hotel on its way to joining a system of canals crisscrossing the state. Its first boat launched from New Hope on December 7, 1830. There was much fanfare, so let's say that bands played. Horns blew. Orators speechified. Spectators waved handkerchiefs as the boat pointed toward Bristol.

And the Delaware Canal was a dud. Canals aren't supposed to leak, but inexperienced contractors pressured to work quickly had used bad materials to line the trench. One year went by, and repairs were completed—just in time for the doldrums of winter to set in.

Spring of 1832 would have been a good time to get the canal busy, except that an unusual ice freshet hacked out "a considerable portion" of a section, "which was proved to have been constructed in a very unskilled manner." More delays followed. Canal leaks and inexperienced lock keepers kept waters low. Boatmen refused to travel the canal "on account of the Cholera, which carried off a number of the individuals who were engaged in the repairs."

It would be 1834 before boats loaded with cargo—mostly coal—were regularly traveling the canal. Original cost estimates of a little over $11,000 per mile had nearly doubled.

Now, the Black Bass was welcoming a new clientele. The "brigandish guise" of the canal boatman, with "his slouched and gaily-ribboned hat" might go "unshunned in cities" but struck "terror to the smiling innocence of the villages through which he floats," said a character in Herman Melville's "Moby Dick." "But it is often one of the prime redeeming qualities of your man of violence, that at times he has as stiff an arm to back a poor stranger in a strait, as to plunder a wealthy one."

Boatmen would stop at taverns like the Black Bass for pinochle, drinking, and fisticuffs. Sometimes, a boat captain would put up his best fighter against another captain's best fighter, providing bare-knuckled, feet-kicking entertainment.

The Delaware and other Pennsylvania canals helped build communities and create jobs. The children of the canal diggers grew up to start businesses and fight for the Union in the Civil War. But in just 30 years, and after all those deaths during construction, Pennsylvania's canals were obsolete. The inefficient, unprofitable system was losing business to railroads chuffing across landscapes and over mountains. The state sold the Delaware Canal to private operators in 1858, who kept it going until the final paying barge plied the waters in 1931.

A tale of three bridges: On March 25, 2017, about 100 people—Millennials, Boomers, even a preschooler—marched across the Lumberville-Raven Rock Bridge. They held signs saying, "Love Your Mother" and "Save and Support the EPA."

While the history of American protest is usually a saga of people against government, this day's rally supported the U.S. Environmental Protection Agency, a D.C. institution being gutted by a new presidential administration. "We all are here because we all know there is nothing more honorable than stepping up for what you believe in and protecting the world we live in," said a young woman who told the crowd she could never, just one year before, have pictured herself here.

I don't know what story arc brought that woman to this spot, but the Lumberville-Raven Rock Bridge exudes a mystique that draws people in. The river, the hills, the island, the sleepy hamlet frozen in amber—they all seem to converge at this curious little span.

You might look at this bridge and think, "If the Brooklyn Bridge and the Golden Gate Bridge had a baby . . ." In a sense, the United States' two most famous bridges, bookending east and west coasts, really are the proud parents of this baby bridge, but its story begins before their time, in 1856.

The first, covered bridge here connected Lumberville residents to a railroad station across the river. The only way to escape

Lumberville-Raven Rock Bridge

paying the toll was to be going to and from church. An 1862 flood wiped out a span on the Lumberville side. The owners replaced it with a steel span, creating a sort of bridge turducken—steel span sandwiched by covered spans, all crossing the canal and river.

In 1932, Pennsylvania and New Jersey jointly purchased the bridge, only to discover severe rot in the wooden portions. In 1944, the U.S. Army Corps of Engineers rumbled into town, deciding this spot was ideal for testing the pontoon bridges that would help win World War II.

Army vehicles took the final toll on the rattling old bridge. The bridge was condemned. Pennsylvania and New Jersey had no interest in rebuilding, and besides, steel was scarce in wartime.

Post-war, along came John A. Roebling's Sons Company. John Augustus Roebling was an Austrian immigrant and engineer who invented a revolutionary form of wire rope for hauling canal boats over the Allegheny Mountains. Quickly, he began applying his cables toward his passion for building suspension bridges, culminating in his design for the most monumental bridge of all, the Brooklyn Bridge.

Roebling's three sons founded John A. Roebling's Sons Company and became the world's leading producer of wire rope. In 1933, their wire found its way to another behemoth, the Golden Gate Bridge. After World War II, their fortunes foundered. The company left family hands in 1953 after they refused to take on the massive debt needed to upgrade their plants.

So maybe, in 1947, the idea of offering to demonstrate an economically designed and constructed suspension bridge made sense. Here, it is a doll-sized walking bridge balanced on the oversized stone piers from the original, 1856 covered bridge. It is one of only two pedestrian bridges operated by the Delaware River Joint Toll Bridge Commission, and a rare multi-catenary pedestrian suspension bridge, meaning you get the unique opportunity to walk across a suspension bridge of several curving cables (that's the multi-catenary part) without traffic whizzing past. You can stop and watch the fog lift off the river, or wave back to your friends enjoying Charleston Meeting Street Crab at the Black Bass.

The giant American flag fluttering below the span is maintained by Tinsman Brothers Lumber and lit at night by a 10,000-watt spotlight owned by the Black Bass.

And just by coincidence, the spiffed-up bridge was rededicated after extensive renovations in a ceremony on May 23, 2013,

130 years and one day before the Brooklyn Bridge opened on May 24, 1883. Two Lumberville-Raven Rock Bridge steel components salvaged during rehab—wire-rope sleeves that protect the cable from wear, and suspension hanger plates that connect suspender ropes to the walking deck—were donated to the Roebling Museum in Florence, New Jersey, filling a hole in the artifact collection of the museum dedicated to all things Roebling.

Grover Cleveland slept here: Okay, so Grover doesn't go down in history as one of the greats. Still, there are thousands and thousands of inns and hotels in the United States. How many can claim to have hosted at least one of the 45 presidents? (Although on that 45 thing—Cleveland jumbled the count, serving non-consecutive terms at 22nd and 24th. In my book, that means we're in POTUS 44 and Administration 45, but I seem to be swimming against the tide on that point.)

Back when America's fight over the gold standard versus silver was simply a Gilded Age reboot of the never-ending clash of tone-deaf privilege versus seething working class, Grover Cleveland was in the thick of things. When he needed to get away, he would come to Lumberville for the fishing, and stay at the Black Bass. His favorite room is named after him, the Grover Cleveland Suite, complete with the same bed that he slept in. Though he was famously known as a family man who had five children with his beautiful young wife, he slept apart from the wife and kids, who shared an adjoining room. The 275-pound Cleveland, it seems, preferred to sleep alone.

"Don't be good!": For the view that draws people here every day and every night, you can thank Herbert Ward and his stubborn insistence that the Commonwealth of Pennsylvania correct a wrong done to the Black Bass.

Herbie Ward's renown endures beyond his death in 2003. Heir to two fortunes. Toast-of-the-town restaurateur in New York's theater district of the 1920s and '30s. Philanthropist. Broadway angel. An artist who found a home in beautiful Bucks County. Lifetime mourner for his partner, Larry Bemis, killed in a Christmas Eve 1960 wreck of a sports car gifted to him by Ward. An animal lover who buried his beloved Tallulah Wiggle and 11 other pets in the landscaped, stone-walled pet cemetery (now behind the parking area). A friend whose signature goodbye was, "Don't be good!"

Grover Cleveland Suite at the Black Bass Inn

Ward and Bemis acquired the Black Bass Hotel in 1947 when it was becoming a rundown roadside bar. They renovated and turned it into a renowned haven for fine dining, the kind of off-the-beaten-path but fashionably trendy inn you see in old movies.

With his independent wealth, Herbert Ward didn't answer to anybody. In 1989, he tried to sell the hotel, figuring that "40 years was enough." He didn't want to sell to someone who would "come in and tear it down or redo it and have plastic walls and Formica tables and chrome all over."

"This is an old inn, and I'd like to have it kept that way," he said.

But there was a problem. Buyers recoiled at the sight of the crumbling retaining wall between the inn and the canal. Neglect by the state, keeper of the canal and that deteriorating wall, was causing the inn's roof and floors to crack, columns to slide, and windows and doors to warp.

"If they don't give a damn about keeping the inn, it's going to fall into the canal," Ward told the Philadelphia *Inquirer*.

So he took the state to court. After all, the Black Bass was not just any inn. Take the night when a vivacious woman from a party of six stepped up to the piano and sang into the early hours.

"It was Liza Minnelli, and she had stopped here on her honeymoon to dine," Ward said. She was just one of an "endless number" of showbiz types who frequented the inn.

Ward's lawsuit and the negotiations dragged on because state officials "do nothing but talk," he told another newspaper. No gag order could hold him, I suspect. Ward was suing for $2.2 million, the full value of the inn. The struggle made headlines. Congressional opponents accused each other of trying to score political points over the case.

In 1992, Ward won. The state capitulated, rebuilding the wall so strongly that it withstood floods and, thankfully for diners who love a beautiful view, supports the river-view dining room. With what it cost to pour many thousand tons of concrete and reinforce it with rebar drilled straight into bedrock, the state "could have bought the building three times," but Herbie Ward stood his ground, said Grant Ross. "Herbie was a character unto himself."

SECTION III

Touch history

Whether you're in the tight confines of the Canal Pub or watching the river through plate-glass windows, the Black Bass Hotel seems to carry you through a continuum of time.

Burned beams: Work hard, party hard. River boatmen and canal engineers knew how to have a good time. On January 17, 1833, watermen and locals carousing at the Black Bass were doing the kind of thing that candlelight-era mothers probably warned against—mixing drunken revelry and open flames.

Black Bass owner Major Anthony Fry was half a mile away when the fire broke out. By the time he arrived, the main part of the building was burning. And then, he "recollected"—the word used in a newspaper account—a favor he was doing for canal contractors. "Oh, right," he might have recollected. "I put a keg of blasting powder in the basement." With that, Fry rushed toward the flames, broke down the cellar door, seized the keg, and hustled it out of the building. An explosion was prevented and lives were spared, and the Black Bass, rebuilt on its sturdy foundation with a new addition, survives for us to enjoy today.

"You can see the residue of the fire," Grant told me. He was patting a blackened beam overhead in the Canal Pub, parallel to the fireplace. "All this had to be stress-tested to see if it was still doing what it should be." Wood, he said, "gets stronger and stronger and stronger when it heats up—to a point."

The wood passed the test. It is, thankfully, "still functioning the way it should."

The cooler: Chances are, you have never used a bathroom that doubled as a morgue. But welcome to the Black Bass. Remember how the cool, stone-walled tavern was perfect for storing bodies waiting for the coroner?

Excuse yourself to use the stone-walled men's or ladies' room behind the Canal Pub, and you're walking into the 19th-century version of a morgue drawer.

Dinner and an autopsy: Try to act cool when you stroll through the dining room. It's probably bad form to announce to groups gathering at the long, narrow center table that they're dining on an autopsy slab.

"Look at the edge of it," Grant told me. He pointed to hack marks in the wood. "That's where they cut too far into the table." Yeesh. A disconcerting image, but there's more.

Unless a canal builder died from, say, premature charge of blasting powder, or was crushed by a falling rock, or smothered in a procedure called "pooling-in," when trees were undercut and allowed to fall in on themselves, the coroner had a mystery to solve, and he wanted to see the deceased's innards. Heart, lungs, intestines.

"The table is narrow," Grant pointed out. "The man is bigger than you, smaller than me."

"They were workers," I said. "Not tall, but hefty." So now I'm wondering why an autopsy table would be narrower than the average, um, guest.

"What you don't want to do is tighten me up," Grant said, "me" being the body in question. "You want to cut open my chest and let my arms swing off the table so it all stretches out."

Another unsettling image, and there's one last, queasy thing to learn about this table. The legs have been evened up. Before, one pair of legs was taller than the other. "It would have been at an angle, and bodily fluids would have run off. This is the original coroner's table."

"That's where Hans was murdered": Grant offered this tidbit with a casual gesture to the end barstool in the Canal Pub. The killer may have been incensed over a woman. He could have been a disgruntled canal worker. Maybe he was in a drunken brawl, just letting off steam until things got out of hand. No matter the story, the end result was the same. Hans was the innkeeper, and a knife caused his untimely end. I imagine this was a hazard of innkeeping in an age of hard drinking by hardened men. Keep an eye out for him. It's said that Hans still hangs out at the spot where he died.

Take me to Maxim's: Surrounded by Anglophilia in the upper bar, you're actually enjoying your drink at an icon of French history. The pewter bar top came, it's said, from Maxim's, the cherished nightspot of Gay Paris. The cream of society came to dazzle and be dazzled amid sensuous Art Nouveau artwork, mirrors, and stained glass. The dining room was never empty because, said its owner, "I always have a beauty sitting by the window, in view from the sidewalk."

How this bar came here is another story that can be neither confirmed nor denied. Somewhere in a scene of "Singin' in the Rain" is a pewter bar—the bar in question, and apparently, Gene Kelly owned it. A Kelly granddaughter who lived up the street from the Black Bass—Bucks County is no stranger to celebrities and artists—inherited it. She put some items up for auction, "and it was bought about 40 or 50 years ago," said Grant. "Could be."

I've been obsessively watching "Singin' in the Rain" now. Haven't spotted it yet. Didn't catch it in the "Gigi" Maxim's scenes, either.

I'll keep looking. One distinctive feature should make it easy to spot. I asked Grant about it, the tower with spigot sculpted into the pewter.

"You know what absinthe is?" he said. "That's an absinthe tower. Absinthe would be pumped in underneath it, and the absinthe would be poured from there."

If you're ever tempted to install a vintage pewter bar, take a lesson from Grant. "We had a lot of trouble getting permission to use this," he told me. "Pewter you buy these days is very different than pewter you'd get 50 years ago. It's got a high lead content. Plus, it's very, very soft, and the lead dissolves out."

Bar with Maxim's bartop

So, "they"—you know, government regulators who have been immovable forces since the Pilgrims had to put guide rails on Plymouth Rock—"said the lead could dissolve out and give somebody lead poisoning." Grant made a skeptical face. "Really? Really? Come on. And they said, 'Well, okay then.'"

"Fun stories about the building": Grant enjoys spinning a tall tale or two about the resident artifacts, but he also relishes the tiny details that illustrate the building's craftsmanship.

"See this here." He pointed to a spot of brick in the Canal Pub's stone walls. I could see others dotted amid the rock, red amid the gray. I could also see slats of wood in the mix. Wood rots, Grant explained, so when it deteriorated, they would shove a piece of brick in the hole and insert mortar around it. "A piece of fieldstone wouldn't be possible, but a fired brick fits nicely."

The wood is there in the first place because it was scaffolding. Lay lengths of lumber perpendicular to the stone, parallel to each other, all at the same height and protruding about three feet. Build the wall around them. You now have brackets for holding planks. Stand on this built-in scaffolding until you need to reach the next level. Do the same thing a few feet up, cut off the brackets at the lower level, "and you're done."

Ingenious.

"We only build with what materials are local and available," said Grant, who would sometimes slip into talking about the past and its people as if he were there. "In this neck of the woods, it's wood and fieldstone."

Chimney breast: "Let's hang out in the ladies' for a while."

We were back in the morgue—that is, the basement women's restroom. There's a curious stone cubbyhole beside the toilet that explains how the Black Bass found its location. Seems that the original builder approached local Native Americans, asking for their thoughts on a good spot to build "this thing called an inn."

They suggested going a few miles downriver, where floods—a fact of life here—always flowed to the other side. Nice and dry, but the building would have required a deep, expensive foundation. Solid bedrock sold the builder on this location. God's foundation saved a lot of money, even though with every flood, "we'll be standing in three or four feet of water," Grant said.

Which gets us to the chimney breast. A good, strong foundation could have supported a chimney with fireplaces stacked on the upper floors. The Black Bass was built with minimal foundation. The thing holding up the chimney and its fireplaces above is a looming slab of black, asphalt-looking lodestone built into the basement ceiling and supported by the stone walls of the ladies' room cubbyhole.

Sewing machines: Have a seat, and knock your knees on the angled table support. Sorry about that. Grant admitted that

Ladies' restroom morgue

treadle sewing machines make "terrible table bases" because you can't pull in your chair far enough to sit at table's edge. But they look great, these tables with the ornate wrought-iron bases. Textiles were once a huge slice of the Philadelphia economy. Women sewed clothing in factories and in the grueling business of at-home piecework. Modernization took over, and treadle sewing machines found their ways to basements and antique shops throughout the region. When the refurbished Black Bass needed tables, there they were. "We've brought everything back that we could," Grant said. "It may have had no value, but we reused it."

"On the Waterfront," written on the waterfront: Again, neither confirmed nor denied, but this one's awesome. An elderly local once told Grant she'd tell him a few stories if he bought her a drink. So he did, and he learned that Marlon Brando and director Elia Kazan holed up in the room that's now the River Suite. There, overlooking the river, they worked on the heart-wrenching script for "On the Waterfront," their 1954 exposé of corruption on the New Jersey docks. I'm not sure where screenwriter Budd Schulberg was during all this. Perhaps director and method-acting star were refining Brando's character, the one who sits in the back of a cab and says, "You don't understand. I coulda had class. I coulda been a contender. I coulda been somebody, instead of a bum, which is what I am."

All the while, Brando and Kazan ate pastrami sandwiches ordered from Doylestown.

"Great story," said Grant, "and it cost me a drink."

Any ghosts? Grant Ross always turns down paranormals who ask to do ghost hunts at the Black Bass.

"I don't want the publicity to say one thing or the other," he said. "Never seen one myself."

Then again, he doesn't stop a server named Jill from relating one of the "very strange little things" she said happens all the time. New Year's Eve, 2017 yielding to 2018. Suddenly, Champagne bottles popped their corks, unbidden, and the music stopped playing. Jill looked toward a table that had been empty a few seconds before, and there sat an old woman. "She was very old. She had a very high collar, white and frilly, and some kind of pin. Seriously."

Beverage manager Clayton Deering also shared the story of the guest at the autopsy table who was, shall we say, particular about her drink order (okay, annoying). He ended up making a sort of cranberry-based cosmopolitan and put it on the table, "which is, like, 400 pounds, so it doesn't move."

I can confirm that.

Anyway, Clayton was serving another table when a ruckus erupted. The autopsy table guests were screaming. They were looking up, down, and around. The woman's red cosmo had splashed all over her white shirt, and no one could see how it happened. Even one straight-shooter in the group could only say that "the drink just leaped out of the glass," said Clayton. "It was like somebody came up and flicked the glass. There wasn't a drop of anything around the table. It was only on her shirt."

Later, a woman from the group approached Clayton. "I'm not a medium, but it's a hobby," she told him. "I sense there's a woman's presence here, and she really doesn't like change, and she doesn't like negativity."

So beware. The Black Bass ghost has a vendetta on persnickety guests.

Of course, Clayton also told the tale of the regular overnight customer who came in late one night, slipped down the secret backstairs for an honor-system cocktail, and went back up to his room.

The next morning, he came down for breakfast just as another overnight guest was gushing to the server, "And we heard the ghost walking up and down the hall and down the stairs!"

The guy didn't have the heart to tell her. And that's how ghostly legends are born.

The food scene: Executive Chef John Barrett was hired in 1997 by Herbert Ward, the Black Bass' longtime owner. After Ward died in 2003, the area was hit by back-to-back-to-back 100-year floods (which means none are due for 300 years? They can only hope). Keeping the restaurant in business became a challenge, and it went to the auction where Jack Thompson bought the building, and Grant Ross got a job.

As the Black Bass was rebuilding, the Thompson family asked John to return. He called his old kitchen brigade, including sous chef Corey Price, and reassembled most of the team.

John got his start at as a vegetable food runner at the Fairmont Philadelphia, just out of high school, his mother "pushing me out the door." He trained at Culinary Institute of America, worked for Chef Tell, and had a "brief stint" in New Orleans.

Coming to the Black Bass, he noticed that "though we were in this small little town, I would read the guest book, and people were from all over, whether they were from New England or Washington or across the states."

"This is an international kind of scene here," he thought.

The menu features a lot of fish, "since we're on the water." Seafood is all local, provisioned from one of the East Coast's best seafood purveyors. It's all scratch cooking, so the red Thai curry sauce starts with the Black Bass Hotel's own curry paste.

A favorite dish is the Charleston Meeting Street Crab, on the menu even before John started here.

"It's basically a crab au gratin, so it's crab, reduced cream, sharp cheddar cheese, and sherry," John said. "That's it."

Desserts come from the General Store, the Black Bass Inn's casual sister establishment across the street. Pastry chef Alison Seelaus bakes everything there, maybe the banoffee bread and butter pudding, or the apple crisp, or the maple crème brulée. It's all carted across the road daily.

I tried: The fish and chips. Battered in American pale ale and served with a tasty herb tartar sauce, the fish was yummy and

The Canal Pub fish and chips

The Canal Pub bartender Clayton Deering

satisfying. The red cabbage slaw on the side was so good I could have eaten another serving for dessert. I ate there late in the afternoon before the Charleston Meeting Street Crab was being served. When I come back, it's on my list.

The beverage scene: Grab a bench seat at the bar, ask Clayton what he recommends, and he will answer, "I recommend you tell me what you want, and I will make you a very, very good drink."

Good answer. Clayton is a classic bartender, with a repertoire of stories and a facility for pleasant banter. He enjoys making "not necessarily complicated drinks, but drinks with some complexity that people can appreciate. Even if it's a cosmo or a margarita, if you know what you're doing, you can make a really good one."

So what constitutes knowing what you're doing?

"Love," he said. "Love, and a few little secrets that we have."

The Black Bass taps pour a nicely balanced, compact selection, with local offerings from Yards and Neshaminy Creek rounding out Guinness, Sam Adams, Bass, and Stella Artois.

"I love Yards," I commented. "Anything they do."

View of river from the River Suite

"So true," said Clayton.

Wow. Like I know something about beer. Thank you for the affirmation.

Lodging: Each of the Black Bass Hotel's nine stylish suites suits unique tastes.

The elegant, two-level Suite Loraine's floor-to-ceiling windows frame the stunning view of river and bridge. The Fieldstone, with a narrow staircase winding to a second level, offers views into the village and over the river. Four suites offer private decks overlooking the water. The pet-friendly Baxter Suite tucks into the hillside. The River Suite, where Brando and Kazan reportedly holed up, feels like a cabin, with dark wood paneling, walls of stone, and a sitting room overlooking the water.

PLAN YOUR VISIT

The Black Bass Hotel
3774 River Road
Lumberville, PA 18933
www.blackbasshotel.com, (215) 297-9260

WHAT'S NEARBY

Lumberville General Store: It really was the Lumberville general store in its day, complete with a pot-bellied stove where locals gathered to solve the problems of the world. It's now refashioned as a casual, BYOB café-deli-bakery, with sales of local books, art, and Black Bass merchandise. Special events include four-course "Supper Club" dinners ("All the fun of a dinner party . . . without the clean-up!"), holiday brunches, and '70s Rock Music Bingo. (www.thelumbervillegeneralstore.com)

Delaware Canal State Park: The park winds for 60 miles along the Delaware River from Easton to Bristol. Follow the towpath trail under bridges and past existing locks from the original canal. (www.dcnr.pa.gov, www.fodc.org)

Michener Art Museum: Lumberville resident Fern Coppedge was among the 20th-century artists inspired by the beauty of Bucks County to produce breathtaking landscapes. Find the shimmering works of these Pennsylvania Impressionists, plus contemporary works and Bucks County Arts and Crafts-style furniture, at the Michener in Doylestown. (www.michenerartmuseum.org)

8.

THE DOBBIN HOUSE TAVERN

Gettysburg, Pennsylvania

Underground Railroad safe harbor

Misbehavior makes history: The Dobbin House Tavern

■ Long before two armies clashed in surrounding fields and soldiers barged in looking for snipers, the Dobbin House was home to a minister with radical ideas about making democracy stick.

■ Tiptoe up the stairs and crawl into the space hidden by a sliding cupboard. Freedom seekers following the Underground Railroad to cross the Mason-Dixon Line found refuge with an abolitionist so fervent that even in old age, he led a rescue effort to free fugitives from low-down slave catchers.

■ Of course, Dobbin House has a story or two to tell about three days in July 1863 and the grueling, gruesome aftermath. Some of its farmland went to a cemetery. President Abraham Lincoln rode past on the way to dedicate it.

■ Sweet Mamie Eisenhower sometimes dropped by the restaurant for dinner with friends.

■ Today's scene: Dining amid historic curiosities, and a dark cellar tavern ideal for losing a Sunday afternoon.

Built: 1776 by the Rev. Alexander Dobbin, Scots-Irish immigrant and a founder of Gettysburg.

Meet the owner

Welcome to Dobbin House Tavern. Your bar stool might wobble on the brick floor. Hold tightly to the railings as you wind up and down crooked stairs. The candlelight might seem dim in the

The Dobbin House

basement tavern, but imagine how the original occupants managed without even a cylinder light tucked discreetly in the ceiling.

All this perfect imperfection dates to the day in 1976 when the
Dobbin House was undergoing a whirlwind restoration, preparing
for its debut as a restaurant. A woman walked in and asked what
was happening. We're restoring the building, she was told.

"I'm sorry to hear that," the woman said.

Jacqueline White, restorer-in-chief, just looked at her. What?

The woman answered, "Every house I go into that's so-called
'restored' looks like it was just built brand-new, and you lose that
beautiful character of the original."

Jackie was gobsmacked, but she has never forgotten that day.

"I have no idea who that lady was, but she has no idea how
much influence she had on me," Jackie told me in her delightfully
expressive way. "From that day forward, I would say to everybody,
'Make it look old. Make it look old.'"

Need an example? Look up at the ceiling of the Springhouse
Tavern. The plasterers were at work when Jackie came downstairs to find it smooth as glass.

"So I got up on the ladder, and I'm doing all this to show them
how it should look, and when I looked down, they were all"—she
rolled her eyes, aping their expressions—"and they said, 'You do
it. You know how you want it.'"

You know how this ends. "So I did the whole ceiling," she
concluded.

The Dobbin House owner Jacqueline White (center) giving a tour

We were sitting at the bar of the restaurant's tavern portion. Jackie was still wearing the Colonial dress and cap she wears to give tours of the house and restaurant. Servers, too, were all dressed in Colonial garb.

Jackie's Dobbin House journey started with her then-husband, the late John White. He was an attorney. She was an art teacher. He heard that the Dobbin House—200 years old, falling down, housing a DAR museum including a diorama of the Gettysburg battle—was for sale. What a restaurant it would make!

Jackie was skeptical. Her parents owned a storybook theme park in Gettysburg, the fondly remembered Fantasyland (I started singing the advertising jingle when I learned this. "Fantasyland, oh Fantasyland, there's so much to see and do.") She knew the ceaseless toil of business ownership. But her husband had this farfetched idea, and then she said the words that start the journey of every crazy old-house person—"We went to see it."

"It was love at first sight," she said. "I loved it from day one."

Of course, the stone building was about to collapse under its own weight. "It was in pretty bad shape," Jackie said. "You don't realize that when you walk into it with a realtor." Still, it had its advantages, including authenticity. When Jackie gave a tour to Frank Auspitz, the York-based artisan of Colonial-style woodwork contracted to help revive the interior, he kept saying over and over, "You are so lucky. You are so lucky."

Lucky to buy a 200-year-old money pit? Sure. The fireplaces were intact. Enough of the woodwork was in place to provide models for replicating. Many of the rough-hewn plank floors were original. All the Whites had to do was jack up the whole structure and spend the next 11 months of their lives amid the dust and damp and earth-moving equipment.

In the basement crawlspace that is now the Springhouse Tavern, the contractor advised against displacing any of the original dirt behind the foundation, for fear of bringing the house down on itself.

"We didn't touch it," Jackie said. "I guess it worked because we've never had a problem."

Scraping paint down to the original colors revealed a comforting yellow, a popular tone in Colonial America because much of their paint was milk-based.

"I did a lot of trips to Harrisburg, Annapolis, of course Williamsburg, Philadelphia, any place that was Colonial," Jackie said. "I think they had a lot more exciting and colorful lives than we think they had."

The Dobbin House Tavern has been a restaurant since Jackie opened the doors at the end of 1977. For some visitors, including an extended family of upstate New Yorkers I met there, it is a regular stop on annual trips to Gettysburg.

How has it lasted this long? Good atmosphere, good food, and good service, Jackie said. Even the restaurant kitchen is included in the tour. That seemed like a crazy idea when Jackie first hatched it, but it's become a mainstay, opening the mysterious backstage world of the kitchen to visitors, and giving staff a chance to show off their smiling faces.

Jackie didn't know anything about running restaurants when she started. She just took the leap. Joining the National Restaurant Association and Pennsylvania Restaurant Association taught her the intricacies of running a successful establishment. The staff are like family, "the salt of the earth. They work very hard, and they're friendly people. We smile a lot. People who aren't like that, they don't last very long."

Jackie also started out knowing little, if anything, about the originator of all of this—the Rev. Alexander Dobbin. One day, she walked into the Adams County Historical Society, and it became

Cross-stitched sampler hanging above the mantel in the kitchen

her starting point for insight into the man who left an apparently comfortable existence in Scotland for adventure in the treacherous New World.

She calls the Dobbin House Tavern her home and all its clientele guests of Rev. Dobbin. In the home's original kitchen, a cross-stitched sampler hanging above the mantel recalls a story written by a colleague of Dobbin's. Seems Dobbin was at a synod meeting in Philadelphia when the colleague apologized for mistakenly sipping wine from Dobbin's goblet instead of his own. Dobbin responded, "I am glad to share in anything that will promote your enjoyment."

Two centuries later, nothing has changed, Jackie said.

"They're still Rev. Dobbin's guests," she told me. "We look at it that way. He just asked me to take care of the place."

Tour the Dobbin House Tavern

The Dobbin House is a sprawling collection of dining areas on three levels where families lived for centuries.

First-floor library, study, living room, and parlor: All are snug and cozy and, per Jackie's insistence on staying old-looking, pleasingly off-kilter.

The parlor

The library

Second-floor family bedrooms: Long ago, the walls were knocked down and the upper floor opened into a single space. Today, it features one of the Dobbin House's signature looks—tables and seating under curtained canopy beds. Colonial sleepers would have pulled the curtains tight to protect against night air they believed was poisonous. Jackie White's mother suggested the "beds" as dining tables. "I said, 'Whaaaat?'" Jackie told visitors taking the tour. "So, at the Dobbin House, you can actually have dinner in bed. I can't believe how many people call to make reservations and say, 'I want to eat in the bed.' But please, don't get crumbs in our sheets."

Springhouse Tavern: Descend a narrow staircase punctuated with a 90-degree bend, and step into the dimly lit, stone-walled Springhouse Tavern. On the day of my visit, it opened at 11:30 a.m. and filled within minutes. A few ceiling lights illuminate the room, but the booths, tables, and bar are lit with real candles, offering diners the rare chance to experience lighting as it was—almost—in the centuries before electricity. No one seemed to mind the dim coziness, including the woman beside me on a warm Friday afternoon. "It's still daylight out there," she told her companions. "The windows upstairs say so."

When Jackie acquired the Dobbin House, the area destined to become the tavern was a crawl space, about five feet high, gauging from the ledge indicating the base of the original foundation. This is where the Rev. Dobbin's wives, first or second, stored potatoes, carrots, onions—anything needing cool storage to stay fresh.

A highlight of the seasonal Dobbin House tours is Jackie's story of acquiring the tavern's bar, one of those meant-to-be tales. She was restoring the building when someone said they knew of a bar at a nearby antique shop. Once again, it was love at first sight of this 17-foot long, early 19th-century beauty, hand carved from chestnut. Jackie asked the antique dealer, where did you find this thing? Seems he had been to a public sale in Clear Springs, Pennsylvania. It was at a general store that was going out of business, a store owned by the Dick family.

"Well, my heart took a little flip," said Jackie, "because my ancestors were from Clear Springs, Pennsylvania, where they owned a general store, and my maiden name was Dick." As she got to this part of the story, the crowd oohed. "So right away, I'm thinking, this could be my ancestors' bar, but if you've ever dealt with an antique dealer, I didn't want him to know that."

Casual-like, she asked, "How much?"

"Well," he said, "I'd have to have at least $100."

The crowd oohed again, this time with a laugh. Recalling that moment, Jackie's hand shot up, and she said in a sing-song voice, "I'll take it."

Wait. There's more. The bar top comprises two pieces of solid wood, secured with dovetailing. After its installation in the tavern, Jackie's grandfather came down and instantly recognized the dovetailing from his days as a young man in the general store. The bar was built in 1818 by his great-great-grandfather, George Dick, "my three great-grandfather," said Jackie. "So it's back in the family again. We're thrilled to have it. That was definitely the find of a lifetime."

I'd call that an understatement.

SECTION II

The history of Dobbin House Tavern:
Rebellion and sanctuary

The pivotal conflict of the Civil War didn't just occur at some anonymous intersection. By 1863, Gettysburg was known as a county seat, a town founded around 1786 at a crossroads of several major transportation routes that would fuel its development. Farm goods grown here and carriages built here were shipped to surrounding regions. Scholars studied at the Gettysburg Lutheran Theological Seminary and at Pennsylvania College, today's Gettysburg College.

So when Abraham Lincoln intoned that our forefathers brought forth a new nation "four score and seven years ago," he coincidentally hit on the year that the Rev. Alexander Dobbin built a home on 300 acres of prime but still wild land in the American frontier.

Alexander Dobbin, wilderness minister: The Rev. Alexander Dobbin was a foot soldier of democracy, doing the hard work needed to make this experiment in self-governance succeed.

The Alexander Dobbin story starts with the story of another rebel you might have heard of, a guy by the name of William Penn. The English nobleman served jail time rather than renounce his adopted Quaker religion for the Church of England. The same king who had imprisoned him, Charles II, also paid a debt to Penn's family with 45,000 square miles of land in the New World, where Penn had the novel idea of setting up his colony as an oppression-free haven for fellow Quakers.

In the meantime, Alexander Dobbin was born in Ireland in 1742. He was Scots-Irish. So was he Scottish, eating haggis and wearing kilts, or was he Irish, guzzling whiskey and cracking heads with a shillelagh?

Actually, the Scots-Irish were a unique breed. They were Scottish residents planted by the British crown on confiscated land in Northern Ireland, beginning in the 16th century, in hopes of quelling the restless Irish by outnumbering them with loyalists. Only one problem. After a generation or three, the Scots-Irish didn't like the English any more than the Irish did. That pesky British habit of religious oppression got under their skin. Trekking to the New World and landing in Maryland and Virginia, they kept moving, some settling in Pennsylvania's wilds while others followed the Cumberland and Blue Ridge valleys south to form the basis of Appalachian culture.

Those who settled in the rugged southcentral part of Penn's Woods sent out the call for a pastor. Alexander Dobbin, ministry student fresh from the University of Glasgow and University of Edinburgh, answered. He arrived in America in December 1773 to serve as pastor for Rock Creek Church near Gettysburg.

Soon, he bought 300 acres of Penn family land. In 1774, construction began of an impressive home in "rubble stone" style, with stone collected from the fields, not neatly chiseled into perfect squares and rectangles but mortared together in their natural shapes.

In 1776, the home was ready for occupancy. Dobbin and his Irish wife, Isabella, moved in. She had 10 children and died in 1800, probably from exhaustion. Soon, he married Mary Agnew. She and her nine children moved into the home. Yes, in a home that was spacious then but would be a two-car garage in today's suburban America, 19 kids slept in three bedrooms.

In 1776, something else of importance happened 130 miles away, in the Colonial capital of Philadelphia. Word spread throughout Pennsylvania that the Continental Congress had issued a Declaration of Independence. How did Rev. Dobbin feel about breaking away from the British? Three things, said Jackie.

■ First, he was Scots-Irish. As noted, not big fans of the British.

■ Second, among the 300 books Dobbin owned was a copy of "Two Treatises of Government," John Locke's essays arguing that government could only rule with the consent of the people. "Tyranny," Locke wrote, "is the exercise of Power beyond Right."

■ Third, Dobbin probably came from means. After all, it took money to study at universities and buy a large tract of land practically on arrival. And yet, he forsook it all for this New World adventure. When he came to America, it was probably for the religious freedom he was denied under British rule.

"Just to leave your home, your parents, never to have a support group around you ever again—oh, my goodness," said Jackie. "You have to really be a believer in your ideals." Put it all together, she said, and he was probably a backer of revolution.

Dobbin was a man who embraced fresh thinking and revolutionary ideas. He was known to loan out his books, so "we like to say that the Dobbin House was the first library of the area," Jackie said.

Dobbin also founded the first classical school west of the Susquehanna River, where boys studied Latin, Greek, history, and philosophy. His students became leaders of their generation—ministers, doctors, lawyers, college professors, and a college president. One became the governor of Ohio. One joined the House of Representatives and later the U.S. Senate.

"They must have gotten an excellent education right here in this house," said Jackie.

As a civic stalwart, Dobbin also led the drive to carve Adams County as its own entity, separate from York County. Until that time, any trip to the county seat of York City, 35 miles away, could take more than a day. Dobbin may have hosted meetings on the matter in the Dobbin House parlor—a dining room in the restaurant today. When their campaign succeeded in 1800, they named their new county after President John Adams. Then, Dobbin was one of two commissioners tapped to decide on the county seat. They chose Gettysburg, making any trip for official business a mere walk up the road from his home.

After a lifetime of civic and spiritual service for the people in and around Gettysburg, Dobbin died in 1809.

"You won't find Rev. Dobbin in the history books," said Jackie. "He was just an immigrant who came to this country, much like my ancestors did around the same time. He worked really hard to build America to be strong and into the country it is today, with those Colonial ideas of self-government, the principles we must always remember. So we at the Dobbin House are very proud to be part of the Dobbin House and to preserve the reverend's legacy."

Matthew Dobbin builds an addition: Even before southern plantations began growing tobacco, rice, sugar, and eventually cotton, there were slaves in North America. Before the 18th century, many held property, married, and raised families, but were, nonetheless, enslaved by owners for their labor and services. With the political rise of planters, any rights once given to people of color were gradually stripped away, and increasingly, plantation owners imposed order through brutality.

Some slaves, about 1,000 a year, decided to flee their oppressors, despite certain perils ahead. They could be caught by dogs trained to tear them apart. They endured hunger and thirst. They risked capture by bounty hunters seeking the rewards made known in newspaper advertisements ("Run away from the subscriber, in Albemarle, a Mulatto slave called Sandy," began a 1769 ad in the Virginia *Gazette* signed by Thomas Jefferson). Even the natural world conspired to put alligators and poisonous snakes in their paths.

For the escaping enslaved person, "all that he has is at stake, and even that which he has not . . . The life which he has, may be lost, and the liberty which he seeks, may not be gained." The man who said that should know. He was Frederick Douglass, who escaped from bondage and made it to New York in 1838.

But there was aid through a network bound by civil disobedience. After all, not every American supported slavery. As Thomas Paine asked in 1775, how could Americans rail against "attempts to enslave them, while they hold so many hundreds of thousands in slavery?" By the 1840s, everyone knew of the passage to freedom, and the people who surreptitiously manned it, as the Underground Railroad.

Matthew Dobbin, Alexander's eldest son, inherited much of his father's property, including that rubble stone house. Though the imperative secrecy of Underground Railroad hideouts makes them difficult to document, the evidence that Matthew Dobbin ran an Underground Railroad stop is convincing.

Consider:

■ Matthew added the second floor above the kitchen, but with a twist. He inserted a space between floors, about three feet high and hidden behind shelves that rolled back like sliding doors.

■ One of Cumberland County's longest-living Underground Railroad conductors wrote a memoir of being introduced to the movement by "enthusiastic abolitionist" Matthew Dobbin.

■ The Associate Reformed Presbytery Church jumped feet first into social causes, and one of its first was the abolition of slavery. Alexander Dobbin, that enlightened idealist, was an Associate Reformed minister. Son Matthew was an ardent abolitionist. Looks like he inherited his dad's passion for equality and freedom.

"We don't know how many slaves made it through the Dobbin House," said Jackie, "but we hope that it was a lot."

Pennsylvania abolished the import of new slaves in 1780, but that didn't make the Keystone State a friendly haven for runaways or those who harbored them. While escaping slaves risked life and limb, anyone caught shielding them faced fines, loss of property and livelihood, and imprisonment.

As a gateway state to the North, Pennsylvania was lucrative territory for slave catchers. They preferred patrolling the borders of free states, which forced escaping slaves to look carefully for their hideaways. Maybe a crawlspace not far from the Maryland border, offered by a minister's son and hidden behind a sliding pantry, was just the thing.

"At night, Matthew would slide open the cupboard, have the slaves crawl out, and give directions to the next station or the next safe house," said Jackie. "By the time they got to the Dobbin House, they must have been pretty happy, because they were over the Mason-Dixon Line. They were in the North, and they were in Pennsylvania, and Pennsylvania was a free state. That didn't mean they couldn't be caught and sent back, but it must have been a good morale boost."

Matthew gave the fugitives directions for going north to Canada, "or they might have tried to go east and get to Philadelphia, where abolitionist groups would help them with new jobs, new places to live, a whole new life of freedom," she said.

Naturally, Matthew "had to keep it extremely hush-hush," Jackie said. But in 1837, he went to live with a family named Wertz in nearby Waynesboro, Pennsylvania, and that's why we have an account of his activities.

Seems that the Wertzes had a son, a lad named Hiram, and in 1911, the aged Hiram put his memories into a newspaper account. In 1845, Matthew Dobbin, still a Wertz household boarder, confided to Hiram that he "had been engaged for several years in helping runaway slaves escape to the north." He was now too old and feeble for the work. Would Hiram take up the mantle?

"I readily assented to this, and became the captain of one of the stations of the remarkable Underground Railroad," Wertz wrote.

Not that old Matthew was, by now, too decrepit for an abolitionist rumble. When he learned that slave catchers were detaining five African-American men at a Waynesboro hotel, he "rallied some of the citizens of the better class, saying that with them at his back he could demand the liberation of the fugitives. If the demand was not granted, then he proposed to use force."

Word got out, though, and the captors spirited their captives away, presumably back to lives of enslavement. These captors were "citizens of the village, but not of the better class. Their occupations were card playing, horse racing, etc."

Dobbin's legacy lived on in the 50 or so slaves that Wertz sheltered in his father's barn by day and guided about eight miles north by night, to a settlement near the Caledonia furnace called Africa. Many were motivated to escape by the declining financial fortunes of their slaveholders, fearful of sale into even worse conditions. They were hungry and tired. Some were "startled by every noise." Others "were full of confidence and in high good humor over having crossed the Mason and Dixon line."

"But all were willing to secrete themselves and keep very quiet for they knew that rewards were offered for them and that men, anxious to win rewards, would stop at nothing to take them into the Southland."

Today, Dobbin House Tavern visitors walk up the narrow stairs from the original kitchen and look to the left. There, the sliding shelf is halfway open, revealing the crawl space where, as mannequins of two men and a woman attest, escaping slaves could shelter. Matthew Dobbin died in 1855, but as Wertz wrote, he would have been proud to know the fate of his father's farm, where a momentous battle "settled the principals he taught with such insistent earnestness."

A few days after the Battle of Gettysburg, Wertz stood on Cemetery Hill. To the west, he could see the stone homestead where Matthew Dobbin was born, now "defaced with shot and shell, with devastation all around it."

"It came upon me in an overwhelming manner that if Mr. Dobbin could have seen this and have known that there the backbone of slavery's defenders was broken he would have lifted up his voice and in fervent tones repeated the language of the Prophet Simeon when the Christ Child was placed in his arms: 'Lord, now lettest Thou Thy servant depart in peace according to Thy word, for mine eyes have seen Thy salvation.'"

Burying the dead, recommitting to freedom: On June 30, 1863, Gettysburg was a busy but unremarkable Pennsylvania town of 2,400 people. By July 4, 1863, it was the site of 10,000 dead or mortally wounded men, 30,000 injured, and 10,000 captured or missing.

The Dobbin House and its residents witnessed it all.

In 1863, a family named Ziegler owned the house and farm built by Alexander Dobbin. John Ziegler was away, fighting for the Union. Elvira Ziegler and their five kids stayed behind. "Like so many Civil War women, here she was, left alone to take care of this great, big, huge farm," said Jackie. No one knows if Elvira and the children sheltered at home during the battle, or if they fled. If they stayed, Jackie tries to imagine the scene:

Union soldiers marching into town. "Maybe they thought, 'Hallelujah, they'll protect us,'" Jackie said. From Seminary Ridge, only a mile away, the sounds of battle—cannons booming, muskets roaring, bugles blowing. The sounds come closer until the battle is raging on Elvira's own land. The Confederates keep pushing, and soon, the same Union troops that marched into town that morning are "running back the way they came. Not a good sign."

The Union dug into the hillside across from the Ziegler home, on the outskirts of town. Confederates occupied the town itself, "and here's the Dobbin House, right in the middle of everything." Rebel snipers took potshots from attics. An Ohio company occupied the Ziegler home, shooting back from the attic and the rafters of the barn.

"This made the Confederates angry, so they snuck into the Dobbin House and they captured all the Union soldiers in here," Jackie said. At least one bullet probably flew through the house. You can see the apparent bullet hole in a door on the top floor.

July 1, 2, and 3 were hot and humid. The wounded and the dead, human and equine, lay on open fields in the sweltering sun. On July 4, Independence Day, the skies opened, and the rain came down. The town was finally quiet, but as Jackie put it, "the worst was just beginning."

One farmer's son described "a trodden, miry waste, with corpses at every step." A Union soldier said "no words can depict the ghastly picture," but he left us a pretty good description when he described Confederate soldiers left on Cemetery Ridge, where "the men lay in heaps, the wounded wriggling and groaning under the weight of the dead among whom they were entangled."

Jackie imagines those wounded "so thirsty from that hot sun. You're hungry and you just want to get help. You look over in the distance and think, 'There's a house. There's a barn. Maybe there's someone there who can help me.' You're gonna walk. If you have to, you're gonna crawl over there and say, 'Can you please help me?'"

So, the Ziegler home became a sanctuary, like so many homes converted to shelter. Jackie has no doubt that the floors of Dobbin House, including the top floor where today's guests dine under bed canopies, "would have been full of Union *and* Confederate boys. We townspeople didn't care. We wanted to help everybody, whoever we could."

But when thirsty, weak, hungry, wounded soldiers beg, "Please, Elvira, can you help me?" what's a Civil War homemaker-turned-humanitarian to do? A few provisions arrived from the Army, and some were available for purchase from farmers in the surrounding countryside who earned an undying reputation for profiteering.

In the town, it is said, better angels presided. Women and their maids cooked food. One young woman was heartbroken by the anguish of the suffering men, who would accept one spoonful of food and mutter, "God bless you."

"Devastation" is the word that comes up, over and over, to describe the impact of a battle fought not just in open fields but in the center of town. Crops were trampled. Gardens were ransacked. Horses were confiscated for battle and transport. Sheep and cattle were slaughtered for food. Fences were dismantled for firewood.

Here's where technology enters the picture. Word spread about the town's plight via the latest word in communications, the telegraph. People started arriving immediately. Nuns from the Sisters of Charity in Emmitsburg, Maryland, traveled from 13 miles away. Others arrived under such names as the Hospital Corps of Adams Express Company, the Fireman's Associations of Baltimore, the Patriot Daughters of Lancaster, the Ladies' Aid

Society of Philadelphia, and the New York Soldiers' Relief Agency. The U.S. Sanitary Commission, established in 1861 to help the military tend to its sick and wounded soldiers, arrived with four wagons of supplies even as the battle raged.

Donations from ordinary citizens also streamed into town, said Jackie—"clothing and food and medicine and blankets and whiskey, and thank goodness they did, because with their help, we townspeople were able to save many, many lives." One African-American Adams County resident named Lydia Smith gathered donations via a rickety cart for delivery to hospitals south of Gettysburg.

While other Gettysburg residents packed up and moved West after the battle, John Ziegler and his family stayed and continued farming. In the battle's aftermath, there was also the horrible question of what to do with the bodies of 10,000 dead. Graves marked by names scratched on fence posts or the lids of cartridge boxes were scattered around farms and fields—locations recorded by surgeons and comrades as "back of Privy, Sargt. Alfred Bird, Com F 50 Ga," or "near Forney's place in a field under an apple tree."

Many bodies of the Union dead were exhumed and relocated by grieving relatives. The bodies of Southern soldiers were gradually sent home in the months and years after the battle until a movement in the early 1870s mobilized states and Ladies' Memorial Associations to return all the dead—or as many as possible—to Southern soil.

Today, step out of the Dobbin House front door, and a bit of green peeks out from behind the coffee shop across the street. That is a corner of the Gettysburg National Cemetery, one of the first national cemeteries created in 1863. During the desperate race to inter bodies before pestilence broke out, Gettysburg's leading lights had the idea to create a cemetery for the Union dead, under an 1862 federal act authorizing the creation of soldiers' cemeteries. Pennsylvania Gov. Andrew Curtin approved the idea, possibly because his buggy tour of the battlegrounds and town revealed the blackened arms, legs, and hands of the dead reaching from their shallow graves, "the devil's own planting . . . a harvest of death."

Even in the wake of catastrophic loss and suffering, Gettysburg's leading lights didn't entirely put aside their egos or thoughts of personal enrichment. One promised to give the state an existing cemetery and adjoining lands for the hallowed ground, only to learn that the man who had originally proposed the idea had already locked up those adjacent plots. Letters, bickering, squabbling—this is Pennsylvania, after all. The warring parties, pressured by fellow townspeople, finally came to an agreement that the existing cemetery and adjoining land would be sold to the state.

At least some of that land, Jackie knows, was part of Ziegler's farm, "but we don't know to what extent," she said. Her vivid imagination describes the scene from Dobbin House on consecration day, Nov. 19, 1863.

"If you were standing here in November of 1863, you would hear a lot of commotion, and if you looked up that hill, you would see 12,000 to 15,000 people milling around. What are all those people here for? They're here to have a dedication of a brand-new cemetery. A parade came down the road right in front of the Dobbin House—soldiers marching, bands playing, dignitaries on horses, and one of those dignitaries, of course, was President Abraham Lincoln, so the people who lived at the Dobbin House might have stood up on that balcony and waved to President Lincoln as he went by."

And President Lincoln, of course, would make his own bit of rabble-rousing history there, with the radical notion that a divided nation could recommit to its founding principles of equality for all. Just for the chance to go back and see that moment from the Dobbin House, Jackie said, "is when I wish I had a time machine."

SECTION III

Touch history

So much of the original Dobbin House remains intact that Alexander Dobbin would probably walk in and take a seat in the parlor, settling in to write his next sermon.

The spring in the basement: Alexander Dobbin built his family home directly over a spring. Not *near* a spring. Directly over, with access by stairs from the kitchen. There were two reasons for building on top of running water.

■ If either of the Mrs. Dobbins wanted to keep the milk or leftover soup cool, she could float a container in the spring, for year-round, 55-degree refrigeration. Wait a second. Nineteen kids and there was leftover soup?

■ In case of attack by Native Americans, the family would retain a fresh supply of water. In 1776, this was frontier, only thirteen years distant from the end of the French and Indian War, when French allied with Native Americans to fight for territory in the New World. Hostilities ran deep.

The spring still flows below the house, where you can see it. Step up the stairs from the tavern toward the house museum, and peek into a window overlooking a walled cistern. The glassy water is almost impossible to see until the pump starts running and breaks the water's surface.

Outside, the house's first-level shutters—not repeated on the second floor, as they would be today—also were meant to turn the house into a fortress in case of attack. Dobbin and his family would have known about the 1755 kidnapping of local girl Mary Jemison by hostile Shawnee and their French compatriots. (Interestingly, Mary gained fame for assimilating into Native American culture and turning down her chances to return to British Colonial culture. Could it be she disliked the ideas of giving up the property she owned and not having a say in her own governance? You can read her story in "A Narrative of the Life of Mrs. Mary Jemison," available in the Dobbin House's Country Curiosity Store.)

The spinning room: In a town full of Civil War-costumed re-enactors, Jackie likes to spotlight Dobbin House's Colonial history. The "spinning room" follows fiber from dying to spinning to clothing. A giant spinning wheel hanging on the wall is called a "walking wheel," which turned fiber into yarn by virtue of a woman walking back and forth instead of pumping a pedal. (I watched YouTube videos of artisans operating these "great wheels." Good grief, they look exhausting.) The cotton, wool, and linen yarn was dyed with tree bark, onion skin, "and even some bugs to make a little color," said Jackie. Then it was loomed into cloth, and finally, the fabric was sewn into clothes. No closet here. Just pegs on the wall to hang the two or maybe three outfits you owned.

The half-walled dining room: I like to think that Alexander Dobbin was a social man. The names of more than 200 brides and grooms for whom he officiated are known, and it's possible that his spacious dining room hosted wedding receptions. For a 1787 wedding, he did something new—he wrote the location on a marriage license as "Gettystown," the first reference to the town founded by and named after his good friend James Gettys. In

The dining room with a hanging half-wall

that dining room, look up, and you'll notice wrought iron hooks dangling from the ceiling. You'll also notice a hanging half-wall separating the dining room from a corridor to the home's original kitchen. Need to expand the space? Swing the wall upward and attach it to the hooks, and the room is now bigger. Resourceful folks, these Colonials.

Cooking up a county: The Dobbin House's original furnishings are long gone, but Rev. Dobbin's will meticulously detailed his belongings, so Jackie scoured antique shops for furniture matching the items where Dobbin, family, and friends would have sat and dined. In the cozy parlor where Dobbin possibly mapped out the creation of Adams County, diners can sit in wing-backed armchairs. A close look at the fireplace reveals that not everything was serious and bewigged in here. Seems a stepson of Alexander Dobbin, Smith Agnew, carved his initials in

Smith Agnew's initials carved into the mantel

199

Windsor chairs in the upper dining room

the mantel, "S A". Sighed Jackie, "I can only imagine the trouble Smith received after his parents found what he had done."

Candles burning: Throughout Dobbin House's dining areas, the candles stand in what look like iron springs. These spiral candleholders are called "courting candles." If a Colonial girl's suitor appeared, her father would size up the guy and announce that the potential beau's visit must end when the candle burned to the candleholder. If he liked what he saw, a wooden dowel would go in the spiral first, propping up the candle for a longer burn. If the guy looked like a bum, the candle would go straight into the holder and burn out quickly, for a short night.

Since dads never change, you can get your own courting candle in the Dobbin House Country Curiosity Store, along with old-fashioned candy sticks, Dr. G's sarsaparilla and orange cream sodas, jewelry, Vera Bradley bags, and Cat's Meow figurines. And by the way, the Dobbin House candles are hand-dipped by Lancaster County Mennonites, dripping into intriguing sculptural shapes as they burn.

Mamie in the house: After leaving the presidency, Dwight Eisenhower and wife Mamie settled on a farm in Gettysburg, their first permanent home in 41 years of marriage. Jackie remembers Secret Service agents in the school she attended with the Eisenhower grandchildren. She would see Eisenhower himself in church. Ike died in 1969, but the beloved Mamie lived long enough to dine with friends at Dobbin House after it opened in 1977. They would tour the house, Mamie's hand touching the rail in the central stairway, original to the building. "I don't know how people knew," said Jackie, "but there'd always be a big crowd out front that wanted to meet Mamie."

Spiral candle holder

Any ghosts? Jackie has heard a lot of cockamamie stories from the ghost tours stopping outside the Dobbin House. No, this was not a Confederate hospital, and amputated limbs did not pile up in the spinning room. No, the house was not built by slaves. Jackie has never encountered a ghost. If the Rev. Alexander Dobbin did flit past, she said she would grab him and order him to take a chair and prepare for a grilling, "because I have a million questions. What kind of clothes did you wear? What kind of food did you eat? Tell me what your life was like. Tell me about your sermons. Tell me about your feelings toward slavery, and toward the revolution. So, I say I scare the ghost."

The food scene: The woman at the bar beside me appeared to be eating a platter loaded with vegetables.

"How's your salad?" asked Linda Sheffield, my server on this day and a longtime Dobbin House assistant manager.

"The more I eat, the more it grows," said the woman. "And I've been eating for 10 minutes."

At Dobbin House, classic fare and generous portions assure that no one leaves hungry or unhappy. Hot beef sandwich, Maryland Colony crab cakes, char-grilled marinated chicken breast, the Mason's Mile High, piled with deli meats "almost as high as the stone walls of the Dobbin House." It's all presented in a delightful menu laid out and written with a nod to Colonial dining habits and lingo. Try the homemade herb "dreffing" on your "sallade." Have a "gill" of "porridge"—known as a cup of soup to you and me. Your freshly ground Dobbin's hamburger is "char-grilled to the strength of fire you prefer."

What to eat? If you bring your appetite, there's "Of Flesh and Fish," a.k.a. surf and turf, "a favorite among Rev. Dobbin's houfe guefts." The Seafood Isabella features fresh veggies and scallops, shrimp and crabmeat in wine sauce "simmered over hot embers 'til tender." Since you're in the heart of Adams County apple country, try the Roast Duck Adams County, "served up juft right with a delicious cyder sauce," or for dessert, the Adams County Apple Pye.

I tried: Just had to try the Maryland Colony Crabcake Sandwich. Crab meat piled high, with minimal filler, just as a crab cake should be. Served on fresh French bread, with a unique and tangy Dijon balsamic mayonnaise. Tantalizing. And no matter what you eat, do not miss the Baked King's Onion Soup. Try it as an appetizer, or pair it with a sallade for lunch. Oh, that bubbling cheese! And inside, surprising bits of beef. It's famous, and justifiably so.

The beverage scene: Linger over three drink specialties of the house.

■ Rum Bellies Vengeance mixes light and dark rums, liqueurs, and fruit drinks. Only two per customer. Really. Jackie said she can't even drink one without her head sinking down onto the bar.

■ The Philadelphia Fish House Punch is a nod to Rev. Dobbin's occasional trips to Philadelphia. The Dobbin House's version of Philadelphia City Tavern's punch features rum, brandy, peach brandy, and fruit juices.

■ And then there's Don's Derring Do, invented by one of Dobbin House's first bartenders. The name called to mind the dashing heroes of old-time melodramas, and I wasn't about to test my limits with a Rum Bellies Vengeance, so this was the one to try. And wow, it is good. Apricot brandy, orange and pineapple juices, and—for that little Civil War touch in this Colonial home—Southern Comfort. Tart and refreshing.

Don's Derring Do

Lodging at Gettystown Inn: The Rev. Dobbin's hospitality extends to three Dobbin House-associated inns nearby, all Civil War-era homes with rooms decorated in 19th-century antiques. Fuel up on a hearty breakfast served at the Dobbin House. (http://www.dobbinhouse.com/innrooms.htm)

PLAN YOUR VISIT

The Dobbin House Tavern
89 Steinwehr Avenue (Business Route 15 South)
Gettysburg, PA 17325
www.dobbinhouse.com, (717) 334-2100

For an insider's look at Dobbin House's history and restoration, take one of the tours offered throughout much of the year. Check ahead to see if they're offered during your visit.

WHAT'S NEARBY

Federal Pointe Inn: It's back to school, but there are no pencils, books, or teacher's dirty looks at Federal Pointe Inn. Gettysburg's first high school, built in 1897 and named after Gen. George Meade, just had to become a boutique hotel, an Ascend Hotel Collection member. Bright, spacious suites with tall ceilings and luxury baths. Wide hallways furnished in elegant side chairs and a giant armoire. Photos of generations of graduating classes hanging on the walls. Mosey down to the basement and the fun Federal Pointe Pub, where the pub fare is decidedly more enticing than school-cafeteria Jell-O, and the blackboard offers today's assignment—deciding which craft beer to choose. (www.federal-pointeinn.com)

Farnsworth House entrance

9.

HISTORIC FARNSWORTH HOUSE INN AND SWENEY'S TAVERN

Gettysburg, Pennsylvania

Bullets and bravado

Misbehavior makes history: Historic Farnsworth House Inn and Sweney's Tavern

■ One hundred bullet holes tell the story. Confederate sharpshooters fired from their nest in the attic. Union sharpshooters fired back.

■ While families sought refuge in the basement, Confederate occupiers cracked open the larders and liquor cabinets of these fine homes.

■ On a day in November 1863, a grand procession paraded past. The tall man at the center, tipping his trademark stovepipe hat to the cheering throng, smiled graciously, but homeowner Harvey Sweney could detect "the dreadful responsibility that this nation and this wicked rebellion has cast upon him."

■ The Blue and the Gray returned to this sleepy crossroads town in 1992—filming a movie on Ted Turner's dime. This time, the carousing warriors looked a lot like Sam Elliott and Tom Berenger, and the house liquor they were swilling came from behind the bar at Sweney's Tavern.

■ From a bloodied glove to a severed horse hoof (fake, we hope), see the movie props and costumes purchased by the Farnsworth House owner and now a tavern focal point.

■ Today's scene: Victorian elegance in the Farnsworth House, and pub ambiance in the connected Sweney's Tavern. Plus, a sweet beer garden amid statuary and a koi pond.

Built: Pre-1810, with a brick addition in 1833, and a circa-1940s garage converted to Sweney's Tavern in the 1980s.

Meet the owner

I have nothing against Dunkin' Donuts. Love me a good éclair. But the Farnsworth House Inn as a tourist-town Dunkin' Donuts? Heaven forbid.

So let's thank that same heaven for Loring Shultz. When the historic Farnsworth House, long a restaurant and inn, went up for sale in 1972, he swooped in before others eyeing the building could turn it into a Dunkin' Donuts. In one move, he simultaneously preserved a Gettysburg landmark and deprived Nixon-era battle-field visitors of the year's new taste treat, Munchkins donut holes.

Shultz was a Gettysburg native and Air Force veteran when he started working for former Baltimore Colts defensive end Gino Marchetti. The Pro Football Hall of Famer found a second career, collaborating with former teammates to launch Gino's, which pretty much owned the Mid-Atlantic fast-food scene in its day. (Suddenly, I can't get the jingle out of my head. "Everybody goes to Gino's, 'cuz Gino's is the place to go.")

Mr. Shultz rose to Gino's commissary manager, but he and his wife, Jean Bible Shultz, dreamed of a restaurant of their own, devoted to a historic dining experience, Williamsburg-style. The house steeped in Battle of Gettysburg lore and known as Sleepy Hollow Lodge needed some work, but the Shultzes dug in.

Really, they dug in. They literally dug out the basement. Also sandblasted the exterior and redecorated the interior. All while living in the upstairs rooms with their four kids.

That's what I call a leap of faith.

Since then, the property has never been stagnant, and growth has been organic. The family rooms were converted to B&B lodging. A bookstore, tavern, beer garden, and Civil War camp for kids have all been added. Mr. Shultz still works in the kitchen of his dream establishment.

The pub is Sweney's Tavern, named after the house's Civil War-era owner, and pronounced "Sweeney." A tannery probably stood here once. Mr. Shultz built this atmospheric spot, a secret getaway off the street but linked to the main house.

Mr. Shultz "respects the history and values the history," Sarah Dull, director of group sales and marketing, told me as we sat in Sweney's Tavern. "A lot of other places are fabricated to make them

Entry

look old. Even though it's not the cheapest or the easiest option to maintain it at its natural state, it's the best. Everything he's added has a different element that just adds to what the Farnsworth has. It all plays off the house, and it's all intertwined together."

Tour Historic Farnsworth House Inn and Sweney's Tavern

Time travel. We all know what it means, and yet, it's not a real thing. Until physicists figure out how to dial ourselves into the past, a pub that was once a home caught up in a fierce, water-shed-moment-in-history battle will have to do.

Farnsworth House: Enter the front door, and you are entering another dimension known as Victorian America. This front section is the addition built in grand style befitting owner John

207

Vintage sign hanging inside the Farnsworth House

McFarlane, prominent citizen and, ironically for what's now a bar, temperance activist. Hang your coat on the ornate oak hall mirror. Note the sign from the Farnsworth's days as Sleepy Hollow Lodging, the one proclaiming "BULLET HOLES IN HOUSE." And there's the framed map of circa-1860 Adams County, loaned out as a prop from the Farnsworth House bookshop for the filming of "Gettysburg."

Take a right into the dining area, and you're in the Meade Room, all dark wood and elaborately carved mantelpiece clocks and heavy drapes over tall windows. Pay your respects to Gen. George Meade, in portrait form over the brick fireplace. Tucked beside the fireplace is a clever shoe cabinet, with cubbyholes for drying wet shoes. Must have been nice to put frigid toesies in warm boots on cold mornings. Another painting, Larry Selman's "We have come to dedicate," depicts the day Abraham Lincoln rode past this house on his way to dedicate the Soldiers' National Cemetery. The

Exterior bullet hole

Meade Room

man depicted on the porch is Harvey Sweney, soaking up the pageantry and solemnity of the moment.

Step through the columned arch into the Lee Room, named after you-know-who, also with a portrait here. Take a closer look at the divider concealing serving staff as they pop in and out of the kitchen. It was once the front door of the home. And there's a bullet hole just over the wrought-iron bolt lock.

Sweney's Tavern: Comfortable and cozy. Low-ceilinged and friendly. Sweney's Tavern was made for retreating from the real world for a few hours. Décor ranges from a wagon wheel and saddlebags to a mounted deer head and a photo of Sam Elliott as Gen. John Buford. The whole space wraps around the bar, creating quiet corners for intimate conversations. Those props from

Sweney's Tavern

Sweney's Tavern bar

"Gettysburg," the movie, are carefully displayed in a glass case spanning the length of one wall. In a nook behind the bar, a battle-scene print is encircled by signatures of the actors who made Sweney's their hangout. Apparently, the rowdy thespians stirred up a bit of trouble. I don't know who instigated what, but actor Tim Ruddy, playing Lee aide de camp Major Charles Marshall, signed, "Thank you Farnsworth. It was Stuart's fault."

SECTION II

The history of Historic Farnsworth House Inn and Sweney's Tavern

From factual Gettysburg to historic-fiction Gettysburg, the Farnsworth House Inn and Sweney's Tavern have seen it all.

McFarlane home: If you read the Dobbin House chapter, you've already met the Rev. Alexander Dobbin. He was a pastor, schoolmaster, revolution supporter, and all-around civic light. Now, I learn, he was also a canny businessman. When his friend James Gettys laid out a town of 210 lots around the intersection of Baltimore and Shippensburg roads, Dobbin realized that this town-aborning came near his farm. Around 1803, Dobbin subdivided a section of his property into lots. This puts a new spin on Rev. Dobbin's drive to form Adams County and get Gettysburg named the county seat. Of course, he wanted Gettysburg to be the county seat. It meant higher property values.

Businessman and politico John McFarlane bought lots #5 and #6. Somebody had already built a frame-and-log building there, possibly associated with a nearby tannery. By 1812, McFarlane owned the tannery. Business must have been good because in 1833, he built a substantial brick addition to the log home, a street-facing edifice announcing that a prominent man lived here.

Then business must have tanked. The bank took over McFarlane's elegant house and held it for 10 years. Schoolteacher and butcher Harvey Sweney—"somewhat stern and of quick temper," noted a contemporary—bought it in 1852. On the first day of July 1863, all hell broke loose. The world remembers the Battle of Gettysburg as a fight for wooded ridges, but for the citizens of the town, war barged through the front doors.

Fleeing: At 7:30 a.m. Wednesday, July 1, 1863, the cannon fire started. By 10 a.m., the bombardment was constant. The streets of Gettysburg jammed with fleeing townspeople, shells screeching as "unearthly yells added to the terror and cries of the women and children." Then came nearly 10,000 Union soldiers surging past the Sweney home to escape the Confederate wave, so many men that an 18-year-old neighbor of Sweney's swore she could have "walked across the street on the heads of soldiers."

For three days, the wounded and dying from the streets and the battlefields were dragged into homes and churches, or they dragged themselves in. Harvey Sweney gave food and bedding and clothing to the Union wounded in his home. In another part of town, Sweney's wife and daughters "found plenty of work to do for suffering men" in the home-turned-hospital where they sought refuge.

In the cellars: Those who didn't flee town scurried to their own cellars or the cellars of their neighbors. Some cellar refugees had fled the outlying farms now engulfed in battle. The Sweney home's basement sheltered the Slentz family, a mother who fled her farm with her five children "bareheaded and without shoes or stockings." They tried herding their cattle before them, but the cattle were lost. At Sweney's, they shared the tiny cellar with a family boarding there, the Weikerts and their three boys, ages 4 to 9.

Huddled in their cellars, the helpless civilians could hear soldiers stomping above. Adding to the dark and damp and fear was hunger. "They took away everything edible, except a small piece of dried beef and some coffee," said a Lutheran Theological Seminary student taking refuge in the home across from Sweney's.

Not everyone cowered. Sweney's 18-year-old neighbor, Anna Garlach, was in her cellar when a Confederate burst in the front door and started upstairs. Her mother emerged from the basement and grabbed the armed man by the coat.

"You can't go up there," she insisted. "You will draw the fire on this house full of defenseless women and children."

The soldier said: I need the house for sharpshooters. Mother said: I insist you leave. Soldier: That would be instant death. Mother: You can stay, but no firing from the house. Soldier: I'll go now. So he opened the door, fired a covering shot, "and in the smoke darted out and got safely across the street."

The sharpshooters: In the home of Harvey Sweney and his neighbors, soldiers climbed "handsome stairways" for deadly purpose. Great armies were clashing in the fields and forests outside of Gettysburg, while Union and Confederate units skirmished

The cellar

in the town's "suburbs"—the fringes where houses gave way to farms.

In the Sweney house, Confederate snipers occupied the garret. Sharpshooters from both sides pinned down their adversaries. Raise your head above a fence rail or let an elbow peek out from behind a tree, and a bullet would whistle toward it. As the mother of Anna Garlach knew, sharpshooter fire drew attention. Confederates would shoot toward Union forces on Cemetery Hill. Union soldiers would shoot back. Soldiers died in the handsome homes—including a Confederate "killed on the spot" in a front room—and bled on the rich carpets.

While sharpshooters took their posts in upper-story windows, and on roofs and behind trees, fellow soldiers retreated into elegant parlors to loll on upholstered sofas and enjoy the wines left behind by their unwilling hosts. One officer ordered a subordinate to rendezvous at "a very handsome house." When the officer arrived, he found the junior officer in the parlor, "playing on the piano, which sounded sadly out of harmony with the roar of the musketry without."

"The awful responsibility": Even the fearless Elon John Farnsworth knew a suicide mission when he saw it. The Confederates were in retreat. The good guys had won.

But Farnsworth recognized his duty. On July 3, 1863, Farnsworth and 65 of his men died in what would be a fruitless attack, mounted after the Battle of Gettysburg had, in essence, ended.

Elon J. Farnsworth was a college man, the University of Michigan Class of—well, here, the story gets cloudy. Maybe he graduated in 1858. Or maybe he was leading "a carousal" when a classmate fell off a roof and died. Maybe Farnsworth and seven others were expelled. Maybe he went to a professor, acknowledging the justice of the expulsion and promising to "make a man of himself."

Adventure followed in the wilds of Utah Territory. When civil war broke out, Farnsworth got a cavalry commission through his Uncle John, a member of Congress. For once, nepotism put the right man in the right post. His men considered him "courage incarnate but full of tender regard" for their well-being. After some time as a general's aide alongside another reckless young spirit named George Armstrong Custer, he asked Uncle John for another favor and was promoted suddenly from captain to brigadier general.

On July 3, Farnsworth received an order, sent from Gen. Judson Kilpatrick, to lead his cavalry brigade through woods and boulders and over heavily defended walls, creating a diversion for Gen. Meade. What we'll call a heated battlefield debate ensued, with Farnsworth essentially putting a curse on Kilpatrick's head.

"General, if you order the charge I will lead it," he said, "but you must take the awful responsibility."

The troopers lined up. Farnsworth led men and horses "into the jaws of death and into the mouth of hell." In the tight spaces between stone fences, there was no escape. The surgeon who found Farnsworth's body on July 5 declared the general's face "as calm and pleasant as in life."

It's said today that Farnsworth fulfilled the pledge he made at college, only five years before, to "make a man of himself." He is one of five Union generals killed in the battle. A monument stands at the site of his death, but another monument, of a sort, stands in town to recall his sacrifice. When Loring Shultz bought the old Sleepy Hollow Inn, he renamed it the Farnsworth

House, honoring the dutiful hero. Elon Farnsworth never visited his namesake inn. I think he'd like it, though. Nice place for an adventurous soul to blow off steam.

"Gettysburg," the movie: I once acted in a searing stage production of "A Streetcar Named Desire" when a student at a talk-back with the cast asked, "How do you get over such an emotional experience after the final curtain?" All nine cast members simultaneously pointed left—northward, to the bar where we gathered after every rehearsal and every performance.

Playacting can never compare to real-life war in danger and stakes, but there are easier ways to make a living—especially when it involves long days in full costume and heavy gear, and the possibility that a musket could be inadvertently loaded, or a bayonet mishandled. The adrenaline high from a day of acting can't be turned off with a switch. Actors and crew need to step it down gradually, and for eons, that has meant occupying the nearest bar.

Gettysburg had endured rumors for years that Michael Shaara's Pulitzer Prize-winning "The Killer Angels," the 1975 novelization of the Battle of Gettysburg, would be turned into a movie. Then one day in 1992, an actor stopped by the Farnsworth House Book Shop and confirmed to Manager John S. Peterson that media mogul Ted Turner's Turner Network Television was launching production. The "TNT Rebs" were closing in.

This particular actor was a Union officer, Brian Mallon playing Gen. Winfield Scott Hancock, but the wave of officers that followed, as their 1992 actor selves researching their characters, included Confederate Gens. Hood, Armistead, and George Pickett himself.

At the decree of Tom Berenger, portraying Gen. James Longstreet, the Farnsworth House was designated the official officers' club, First Corps, Army of Northern Virginia. "As might be expected," Peterson would recall, "the tavern soon became the scene of some of the merriest Civil War parties since Jeb Stuart rode rings round McClellan."

Friday and Saturday nights, Sweney's Tavern was reserved for actors and crew. For one month, "the camaraderie bordered on the Elysian, and Tom Berenger deserved much of the credit." They coerced Peterson to drink Guinness with them. They reached their high-water mark the night Gen. Pickett, a.k.a. Stephen Lang, climbed on the bar and, glass raised in a toast, declared, "At long last, I've taken the high ground."

They tried not to let the actual circumstances of the battle dampen their mood. "Despite the outcome," Berenger said, "we had more fun and our uniforms were more colorful."

The Union arrived after the Confederates left town. They were "slightly subdued" compared to their Rebel counterparts—until the Irish Brigade swept in. Answered Brian Mallon to Berenger's claim, "They may have had more colorful uniforms, but we sang more and better songs and held the field at the end."

In his memories of that summer, Guinness and all, Peterson wrote, "From the brim to the dray, the summer had poured sweet and clear. Whichever side held the tavern, Killer Angels '92 was a very good year."

Historical accuracy check: Even amid the merriment, the actors took their roles as recreators of the past very seriously. Battlefield guide and unofficial Farnsworth House historian Tim Smith often found himself answering questions about skirmishes and characters. It was his job, he said, "to drink with the actors."

"I think I was partly responsible for Sam Elliott's costume," he told me.

Really? How come?

"Because Gen. Buford didn't wear the regular uniform of a general during the battle. He was wearing a hunting jacket. I gave him a description of that, and somebody else had told him about that, so he bought his own outfit."

SECTION III

Touch history

From top to bottom, Farnsworth House contains a microcosm of the battle raging in the town while armies clashed on farm fields and ridges.

In the garret: If bullet holes were legal tender in Gettysburg, which they kind of are, the Farnsworth House would be worth gazillions. Tour the Farnsworth House to see the brick-walled attic and its square, wood-framed window where Confederate snipers knelt to take aim at the Union side. Below and around the window are about 100 pockmarks from shots fired back at them by Union fighters. Some of the bullet holes are inches from the window frame.

From July 1 through the morning of July 4, gunfire filled the daylight hours. On the afternoon of July 4, an eerie silence descended. Soldiers and officers on both sides waited tensely for word on the outcome of a Confederate charge against the Union center.

Frustrated by the defeat of Pickett's Charge, Confederate Major Eugene Blackford, here on the south edge of town, resumed the potshots "with careful aim." He shot 84 times from two guns, one gun cooling while he fired the other. He fired until his sore shoulder made it impossible to continue.

"Now and then the enemy's gunners would turn a gun or two on us, and give us a shot, but this was too destructive of the lives of women and children for even Yankees to stand," he said, "so it was stopped."

In the cellars: In the week before the battle, Confederate raiders marveled that so few Gettysburg residents knew any information on the location and strength of Union forces. "It is a strange thing you people know so little," mused one officer.

Most townspeople didn't hide in that week before bullets and cannonballs started flying, but as the strains of "Dixie" played by a Confederate band sounded through the town, one group of residents fled or hid—free blacks and escaped slaves. Southern forces were rounding up African-Americans and sending them south, contraband to be returned to former owners or sold at auction. From Gettysburg, a refugee trail of African-Americans wound into the hills. One woman swore that "no rebel" would carry her back to slavery. A farmhand hid in a wagon for three days while his employer's son brought him food. Those who couldn't escape were marched past townspeople, crying and moaning on their way to enslavement.

When battle arrived, two families huddled in the Sweney house basement while sharpshooters held the attic, and presumably the fine parlor and kitchen. In this low-ceilinged, stone-walled root cellar, we can imagine they experienced the same terrors recorded by fellow townspeople. One girl recalled "the crack of rifles, the hurried orders, and outside the mingled roar of heavy musketry, galloping horses, yelling troops, and the occasional boom of cannon." And yet, above all that cacophony, "we could hear the beating of our hearts." One family determined who had the upper hand in battle by the "predominance of blue or gray legs hurrying past the cellar window."

When they woke on the morning of July 4, the people of Gettysburg found that their occupiers had, in the memories of one young boy, "folded their tents and quietly stolen away." In days to come, the air would be choked with the stench of rotting flesh and a "plague of flies." The grim tasks of burying the dead, caring for the wounded, and rebuilding the town were ahead. But in the words of one resident, on that day after battle's end, "A happier set of people you never saw."

"Peace to their ashes": On a pleasant Thursday morning in November 1863, a drum roll sounded from the Gettysburg hilltop. Cannons boomed at orderly intervals, one volley every minute as if counting down.

Harvey Sweney stepped onto his front porch, where a "living sea of human beings" surged toward the new soldiers' cemetery and the dedication ceremony planned for this day. Around 10 o'clock, the "dense mass of living beings" parted, and a cavalry detachment rode past. The horses trotted to the accompaniment of a Philadelphia band. Infantry marched in orderly contrast to the chaotic scene down this same street on a steamy day in July. The parade stretched up the road, infantry and mounted men, more bands, and dignitaries riding on horseback and wearing "handsome costumes."

In the middle, behind a bodyguard, rode a tall man on a "beautiful bay charger." The man was a head taller than the other important fellows with him. He bowed left and right, sharing a modest smile with the women, men, and children waving from doors and windows. His self-deprecation endeared him further to those already inclined to love him, and won over the hearts of the rest.

Harvey Sweney saw it all from that stoop, close enough to witness the heartbreak of Abraham Lincoln behind the gentle smile.

"But tho' he looked cheerful and happy on that day an observant eye could see that the dreadful responsibility that this nation and this wicked rebellion has cast upon him has had its marked effect, and that he feels the terrible responsibility that rests upon him," Sweney wrote in a letter to his brother, recounting the day when President Lincoln—having surprised everyone by accepting a courtesy invitation—dedicated one of the first national cemeteries for American soldiers.

"Peace to their ashes," Sweney prayed.

Sweney's letter didn't mention Lincoln's speech. Perhaps he didn't go to the ceremony. He just knew that, even after Gettysburg set about "assuming its usual appearance" on November 20, something unalterable had descended. Their hometown, he told his brother, had become "a place of note since the memorable battle of July and is as you remark, destined to be one of those places which will go down in history to coming generations."

Most bars count down to St. Patrick's Day. Farnsworth House Inn and Sweney's Tavern mark their calendars to Gettysburg's Remembrance Day. Held on the Saturday around November 19, it's an annual tribute parade to the Union dead who, as Lincoln said, consecrated the cemetery "far above our poor power to add or detract." A living history parade passes by, reenactors trooping as soldiers (even a few Rebs) and cavalrymen and officers and wives and bagpipers and dignitaries, including Mr. Lincoln himself.

The Sweney's Tavern Beer Garden stays open through the fall just for this day, so parade-goers can watch, and reenactors still in uniform can gather for a toast or two afterward, no matter the weather. In the early evening, luminary candles light the graves of all 3,512 Civil War soldiers resting just up the hill, as their names are read into the night.

Props: Writer-director Ronald F. Maxwell and the producers of "Gettysburg" lobbied studios for 10 years to turn "The Killer Angels" into a film. Maverick media mogul Ted Turner, visions of his own "Gone With the Wind" dancing in his head, gave the project the green light—and the buckets of money needed to proceed.

"Just as the establishment of CNN in Atlanta challenged (some would say toppled) the long-ruling New York perspective of network television news, Turner's entry into the ranks of big-budget filmmaking could serve as a wake-up call for a creatively bankrupt West Coast industry arrested in an adolescent orgy of sex, sensationalism, and exploding cars," wrote a Washington Post reviewer of 1993.

How'd he do with that toppling the sex, sensationalism, and exploding cars thing? Oh, well. Ted Turner defied conventional wisdom, and for that, he belongs in the Well-Behaved Taverns Hall of Fame. At Sweney's Tavern, see how Ted Turner-kind of money buys the detail that makes history as real as a bloodied glove, a bayonet, a tattered flag, a candlestick covered in a cascade of melted wax, and a weathered wicker whiskey jug cover.

Even if you've never seen "Gettysburg," the movie, it's worth a stop at Sweney's Tavern to see the props and costume collection. Some are reproductions. Some are authentic. Farnsworth House

Sweney's Tavern movie costumes

owner Loring Shultz bought the collection from Turner Network in 1992, after filming was over. Carefully preserved behind glass, you'll find Joshua Chamberlain's (that would be Jeff Daniels') coat, boots, and hat. George Pickett's (Stephen Lang's) coat, sash, and hat. James Longstreet's (Tom Berenger's) shirt. Robert E. Lee's (Martin Sheen's) hat. That checked shirt, so prominent in the display? Brig. Gen. Buford's, as worn by—sigh—Sam Elliott.

Tim Smith, the battlefield guide who helped make Sam Elliott's costume more authentic, originally thought that Loring Shultz's plan to buy a truckload of props "was the silliest thing ever and it would never work."

"And of course, he did it, and people love it," Tim admitted. Come to Sweney's Tavern on any evening, and "Gettysburg" runs in a continuous loop on the TV screen. The guy next to you at the bar might be a reenactor waiting to point out the scene where he marched with Pickett or fixed bayonet for Chamberlain.

"Wait, wait," he'll say as the scene unfolds. "There I am!"

Honored equine dead: Sarah was showing me the props display when I asked her to name a favorite.

"I think the horse hoof is kind of cool and weird," she said.

Yep. Some props person got the direction, "Make a severed horse hoof." Because horses were in the thick of battle, just as much a target, if not more, than their human counterparts. After all, a dead horse couldn't pull a cannon into position or carry a sword-wielding cavalryman above the fray. Horses hauled the wagons that carried the food that fed the troops. They pulled the ambulances that took the wounded off the field.

Estimates of horses killed in the Civil War range from 1 million to 3 million. At Gettysburg, perhaps 3,000 equines joined the thousands of battlefield dead. One widow emerged into the silence after the battle to find 15 horse carcasses in her front yard.

Any ghosts? The Farnsworth House is one of the places where I didn't even have to ask. One of the most haunted inns in America, they say.

"You know that feeling where you think someone is watching you?" Sarah Dull asked me. "I've had several of those. There have been moments when it makes my hair stand up."

There's the little boy who plays with any toys left around, the children who run around yelling, the ghosts who rattle doors and shake bedposts, the soldiers stomping around the attic and up and down the stairs. Maybe you'll catch one yourself at a Farnsworth House ghost tour. Choose from several tours, including the Mourning Theater in the cellar, equipped with lanterns, flowers, statuary, and—yes—a coffin, or the full-blown Paranormal Night, complete with ghost-hunting equipment.

The food scene: Come to Farnsworth House for fine dining and Sweney's Tavern for family-friendly fare. Of course, they share a kitchen, and you can settle into your choice of surroundings to enjoy the famous House Specialty Game Pie. The blend of turkey, duck, and pheasant mixes with mushrooms, bacon lardoons, red currant jelly, and wild rice, under a pastry crust topping, all served in a pewter crock. It's the Farnsworth House's biggest seller and is "very Civil War," said Sarah.

Civil War dishes inspire much of the menu—Grant's Apple and Bacon Pork Chop, or the Slow Roasted Half Chicken. Plus, entrees come with sweet pickled watermelon rinds, Jennie Wade bread with Adams County apple butter, and Southern spoon bread, and a choice of two sides. You don't leave here hungry.

The lunchtime tavern menu is a bit more "something for everyone," with flatbreads and burgers and salads, but if you're in the mood for a hot lunch, don't miss Aunt Ann's Homemade

Meat Loaf, which really is made by Aunt Ann—Loring Shultz's sister Ann, who also makes the Game Pie. In the evening, the same dinner entrees created with Civil War flair for the fine dining side—the Game Pie and roasted chicken and steak and crab cakes—are here in the tavern.

Save room for a classic dessert—the 5th New York Mile-High Cheesecake, Granny Smith Apple Pie, shoofly pie, and even ice cream homemade by Cone Sweet Cone. The apple cinnamon bread pudding is Sarah's favorite. Remember real whipped cream? Get a dollop on your bread pudding, Southern Pecan Pie, or chocolate sundae.

I tried: I'm one of those people who likes fruit on anything, so when I saw the 13th Georgia Gordon's Brigade, one of the Company Cook's Flat Breads, I had to try. It's goat cheese and peaches (hence, the Georgia name and reference to the Georgia troops clustered in this area, and possibly in this house), topped with fresh greens, cherry tomatoes, shredded cheese, and balsamic glaze.

The drink scene: Specialty drinks range from the Confederate Sharpshooter—Malibu Coconut Rum, vanilla vodka, and pineapple juice—to the 3rd U.S. Infantry, an enticing blend of Bushmills Irish whiskey and Champagne. Seasonal fare might include the wintertime Peppermint White Chocolate Martini or the springtime April Rain Martini. One of the specialty seasonal drinks stuck around for its popularity, the Sweney's Lemonade, a concoction of lemonade, vodka (or not, if you prefer), and sweet strawberry topping.

Wines from the local Adams County Winery include the sweet white Tears of Gettysburg, semi-sweet Rebel Red, and Scrapple. I did a double-take on that last one. Turns out, it's sweetly spiced cranberry apple wine, made with 100 percent local apples, from the rich Adams County orchards. Local breweries get the spotlight on tap and at beer dinners, such as one featuring Evolution Craft Brewing Co., of Salisbury, Maryland. The chef prepares a menu, and the breweries pick the beers for each course. "We trust the breweries," said Sarah. "They're the experts."

Lodging: Stay in a Farnsworth House Inn room for a taste of Victorian America. Even better, there are private baths, which was not much of a Victorian thing. The lovely Eisenhower Room honors Mamie Eisenhower, a frequent inn visitor, and features a painting by Dwight Eisenhower himself. Sleep under the canopy

Beer garden

in the Sara Black Room if you dare. People say it's the most haunted room in the house. For Victorian-inspired décor with more modern amenities, select a Garden Room that opens to the Beer Garden.

PLAN YOUR VISIT

The Farnsworth House Inn
401 Baltimore Street
Gettysburg, PA 17325
www.farnsworthhouseinn.com, (717) 334-8838

WHAT'S NEARBY

The Jennie Wade House Museum: Let's not give Confederates the moral high ground on not being "too destructive of the lives of women and children." Twenty-year-old Mary Virginia "Jennie" Wade, or "Ginnie," had a sister who lived on Baltimore Street. The family knew heartbreak. Their father was known for brushes with the law and went to the poorhouse as a lunatic. Jennie and her mother made ends meet as seamstresses. They were raising a 6-year-old disabled boy named Isaac.

When battle erupted, the trio and Jennie's youngest brother took refuge in the home of Jennie's sister, the mother of a 5-day-old son. Now trapped between the Union and Confederate lines, even an artillery shell crashing through the roof didn't send them fleeing. Jennie couldn't be confined to the cellar, sometimes distributing food and water to Union soldiers.

On the morning of July 3, she was in the kitchen, baking biscuits for the troops, when a Confederate sharpshooter's bullet crashed through one door and then another and, still not spent, pierced her back. Jennie Wade died instantly, the only civilian killed outright in the Battle of Gettysburg. The day after her death, Jennie's mother finished making the biscuits.

In the 1970s, battlefield guide Eugene Sickles investigated the path of the bullet and, says Tim Smith, "became convinced that it was fired from the garret window of the Farnsworth House." (https://www.gettysburgbattlefieldtours.com/jennie-wade-house/)

10.

THE WOODEN KEG TAVERN

St. Clair, Pennsylvania

The fighting Molly Maguires

Misbehavior makes history: The Wooden Keg Tavern

■ Did the Molly Maguires congregate here, scheming terror against the coal barons in a desperate attempt to liberate their families from shacks, disease, and starvation?

■ Did Pinkerton spy James McParlan start his campaign of infiltration by buying drinks all around at this bar?

■ Was the basement tunnel meant simply for rolling beer kegs from the brewery across the street? Or could a Molly have occasionally slipped through to escape detection?

■ Today's scene: The ideal spot for hoisting a pint in memory of miners who refused to take the scraps the coal operators were giving, and the 20 who paid the price on the gallows.

Built: Circa 1870, by Irish-born brewer Martin Dormer.

Meet the owner

James T. Croley II appreciates character, and there are oodles at the Wooden Keg. But at age 21, all he wanted to do was buy a liquor license.

It was 2004. He had made a few bucks using his carpentry skills, first for his father's restaurant in Pottsville, and then flipping houses. He saw a newspaper notice about a liquor license for sale. Here was his chance for a little establishment of his own. He also found rental space, but at the last minute, the landlord backed out.

The Wooden Keg Tavern

"Me and my wife were a young couple then," he told me as we sat in the Wooden Keg barroom. "We didn't have a lot of options. Limited money. I got in a scramble."

He called the liquor-license seller and asked, "Where am I buying this license from?"

That was his introduction to a rambling Victorian building so off the beaten path in the coal town of St. Clair that he had never heard of the place, "and I've lived my whole life maybe 10 miles away."

"I came and looked at it and was blown away," Jim said. "It was the strangest thing in the world. I saw there was a lot of potential, and a lot of work, too."

Jim dreamed of turning this "little bar for old guys to hang out at" into a real restaurant. After two years of leasing, he bought the building outright. The paperwork had just been signed when one of the sellers mentioned something Jim had heard whispered.

"By the way," the man said, "there was Molly Maguires in that building."

Jim didn't think much about it at first. They chose the name "Wooden Keg" to honor the brewery that once stood across the

The Wooden Keg Tavern owner James T. Croley II

street. Their slogan was "Where Every Night is Wing Night," because wings were—and remain—their specialty. But old-timers kept wandering in and talking about the Molly Maguires.

"For whatever reason in high school, history didn't interest me, but as I started to get older, it really did," Jim said. He was enlarging the dining space and turning the basement into a dining room. He knew he had to create an Irish pub "and profess that history."

How much of it is true? Hard to say. The Molly Maguires—if they existed, but that's a whole other book—were a secret society, not inclined to take minutes of their meetings. The detective who infiltrated the gang sent regular reports back to his employer, the Pinkerton Detective Agency, and few historians have mentioned this St. Clair bar.

And yet . . .

The brother of the 1870s owner lived here and was a known Molly Maguire. Patrick Dormer was his name. He was a saloon-keeper, purportedly in Pottsville, but descriptions of his bar where he met the Pinkerton spy in 1874 are an excellent match for this place.

And yet . . .

The Wooden Keg's exact construction date is fuzzy, and that matters. The Mollies started rumbling around 1865 or 1870. On the first day of summer 1877, the first group of Molly Maguires was hanged. The land under the Wooden Keg was owned by the Dormer family—the known Molly, and his brother, Martin—in 1866, at the latest. The Dormer brewery was up by at least 1871.

There's no proof that the bar was here in 1874, but no proof that it wasn't, either, and it would certainly make sense to have a bar for selling your own beer. In fact, some sort of building was here—possibly this substantial brick bar and hotel—when the wife of a Martin Dormer business partner was convicted of keeping a "disorderly house." You know. One of those places where loud music could be heard through the night and young ladies tenanted the rooms upstairs.

In his exhaustive "St. Clair: A Nineteenth-Century Coal Town's Experience with a Disaster-Prone Industry," historian Anthony F.C. Wallace wrote that Dormer's tavern became "notorious in St. Clair as a reputed hangout of the Molly Maguires, who allegedly met there on their travels between Port Carbon and Shenandoah." Pinkerton spy James McParlan, trying to ingratiate himself with the AOH and its reputed Molly activity, tracked down Patrick Dormer at the Dormer saloon "just over the (St. Clair) borough line."

It just so happens that the Wooden Keg isn't officially in St. Clair. The borough line goes right down the middle of the street that runs beside it. Step across it toward the Wooden Keg, and you're in East Norwegian Township.

"They used to say the St. Clair Police Department would come through here, and all they could do was wave," Jim told me.

So, I'm convinced. And as Jim Croley put it, "if this was not the original building, then the foundation's original. The site's original." That's as much as many historic taverns, victims of fires and floods through the years, can say. Someday, given time to do the research, Jim believes he will confirm that "James McParlan was here."

Wallace's marvelous book opened Jim's eyes to the Molly connections. "There were probably guys that were hung that were innocent, and there are probably guys that were hung that weren't," he said. Nothing justifies murder, he added, but creation in St. Clair of the Workingmen's Benevolent Association, an early union crushed by the coal barons, was evidence that the miners seeking humane working conditions tried first to "do everything the right way" before launching an insurrection.

Jim started two other Wooden Kegs in the region, in old, atmospheric spaces, but closed them down to concentrate on St. Clair. It didn't make him any less busy. His clientele from those satellites just come here now for their Irish Whiskey BBQ wings and handmade Bufferogies (that's the pierogies deep-fried and tossed with the house wings sauce). Plus, he started a new Ancient Order of Hibernians chapter, the Patrick Dormer Chapter, that meets here and raises money for Catholic churches and schools.

"When I was younger, it was all about the money," Jim said. "Now, I'd rather have more free time and peace of mind, and maybe a little less money. I'm able to focus 100 percent on this location and expanding it. Doing things to make it better and maybe having an opportunity to do more of that research I've always wanted to do."

Tour the Wooden Keg Tavern

A space like this, with penny-tile floors and tin ceilings and a tunnel in the basement, just had to have stirred up skullduggery.

The tunnel: "Watch your head. Watch your head."

Ouch. Too late. Should've watched my head.

The tunnel is a Wooden Keg Tavern must-see. Just be sure to watch your head. Low stone arches can be hard on the noggin, as Jim Croley tried to warn me.

You see it as soon as you come down the stairs to the cellar dining room—a stone arch in a stone wall, with a couple of steps that open to a tunnel section about 12 feet long. A pair of wooden doors closes off the far end.

A tunnel adds an air of mystery to a restaurant. The most utilitarian explanation for this one seems logical. Martin Dormer built a brewery, and he built a saloon across the road that was, at the time, St. Clair's main artery. Easier to roll kegs underground to the bar than cart them across the busy street. Plus, an underground space would be handy for keg storage, "because it would have maintained temperature," Jim said.

He added, "the tunnel had that alibi element. You could come to the front door and leave without anybody seeing."

Ah. There's the intrigue we crave. Is the rest of the tunnel, beyond those doors, intact? Jim doesn't know. One customer, in his late 90s, told him about coming here as a kid to get ice cream.

The tunnel entrance

"Molly Maguires used to come through this tunnel," the elderly gent said, "and then it was collapsed."

On purpose? Oh, to find out. But the unknowns are too, well, unknown. It would be nice to discover that the tunnel is wide open to wherever it ends, Jim said. "Or maybe you start digging and realize they purposely caved it in all the way up." Plus, there are other property owners to consider. The gods of history—and the money it would take to find out—just haven't aligned on this one.

Let's just enjoy it for what it is—a spooky, flood-prone tunnel with weeping stone walls that get stalactites that occasionally need to be brushed off with a broom.

And maybe a Molly Maguire or two crept through here, playing the township-line game to escape detection and live to fight another day in the quest for justice, safety, and the kind of pay that let a man keep his children fed.

The tunnel room: Early in their restaurant days, Jim and Jess Croley had no kids yet. He cooked. She served tables. After taking off his apron and closing the kitchen for the night, he would hang with the locals and have a few beers. The more stories they told, the more he became intrigued by the building's history.

The tunnel room.

Tunnel room bottles

"After five or six beers, I did my best thinking," he said. "Because I was so calm." In the storage area downstairs, he would ponder over the tunnel. "This is amazing," he would think.

Business was going well, and it was time to expand, so the logical idea came to mind. They turned the basement into a dining room. Jim and his father-in-law poured the floors and installed a wall in rough-hewn wood to complement the existing stone. The wing-night slogan gave way to "A Molly Maguire Hangout," taken from Wallace's book on St. Clair. Suddenly, customers had a choice in dining areas. He and Jess were making their own kind of history.

"There are people that love to come in the bar, and they have no interest in sitting downstairs because they want to be where the action is. They want to see people and talk to people," he said. "But there's also a slew of people that don't want to be near that. When I went non-smoking and put in the downstairs dining room, I started getting big tables with grandma and grandpa and the kids. We went from a barroom to a restaurant. It just snowballed."

The barroom: Usually, the trick with vintage photos is finding the tiny details that bring you to the scene's present state. With the old picture of the Wooden Keg barroom hanging on the wall, there's no need for detective work. Any sepia-era person walking in today—a man wearing a boater hat, say, or a flapper in a shockingly short knee-length dress—would feel at home. Tin ceilings. Broad windows. Transoms over the doors.

The hanging light fixtures are gone, but "you can still see the screw holes," Jim pointed out. "It's all original. It's all the same."

The building was once the Atlantic Hotel, and this photo, date unknown, shows the barroom when it was the lobby. In the 1920s, there was a Jazz Age convenience store here, with gas pumps out front (visible on the exterior photo hanging beside the interior, also a dead ringer for its current self) and ice cream for sale. And, as always, a saloon.

"Back then, it wasn't weird to have a bar in a convenience store," said Jim. Later in its history, this building also housed a tobacco shop in the basement, and a television repair business. "I found old picture tubes and stuff in here."

This single room used to be two. It explains the extraneous side door—the former ladies' entrance. It also explains the posts in the middle of the bar, reaching to the ceiling beam. They weren't here originally, but something had to replace that load-bearing wall.

"I did it all, with a couple of friends," Jim said. "An engineer told me how to build the beam, and we did it. It didn't fall down, so I guess it worked."

The Speakeasy: I was sitting at the bar next to an old-timer telling me stories of the Wooden Keg—a Molly doubter, by the way—when he said, "See that bookshelf? Go over and push on the right side."

Whatever you say. That rustic old shelf is built into a brick wall, but I'm a good Catholic girl who does as she's told. Let's see what happens.

I pushed, and the shelf gave way, swinging open like a door. In fact, it is a door, leading me into a long, narrow, breathtaking room in brick and dark wood and exposed beams.

This is Jim Croley's latest upgrade at the Wooden Keg, a private-function space ideally suited to its speakeasy theme.

"No Molly history here," Jim told me. "Dormer used to live in this part. He was laid out here. They did that back then."

Not that this room looked anything like a Victorian-era parlor when Jim acquired the building.

"It looked like an old 1950s apartment," he said. "Flowery plastic stuff was on the wall."

James Croley pushing open the bookcase-style door to the Speakeasy

The Speakeasy

Con-Tact Paper! Instant décor, back in the day.

"There were layers and layers of Formica on the floor," he continued. "I filled eight dumpsters up. Plaster. You just keep finding things. Big, old cast-iron sink like grandma's kitchen."

Oh, and a room in the back. He didn't know about this old addition until he started ripping out those Con-Tact Papered walls. Today, the exposed doorway and window open to a back bar and buffet serving area.

Once again, the work was all Jim's. Carpentry skills come in handy when you own an old building. Be sure to look down at the wood-plank floors here. I asked if he found them under all that Formica. No, Jim said. He built them. Kiln-dried the wood, even.

What??

He knew what he wanted to do in here, but first, he "had to get a lot of ducks in a row." He wanted "straight-up board" for the floors, which is hard to find in a tongue-in-groove world. So he had a sawmill cut a fresh oak tree.

Then, of course, the wood had to dry.

"You layer it all in a big stack in the middle of the floor, and you strap it real tight, and you set a box fan on it, and for five

Speakeasy entrance

months, it just sits here. Some of it warped and we had to throw it away, but you're talking maybe $1,000 instead of $7,000."

And the effect is priceless. It doesn't look like something from a big-box store. For one-seventh the price, he got an effect seven times more beautiful.

"It'll be here forever, too," Jim said. "It takes a beating, but it's hard oak. The more the finish wears off, the more authentic it'll look."

The room design is also his own. He pointed to a door opening to the front porch, made in Mexico with a speakeasy peephole for effect. And since speakeasies are supposed to be concealed, the window displays the building's old Atlantic Hotel sign.

The crowning touch was finding a company that made the bookcase-style door. Everyone who enters this room is "smiling from ear to ear, especially with the surprise element," Jim said, and it's not just the surprise of a bookcase that magically turns into a door. "You bring your wife in for a surprise party, and you see all your friends and family in here. I've had people get engaged in here. People get engaged in the tunnel."

SECTION II

The History of the Wooden Keg Tavern:
The Molly Maguires make a stand

A pub with a tunnel, on a main road in a town simmering with labor unrest. The Atlantic Hotel could have seen Molly Maguires coming in the door. And someone else walking through the door could have marked the beginning of the end.

In the pub: On a day in 1874, the door opened at a saloon run by Patrick Dormer. Some say the saloon was in Pottsville. But it could have been the Atlantic Hotel.

James McKenna strolled in quietly. He wasn't known to the noisy miners here, drinking away and dancing "to a screaming fiddle." McKenna called for his new companions to step up to the bar. This round was on him. With that, he broke out in a jig as the crowd cheered. He sang a rebellious song of old Ireland, celebrating the murder of a land agent by the feared secret society known as the Molly Maguires.

Pat Dormer—6-foot-4 and 250 pounds—was a 30-year veteran of anthracite-region strife, in the thick of things when a strike was called, relief needed for destitute families, or pleas made to deaf ears in the state legislature to outlaw the practice of payment in scrip. Dormer invited the newcomer to a game of cards. Sitting at the table was a thug named Frazer.

"You've got six cards in your hand," McKenna suddenly accused Frazer. "That's too many for a game of euchre."

"You're a li—." McKenna cut Frazer off before he could finish the word.

"Am I?" He grabbed Frazer's hand. A fight spilled into the alley, Pat Dormer lighting the scene so everyone could watch. Little McKenna was far outclassed in height and weight, but with every knockout punch, he stood back up.

Frazer went down six times. On the seventh, he stayed down, and McKenna was cheered as a hero. Pat Dormer, deeply impressed, invited this scrappy new friend to his sister's wedding. There, with all the rest, McKenna got drunk—supposedly—and fell asleep on a bench, where he happened to overhear some Molly Maguires' passwords and, apparently through slitted eyes, caught a few Molly hand signals.

That's one version of the introduction of "James McKenna" to the Molly Maguires. Another says he ingratiated himself by attending Catholic services during a sort of week-long revival, morning and evening, sunshine or stormy. The stereotypically Irish version, with the drinking and singing and jigging and slugging, makes for a more rousing opening.

In any case, "McKenna" spelled doom for the men he would finger as Molly Maguires. McKenna's real name was James McParlan. Working for the Pinkerton Detective Agency, the Irish-born McParlan was spying for the mine and railroad owners. By winning the trust of Patrick Dormer, who held the post of "body master," or secretary, of his AOH chapter, McParlan would be initiated into the Ancient Order of Hibernians and, he claimed, the secret society known as the Molly Maguires.

The Mollies: "Breakfast? Miserable, lukewarm gruel and no milk to wash it down with, and no sugar either." Summer? Coal patch shanties baked "into one big oven. A dozen sweaty bodies bumping, trying to keep out of each other's way. This was how we lived. This was how the Kehoes lived. Children dying like flies of consumption, two of Jack's sisters and one brother. Now can you understand why Jack got bitter?"

With each recession and depression in America's increasingly industrial economy, coal operators preserved profits by slashing pay, doled out in nearly worthless company-store scrip. Deep in the anthracite region, they cut corners on safety, unhindered by any regulatory oversight from a coal-friendly Pennsylvania legislature. In Schuylkill County alone, 600 miners died between 1869 and 1875. Fifteen hundred would be permanently disabled.

Here in St. Clair, Irish miner John Siney founded the Workingmen's Benevolent Association, a union negotiating for fair wages and safer working conditions. After a September 1869 mine fire claimed the lives of 110 men and boys—jumping from the blazing breaker, or trapped behind desperately built barricades while they wrapped shirts around their noses in futile attempts to block the toxic fumes—Siney exhorted protestors, "Men, if you must die with your boots on, die for your families, your homes, your country, but do not longer consent to die like rats in a trap for those who take no more interest in you than in the pick you dig with."

The newly empowered WBA negotiated a minimum wage, but it didn't last. Pay was slashed again in the depression of 1873. The coal barons had crushed the union and snuffed out its pesky agitation.

At the bottom of the coalfield hierarchy, Irish miners turned to organize through chapters of the Ancient Order of Hibernians. But coal baron Franklin B. Gowen counterpunched by pinning all AOH members with a disreputable name, one recalling lawless ruffians of the Old World: Molly Maguires.

In Ireland in the 1840s, it's said that a woman named Molly Maguire resisted English land grabs. Irish Catholics stripped of their land tenancy took to thrashing authorities with the warning, "Take that from a son of Molly Maguire!"

Gowen, president of the Philadelphia and Reading Railroad, used the label to besmirch anyone agitating for reasonable pay and safer conditions. He was a lawyer, born in Schuylkill County, one-time Schuylkill County district attorney. His brother was a Union officer killed in the last days of the Civil War. Gowen believed in order and in engineering. He wrote limericks. He lived modestly while other coal barons built palaces. He paid workers in cash. He ordered the instant dismissal of any company superintendent who fired a worker for religious, ethnic, or even union-association reasons. Ninety-five out of 100 workers, Gowen believed, were "decent, orderly, law-abiding, respectable men."

But let an outside organization make demands or try to control his business dealings—which involved monopolizing coal shipments to Philadelphia, and snatching coalfields to maintain that monopoly—and the urbane Gowen turned vindictive. Molly hooligans, he declared, were behind the mayhem terrorizing Schuylkill County.

"I have to die": Was a murderous secret society targeting coal operators, or were desperate men lashing out against intolerable conditions? Whether or not the Molly Maguires existed, the terror was real. Young mine foreman Thomas Sanger was shot down as he left his home. Gunfights along streets and at picnics sent bystanders scrambling—or left them dead. A police officer who had arrested a purported Molly was dousing a streetlight when a bullet hit his right side. Another tore through his neck. "Give me a kiss," the officer told his wife, who had hurried to the scene. "I have to die."

Miners were murdered, too. "Vigilance committees" subsidized by the coal operators terrorized miners' families. Months after the Sanger killing, gunmen stormed the home of an extended Irish family at Wiggans Patch. A pregnant woman died as she tried to escape. The attackers dragged out a purported Molly, shot him 15 times in the head and set his clothes on fire. To make sure he was thoroughly dead, they shot him in the chest 10 times more.

Day of the Rope: James McParlan wasn't the only spy worming into coal-region labor groups, but working for the ruthless Franklin Gowen, he got what he needed. In 1876, as he bluffed his way out of rumors that he was a spy, McParlan handed over a list of names, and the trials began. Some were in Pottsville, the Schuylkill County seat just a few miles from St. Clair. Some were in Mauch Chunk, the seat of adjoining Carbon County.

When the gavel banged the first trial into session, a familiar person stood beside Schuylkill County District Attorney George Kaercher. It was Franklin Gowen, former district attorney taking leave from his railroad job and volunteering to run the prosecution—never mind the obvious conflict in assigning the task to the person who benefitted the most from crushing coal-field unionism forever.

Gowen's seven-hour closing statement painted the Molly Maguires as the bogeyman of the coalfields. "This Organization we are now for the first time exposing to the light of day has hung like a pall over the people of this county," he declaimed. "Before it, fear and vengeance of their pursuers. Behind it stalked darkness and despair, brooding like grim shadows over all of us."

He chastised the Irish for failing to condemn the agitators in their midst. "Does the Irishman wonder why it sometimes is difficult to get a job in this country?" He declared himself a champion of "the laboring people of this county, people who have suffered more through the actions of these men than any other. I protest against the monstrous assumption that these villains are the representatives of the laboring people of Schuylkill County."

Pity that some of the Pennsylvania Dutch jurors didn't speak English and had to miss this brilliant oratory. No matter. This trial and all the others would end in guilty verdicts for 20 men, all hanged for murder. The first 10 condemned were hanged on June 21, 1877, a day that would be called "The Day of the Rope."

On January 14, 1979, purported Mollies leader "Black Jack" Kehoe, the last of the Mollies to hang, received a posthumous—very posthumous—pardon from Pennsylvania Gov. Milton Shapp.

As for Franklin Gowen. In 1885, the financier and robber baron J.P. Morgan forced the combative, charming Gowen out of the Philadelphia and Reading Railroad presidency. The unions

Gowen had strived to quash were stronger than ever, swollen with anger from the oppressive tactics against the Molly Maguires.

By now, friends noticed that Gowen was no longer quick with a joke. On December 12, 1889, he stepped into a store in Washington, D.C., where he was arguing a case before the Interstate Commerce Commission, to buy a gun. The next day, he sat in his Washington hotel room, put the gun to his head, and pulled the trigger.

Historian Harold Aurand called the Molly Maguires investigation and trials "one of the most astounding surrenders of sovereignty in American History. A private corporation hired a private detective agency. A private police force arrested the suspects, and coal company attorneys prosecuted."

The state, he wrote, "provided only the courtroom and the hangman."

"Cutting Affair at St. Clair": Patrick Dormer was sleeping when Patrick Conry woke him up. This was Dormer's home and saloon in St. Clair, a Saturday night in October 1870, as told in a Miners Journal news story. (Note the date: Further evidence that Dormer the AOH officer had a bar here before James McParlan infiltrated the Mollies.) It seems that Mr. Conry had some business to conduct with Mr. Dormer.

While they were talking, three other men walked in, "one at the time." Soon, the three were fighting. When Conry tried to break it up, a man named Hines drew a knife and slashed a deep gash from the top of Hines' forehead and down his back. A doctor feared the wounds were grievous, but they turned out to be otherwise, "although Conry's face and nose are considerably disfigured." Hines was arrested and imprisoned on charges including "Maihem." Hines' friends "industriously labored to settle up the matter," but the Miners Journal could not ascertain "with what effect."

We'll never know if Hines got busted out of prison by his buddies, or if Conry spent the rest of his life facing the world with a disfigured nose. My question is: What "business" with Dormer brought Conry there in the first place? In the coal regions of 1870, the purpose could have been perfectly innocent. But to me, it sounds like intrigue was afoot on a dark autumn night.

SECTION III

Touch history

Jim and Jess Croley got married in the middle of renovations at the Wooden Keg. "We just went out to Vegas," Jim said. "I'm over here sweeping up some sawdust, and I go home and get in the shower and get on the airplane. We hung out there for a week and came home and went right back into this." All that work shows in marvelous details uncovered, and a few crafted new for future generations to admire.

The bar: Jim Croley built this bar. That blew my mind. Oak sides, maple top, edging made from a trim that he found, footrest made of piping. I'm pretty fussy about reproductions—either look exactly original or make it complementary in an obviously modern way—and Jim nailed the old-looking, been-here-forever vibe.

From sometime in the 1950s until 1998, the man who owned the building "didn't really run a business out of here." He ran—I don't know what you'd call it. He came in every day for a few hours, sitting on a stool at the end of the bar closest to the door. A few customers would sit drinking their beers. Nobody got a fresh

The bar

drink until everybody was empty. That's when the owner would get up from his stool, trudge to the cooler, and pull a new beer for everyone.

"If you drink your beer too fast, you would wait," Jim said. "The same four or five guys would come in every day. It wasn't a business. It was a hobby."

The bottles: Above the bar, old bottles. Along the barroom wall, old bottles and lanterns. On a beam in the tunnel dining room, old bottles.

Saloons run on bottles. That's not news. The difference here is that the old man who served drinks one round at a time also didn't believe in taking the trash outside. Day after day and year after year for 40 years, he dumped his cigarette ashes in the tunnel. When Jim excavated the tunnel, he "took truckloads of ashes out of there." And there they were—"all those bottles were buried in those ashes. We washed them off a little bit and threw them up there."

Most of the bottles are clear or brown, but Jim learned from a "metal detector-type guy" to keep an eye out for blue. Light blue bottles saying "Atlantic Dormer Brewery" are worth hundreds of dollars each. He hasn't found one yet, but the tunnel is slated for new flooring, and metal detector-guy says there's another foot to get to the original floor, so who knows? There might be a blue bottle in the Wooden Keg's future. In the meantime, I'm keeping an eye open at flea markets.

The sculpture: Tucked into a corner of the tunnel dining room is a small, lighted display case. Inside is a figure of a man, about 24 inches high, carved in clay. Look closer, and your heart skips a beat.

A sack covers the man's head. Hands and feet are bound in rope. He is ready for the noose.

With a plan that started in 2002, Mahanoy City—a town steeped in Molly Maguires history, about 10 miles from St. Clair—commissioned renowned Pennsylvania sculptor Zenos Frudakis to create the centerpiece of the Molly Maguire Historic Park. Installed in 2010, the faceless, larger-than-life-size statue represents all 20 miners sent to the gallows and all others who fought for the right to organize.

"It was an injustice to begin with," the sculptor said at installation. "They (coal barons) had a list of who they wanted to get rid of and got rid of them. There were others who were accused of things they didn't do. It would have been another injustice to do a sculpture that didn't show the impact of what really happened."

Now we get to the tale of how this model arrived here. Frudakis made two seven-foot statues and two models, Jim said. That makes four. Keep this in mind. One full-sized statue went to Mahanoy City. The other was destined for the Pennsylvania State Museum, and it stood for a time on the Capitol steps in Harrisburg.

Jim wrote to the sculptor and asked to buy a model. Frudakis agreed to make one, on the condition that Jim did not resell it. Agreed, and here it is.

So, three down and one to go. Where is that other model? You might have seen the 1970 movie, "The Molly Maguires," starring Richard Harris as the spy McParlan. Playing the hard-bitten, doomed Molly leader Jack Kehoe was Sean Connery, an actor versatile enough to play varied roles and smart enough to choose parts that would break him out from James Bond typecasting.

That second model, the fourth of the four statues, is said to be in the home of the honorary chairman of the Mahanoy City Molly Maguire Statue Advisory Committee—the actor now known as Sir Sean Connery.

The church pew: As you approach the Wooden Keg Tavern, the already steep street takes an even sharper climb. Your eye follows, and there stands a hilltop Catholic church. You know instantly that it's Catholic by the shrine to Our Lady of Lourdes on the hillside.

This is—or more accurately, was—Immaculate Conception Church. In 2008, the Diocese of Allentown closed the parish, in a harsh reflection of changing times that deprived parishioners of the beloved church where they had been baptized, married, and buried their parents.

Before the church was here, there was the Dormer Atlantic Brewery. This was the site where Martin Dormer brewed his beer. On the sprawling grounds, others came to enjoy Dormer's Park, also known as Atlantic Gardens, a Dormer-owned grove popular among Schuylkill County residents for picnics, dances and concerts among the greenery.

Martin Dormer died in 1899, and his widow sold the property to a Catholic bishop in 1904, I'm told. The bishop established a church in the brewery building—I like his thinking—but the congregation outgrew the space. They demolished the old brewery and built the church that stands today.

In the Wooden Keg's tunnel dining room, diners sit on a church pew along the stone wall beside the tunnel entrance. How it got around the stair landing is beyond me, but people can get ingenious about such things. Jim is pretty certain that the pew came from that first church, the one in the brewery.

I like the symmetry. Once, parishioners sat along this pew in fellowship, in a Dormer brewery building. The church would undergo many changes and end in heartbreak, but there were fond memories, too. Today's diners sit on this pew and share fellowship, creating memories to be cherished, in a building built by Martin Dormer, the brewer.

As for that shrine on the church grounds, visible from the Wooden Keg porch, it's a reminder not only of the Virgin Mary's appearance to Bernadette in Lourdes but also of one soldier's service in the fight for freedom. In World War II, area native John Sninsky was a G.I., in the thick of the action through the Battle of the Bulge. Never knowing his odds from one minute to the next, he made a pledge to the Blessed Virgin Mary. If she brought him back alive, he would build her a shrine. She did, and the grateful veteran kept his promise.

Any ghosts? "Tell us what year it is," the ghost hunters asked. A whispered voice said, "1870."

Or 1870-something. Jim Croley didn't have the recording at hand. But a question asked and played back on a digital recorder got an intelligent response. The paranormals also asked, "Can you tell us your name?"

"Martin," said a voice.

So, when you visit the Wooden Keg, say hello to Martin Dormer, who may still have an attachment to the place he built around 1870. He especially likes the basement.

The ghost hunters also said they detected a man with a beard. Hardly worth mentioning, except that Jim's daughter, at 1 year old, equated every bearded man with her grandfather, her Pop-pop. Seeing Billy Mays, the OxiClean guy, on TV, she would point and say, "Pop-pop."

One day, she looked up to the landing of the Wooden Keg stairs, pointed, and said, "Pop-pop."

"There's nothing there," Jim said, "but she's saying 'Pop-pop. Pop-pop.'"

The ghost hunters say there's a little girl here, too. Back when Jim and his family lived here, his daughter had a Stretch and Fun

Elmo doll, the kind that would giggle and squeal when you pulled its arm.

"I hear Elmo making this stretching noise and laughing in the next room," Jim said. "I went in there, and the Elmo doll was laughing. You think Elmo is for kids, but in the middle of the night, that sound is the scariest thing in the world."

Then again, an Amazon reviewer noted that Stretch and Fun Elmo was a bit much for younger kids, and "there have been occasions when I heard it talking from the closet." So maybe Stretch and Fun Elmo sometimes takes on a life of his own.

Let's just agree with Jim that the Wooden Keg isn't home to anything "extremely dark. No doors slamming or crosses upside down." Just a good, old-fashioned doll-stretching once in a while.

The food scene: The food at the Wooden Keg is "not super-intricate, but it's basics done to real high-quality," Jim said. He is largely self-taught, chef-wise. He compares the menu selections and their preparation to the dishes on "Diners, Drive-Ins and Dives." Sure, you can get fried mozzarella sticks at any old chain restaurant, but they come from a freezer bag dumped in the fryer.

"If you come here to eat mozzarella sticks, it's a fresh hunk of mozzarella that's battered and fried to order," he said. "It's onion rings that are hand battered. Jalapenos, mushrooms, pickles—all the fryer food is high quality."

Wings, burgers, and French fries—all fresh. Order the fish, "and we're battering it and giving it to you."

"Every time an order comes in for onion rings, these guys are tossing onion rings and batter and breading to order," he said. "We don't have this big whole kitchen where we have racks of onion rings ready to go."

Of course, "you wait a little longer for your food when you eat here, but that's the reason why."

And besides, I asked, what's wrong with slowing down once in a while?

Platters emerging from the kitchen are piled high with wings, potato skins, or "Loaded Irishmen Fries" (get it? "Loaded" Irishmen?) smothered in cheddar cheese sauce, bacon, chives, ranch dressing, sour cream, and Old Bay seasoning. Broiled crab cakes come from a family recipe—must try those in my lifelong hunt for crab-cake perfection. There's Guinness grilled chicken, and the "Keg Paddy Melt" of burger topped with sautéed onions, cheddar and Swiss cheeses, all grilled on marble rye.

The beverage scene: "A little of everything," said Jim. "A little bit of everything, and different draft beers." On my visit, the taps were primed with a fair amount of locals. Yuengling truly is local here, being just three miles down Route 61, and in addition to the ubiquitous Lager, there was a little-known favorite of my husband and mine, Lord Chesterfield Ale. And there with the Miller Lite and New Belgium Fat Tire were a Rusty Rail Swing Tree White IPA, from Mifflinburg, PA, and from Easton's Weyerbacher, a Sunday Morning Stout, the American imperial stout aged in bourbon barrels and described by Weyerbacher as "the perfect cap to a Saturday night or start to Sunday morning." If a 12.7% ABV quaff is your idea of getting a good start to the day.

PLAN YOUR VISIT

The Wooden Keg Tavern
1 W. Caroline Avenue,
St. Clair, PA 17970
www.woodenkegtavern.com, (570) 429-1909

WHAT'S NEARBY

Hibernian House: Follow a narrow side street in the town of Girardville until it crosses a rutted alley, look for the building with the light green siding and the angled corner door, and you've found the Hibernian House. Originally run by Molly Maguires' leader "Black Jack" Kehoe, it's still in the Kehoe family. If you're lucky, the door will be open. Step in and have a beer in memory of the men and their families who stood up to injustice and showed the world the power of solidarity.

Hibernian House

II.

TWO RIVERS BREWING COMPANY

Easton, Pennsylvania

Speakeasy on the Delaware

Misbehavior makes history: Two Rivers Brewing Company

■ "Going to Easton!" Prizefight-goers spilling out of Madison Square Garden knew what that meant. Follow the barker to a waiting bus or car, and the next stop was Easton, Pennsylvania—Sin City on the Delaware, where city officials turned a blind eye to all things illegal and illicit.

■ No mistaking the speakeasy at the Mount Vernon Hotel. The bar was installed in the 1920s, at the height of Prohibition.

■ Why would a carriage house built during Prohibition need a dozen pipes flowing into the steel-reinforced second floor? Perhaps they supplied an illegal brewery.

■ Today's scene: No lawbreakers holing up here, but Two Rivers Brewing Company has taken up the banner of the Brewpub Revolution, creating a force to do good in the community and satisfy hungry souls craving friendly company, tasty food, and fresh beer.

Built: 1855, from an 1810 original structure, and with a 1920s addition

Meet the cast

Troy Reynard broke into his own building. When you buy a wreck at sheriff's sale, no one hands you the keys. There are no keys.

He crawled up the fire escape, busting his foot through a rotted tread. In a stroke of celestial serendipity, the yoga studio

Two Rivers exterior

owner next door also happened to be a restorative mason. Let me fetch a ladder, he said. They reached through a broken second-floor window and opened a door, and Troy set foot in his building for the first time.

While waiting in the lobby for a locksmith, a cop came by. The building's history with police is probably checkered, but this story ends well. The cop seemed to believe Troy's story. He just got Troy's name and contact info, and let him go about his business.

Two Rivers Brewing Company, named after the confluence of the Delaware and Lehigh rivers at Easton, had found its home. The building was so decrepit that a home flipper at the same sheriff's sale, told that Troy and his partners were the sole bidders for the old Mount Vernon Inn, snorted, "That pile of garbage? Good luck with that."

They did have some luck, some bad but mostly good. A team assembled. Troy's "fever dream" persisted. Easton residents and visitors now gather for tasty craft brews in the speakeasy where Prohibition-era visitors once got their hooch.

The idea started with Troy, his wife Kathy, and their friends Brad and Judy Nelson. The couples met through Kathy's work

Co-owner Troy Reynard

and discovered a shared love for good beer. Their travels and vacations centered around beer. Over beer in Cooperstown, New York, the idea popped up. We should own a brewery. The thought simmered. Troy was on the verge of buying a second coffee shop, to complement one he started in Easton in 2005 when he hesitated. They had to make a decision, he told Kathy.

"Fudge it," Kathy said (only she didn't say "fudge"). "Let's start a brewpub."

That coffee shop formed the business model for the brewery.

"When I started the coffee shop, I didn't want to create something to get a quick hit and get my money back out of it," Troy told me. "It was about quality, service, and environment there, and I think we've focused on the same things here."

The downside, of course, is the slower path to profitability, "but it's a way more sustainable model." In fact, with very little advertising, Two Rivers' business skyrocketed from the first year to the second.

"If there's anything I did right in this whole thing, it's hiring the right people," Troy said. "As a partnership, my wife and I and

Brad and Judy, we let these guys do their thing without very much interference at all."

Troy was sitting with staff as he shared his philosophy. He turned to Head Brewer Josh Bushey and Executive Chef Jeremy Bialker and asked, "I get what, three, four wild cards a year?"

That's about right, they agreed. It means that Troy can suggest a beer flavor or a new dish once in a while. In most cases, all agree it's worth a try. "The Nashville hot chicken was my idea," Troy said. Jeremy confirmed that he now sells about 40 pounds a week.

"It's a little more northern," Jeremy said. "The recipe called for 12 ounces of cayenne pepper, but I cut it to six."

It's important, Troy said, "to let your talent do what they're talented at. Jeremy was the only chef I ever wanted. I don't know what I would have done without him."

Therein lie two tales. Two Rivers Brewing Company is a collection of stories.

Jeremy was the chef at the highly regarded Porters' Pub & Restaurant up the street. Troy, a regular who led the Porters' mug club in beer tastings, put so much faith in Jeremy's specials and their pair-ability with craft beers that he rarely ordered off the menu. Asked to consult on this new venture, Jeremy had a feeling he was getting his foot in the door for a full-time position. When they finally asked him to be a chef, "they didn't even have the question out before I said yes," he told me.

As building renovations progressed, Jeremy became a sort of general contractor and handyman.

"I had a platform on the balcony with cinder blocks and a ladder on it, cutting away with a saws-all to make sure the fire escape was safe," he said. "I'm holding on with one hand, and the saws-all in the other. I'm plugging away, and I'm thinking if my mom drove by right now, she'd be, 'What are you doing? Get down from there.'"

Then I turned to Josh. How did he come here?

"I don't know," Josh said. "Head injury, I think."

A saws-all fell on your head, I suggested.

Josh and his wife lived in Washington, DC, where he had "a permanent barstool at a bar called Brickskeller," renowned for its beer selections. Then they moved to the Lehigh Valley. One day, he was supposed to mail their old home's closing papers from a FedEx box in Bethlehem Commons.

"I didn't find the dropbox, but I did find Keystone Home Brew Supply," he said. "So I came back with both the closing papers and a homebrew kit. I got yelled at."

Don't worry. The closing papers got mailed. And Josh delved into home brewing, which led to wins at competitions, which led to an entry-level brewery job. He worked his way up, went to brewing school, and then to another local brewery. He and Troy, who met on a local business coalition, had been bonding over beer. In May 2015, Troy told him he needed a brewer to operate Two Rivers' new brewing equipment.

"Thirty days later, we had beer on tap," Josh said.

The Two Rivers team prides itself on creating an atmosphere that welcomes "a mix of everybody," said Wendy Carroll, front of house and banquet manager. "With the Crayola factory down the road, we get a lot of families on the weekends."

"You always see the sweaty dads pushing the strollers up the hill," added Josh. "Beer is almost in sight."

The enterprise "is trading on the history of the building," said Troy. The Speakeasy Fellowship Growler Club is Two Rivers' beer club. Members get a 64-oz double-wall stainless steel growler, discounted fills and beers and merchandise, t-shirt, and the chance to sample new beers the day before release.

On Prohibition Repeal Day, members are treated to the Annual Speakeasy Fellowship Beer dinner. The event toasts the second-most date that will live in infamy in the 12-year administration of Franklin Delano Roosevelt when a stroke of his pen legalized the sale of 3.2 percent-alcohol beer.

The dinner underscores the club's higher purpose. Months after the first event, members were still talking about it. There were Jeremy's six courses paired with "some special beers we had stowed away," Troy said. And an atmosphere that promoted mingling and joviality.

"People that didn't know each other were sitting together and getting to know each other," said Josh.

The building just has that vibe. Somewhere in here is a friend you haven't met yet. Troy believes he committed "an act of rebellion to save the building because it was in bad shape. A lot of people thought somebody would buy the property and tear it down. There's no way we can do that. Our project is part of the renaissance in downtown Easton."

Tour Two Rivers Brewing Company

The partners' first glimpse of the interior was "a little shocking," Troy admitted. A previous owner, attempting renovations, had stripped out eight dumpsters' worth of plaster. The kitchen was a shell. One wall bowed so severely that steel support rods now hold it in place.

"Bite by bite," renovations took shape over the next 18 months, Troy said. The first floor opened in December 2012. Second-floor dining room in April 2013. Brewery in June 2015.

And lucky for the new owners, the heart of the building—the rich, wood ornate bar—was still intact.

The bar: When Troy ushered me into the bar, we stepped into the perfect sanctuary for this rainy day. A family ate at the center table. Josh, sweeping broken glass from the floor, joked around with the family's three kids. I couldn't think of a better place to be.

"I think the last major renovation was probably done in the '20s," Troy said. In historic buildings, there are things to be said for decades of neglect. Sure, there might be sagging floors, but the bar running the length of the inside wall was here when Troy and his partners bought the place. So were the terrazzo tile floors, the tin ceiling, and the teardrop flush-mount light fixtures.

The interior designer, who holds a University of Pennsylvania master's degree in historic preservation, had plenty of original material for inspiration. The dark burgundy walls create a feeling of protectiveness. Edison-style light bulbs and the new double ceiling fans—"awesome," Troy said, and I agreed—complement those original features with industrial chic.

The bar was installed in 1929. That's right. When Prohibition was still in force and, in fact, the same year a reform mayor took office and started cracking down on Easton's speakeasies and brothels. Obviously, someone still saw a future in sin.

"We didn't try to fix the mirrors," Troy told me as we looked at the bar back. "You can still see the wear and tear on them. And that's the original cash register. It's not functional, but we kept that there."

Signs of the room's original layout seem to say that renovations went along with the bar's installation. Pre-1929 photos show that a corner window was actually a door. The best that Troy can figure from marks on the floor, the front of the bar today is where the back of the bar was then. A hallway led straight from

The bar

Teardrop lights and awesome ceiling fans

Dining room

that front door to the hotel front desk, so patrons could register for a room or buy a cigar without going into the bar.

"What else was weird," Troy said, pointing to that corner with the door-turned-window, "is the subway tile. That's the only place it exists, but I think that's because it ran along the hallway when it was a hallway. Even though it's only visible here, a bit does run behind the bar."

Makes perfect sense. And check this out, I said. The floor tiles here are laid out in a square. That looks like a foyer to me.

The couple drinking a flight of beers at the table on that spot gave us a curious look.

Sorry, folks. Just doing a little architectural CSI.

Brewery: Building additions, I've learned, can be quite handy in times of rebellion. Sometime in the 1920s, during Prohibition, the old inn got an attached garage or carriage house. You can see it in the changing color of brick on the outside.

This addition boasted two features that a typical carriage house shouldn't need. There was the steel-reinforced second floor. And there were the abundant holes for water lines—about one dozen—all leading to that industrial-strength floor.

Troy Reynard and Josh Bushey in the brewing room

The theory, of course, "is that they were doing some sort of bootlegging back there," said Troy. "I don't know if it was beer or liquor or what, but there was no good reason to have that many openings for plumbing stuff back there."

I asked brewer Josh, "If you were doing this illegally, is that how you would do it?"

"Oh yeah," he said. "You have to move stuff inside the building, move liquids around." He turned to Troy. "And there was a concrete slab there, too, right?"

Yes, a concrete slab on the second floor, for no apparent reason.

"You're not pulling cars up there," said Josh. "It needed to support a lot of weight. And it was in the back of a building that already had nefarious activities."

Fortunately for today's owners, that reinforced floor was just the ticket for a modern brewery. If Josh is around when you visit, ask for a tour. He showed me the spotless fermenters, mash tun, hot water tank, and boil tank.

"The building dictated the brewery we got, because of space considerations," he said. Most brewing systems are taller. That's the efficient way, but the low ceilings here dictated seven fermenters and 10 small tanks, which gave Two Rivers "a tremendous amount of flexibility" and allows production of a large variety of fresh beers, said Josh. With this system, the beer gets time to mature to full flavor in the tanks. No one's rushing it into bottles and kegs when all the fermenters are full and one needs to be emptied.

"We can tie up a tank doing a real lager, sitting a beer in there for up to 12 weeks, where usually in a brewpub, every two weeks that tank has to turn," Josh said. "Here, we have smaller tanks but many of them, so the beers can sit in there a while and end up the way they're supposed to be. Everybody else, that tank's emptied no matter what."

The beer made here goes straight into serving tanks and, by way of insulated hoses, to the Two Rivers' two bars. "It's never touching oxygen," Josh said. "It's as fresh as it can get."

The Seven Spirits Club: There's no way to know what the old Mount Vernon Inn's speakeasy looked like, but Two Rivers is tackling its own imaginative recreation. The Seven Spirits Club—named after the seven ghosts that paranormals say frequent the building, with a clever pun on the alcoholic spirits lingering here—is the Two Rivers' upstairs bar. It's a compact room, high-ceilinged but cozy, with doors leading to the balcony overlooking Northampton Street.

The bar in this room was added during renovations, but even without a history of its own, it's part of the building's legacy.

"The front of the club bar is old hotel room doors," Troy told me. "That was the carpenter's idea."

No! Really? But look under the bar top, and it's obviously a door on its side. There's even a hole for the doorknob.

Banquet manager Wendy Carroll, taking the tour with us, tapped on the bar top. "Isn't this slate from the sidewalk?"

"I was getting to that, Wendy," Troy said.

"Sorry," she riposted. "I just wanted to make sure it wasn't a dream."

So, they found sidewalk slates in the basement and had them cut and finished for the bar top. They tried to reuse anything they could find. The back-bar mirror came from the bathroom downstairs. The new frame around it was designed in Art Deco style, with elements similar to the original bar on the first floor. That, too, was carpenter Paul Deery's idea.

"I thought it was so cool that he picked that up," said Troy.

Brewing room

It's the ideal spot for lingering, Prohibition-style, over a cocktail made with local spirits. Maybe a gin fizz or something dreamed up by the bar staffers who enjoy trying new flavors and having fun with processes that our Prohibition-era ancestors would have considered the bee's knees.

"We do a lot of infusions," Wendy said. "Right now, we have fig-infused brandy, rosemary-infused gin, and coffee-infused vodka."

SECTION II

History of Two Rivers Brewing Company:
Brewing up trouble

The story of Easton's days of notoriety starts in New York City. Crowds leaving the prizefights in Madison Square Garden would hear the cries of barkers stationed at waiting cars and buses.

"Going to Easton!" the barkers called. "Going to Easton!" Grab a seat, and your magic carpet ride to a haven of heavenly delights is 100 minutes away. In the middle of it all, at a key trolley juncture, was the 44-room Mount Vernon Hotel.

Prohibition: "If you are soused, Can't drink no more, Go home to mother, Use this door."

Buy a house in the Lehigh Valley, and you just might find a speakeasy in the basement. At least, one family did. From the outside, the Bethlehem bungalow they bought in 1999 looks typically charming, but behind its walls are a cherry bar, secret room, the ever-present aroma of stale beer, and clever ditties painted in Olde English script on the doors and walls.

This is what Prohibition meant in the Lehigh Valley and, especially, Easton—a chance to fling open the doors to anyone craving a drink. Even before 1920, vice was a way of life in this river-junction town. Boatmen needed their diversions. Grain carted into town provided ample supply for breweries and distilleries sprouting along the river. In 1816, the word "wicked" attached itself to the town, probably not for the first or last time.

In the lead-up to Prohibition, David "Blind Eye" Nevin, mayor from 1911 to 1920, somehow overlooked the debauchery around him. Occasionally, he staged "crusades" to appease civic-minded citizens. His 1917 raids, announced on a Thursday in January, would crack down on the city's 27 brothels and seven gambling dens—but not until "Monday next." You bawdy houses and prostitutes listening out there? Advance warning was only fair, Nevin said, as he was disinclined to "drag those women through the streets to the police station and to take their blood money to pave the streets of our city."

Nevin set the tone for Mayor Samuel Horn, his successor who allowed "a fine, juicy crop of crime and scandal" to flourish.

As Prohibition dawned in post-Great War America, Easton rose up in resistance, under the banner of freedom. One Eastonian wailed, "Should we lose our Democratic principles at home right after winning a war to make the world safe for Democracy? Why should we liberate millions of people in other countries, and ourselves be deprived of our liberty?"

The pump was primed. "Prohibition Enforcement in this Section a Huge Farce" lamented the Easton Express/Easton Argus three weeks before the Jan. 17, 1920, ban on the production, transport, and sale of intoxicating liquors. Eastonians would continue producing, transporting, and selling booze, and happy customers—not breaking the law by actually consuming the stuff—would flock to town.

Democrats and Republicans accused each other of shakedown "fundraisers," offering saloon owners protection from enforcement in exchange for "donations." Easton's surrounding mountains offered conveniently inaccessible sites for stills running day and night, earning their operators millions of dollars.

Ten federal agents were dismissed for taking bribes from one Easton brewery. Mayor Wesley M. Heiberger complained in 1924 that Pennsylvania State Police swooped in for raids without the courtesy of contacting him or the police chief, and any arrests rarely led to conviction by juries sympathetic to the brewers and speakeasy operators.

"How can we get law enforcement if the people themselves don't want it?" Heiberger lamented.

To which Pennsylvania's teetotaling Gov. Gifford Pinchot archly replied, "There are cities in Pennsylvania in which the state police have never been able to make a successful raid when the local police know that the raid was planned."

At night, pickets watched for raids while trucks rumbled from Easton breweries ostensibly converted to producing soda water, cider vinegar, and sweet cider. On a Thursday night in 1922, agents swooped down on Easton and the nearby towns of Nazareth, and Bangor, but any hopes for a wave of convictions hit a snag.

"TRUCKLOAD OF SEIZED BOOZE TOPPLES INTO THE DELAWARE CANAL" screamed an Allentown *Morning Call* headline. Seems some of the confiscated booze didn't reach its destination of Philadelphia, "and never will" because "one of the booze-laden trucks fell into the Lehigh Coal and Navigation Company's Canal near Point Pleasant, thirty miles south of Easton."

By accident? On purpose? We'll never know. But "some of the bottles were broken and others were spirited away by the crowd that gathered."

The lack of materials to analyze made conviction unlikely, but the *Morning Call* held that "the strong arm of the law struck some mighty blows in favor of Mr. Volstead on Thursday and numerous profiteers in the oil of joy came to grief." After all, the "oil of joy" profiteers (I just like writing "oil of joy") suffered "the loss of their treasure." The paper reported that "among the places in Easton raided were . . ." Well, the list goes on for quite a while, but there it is: "Mount Vernon Hotel, Sixth and Northampton streets, Robert Seibert, proprietor." Pity that some of its hooch might have met a watery end in the canal. Or, maybe a few bottles got lucky and floated their way to someone who made good use of them.

Remember those pipes found at Two Rivers? Easton brewers—including the technologically savvy Kuebler family, whose brewing company also owned the Mount Vernon Hotel for a time—knew all about pipes. Thirty years before Prohibition, at least one Easton brewer, Seitz Brewery, was piping beer from its production facility to its bottling plant, maintained separately to comply with state law. In Prohibition, the venerable brewer piped its illegal beer, pressured by an electric compressor, under the Delaware River to a gas station in Phillipsburg, New Jersey, to be transferred to kegs.

At midnight of December 4, 1933, the Seitz Brewery gates swung open. Trucks rolled out, but unlike so many previous expeditions, this nighttime run didn't need the cover of darkness. Tonight, whistles blew. Residents cheered. Some danced in the streets.

Prohibition was over. The Mount Vernon Hotel had never ceased pouring beer and liquor, but after 13 tumultuous years, service was once again legal.

"Actress": "What is your profession?" police asked the women brought to the station.

"Actress," said some.

Others ostensibly modeled clothing in department stores. "Mannequin," they said.

Suddenly, a petite redhead wearing an eye-catching hat burst into the room. She had an objection, she told the officer recording the women's answers.

"Put down 'whore,'" she instructed, "and proud of it."

In a town of colorful characters, Moetta Newhart took the prize. Her father was a tightrope walker, fortune-teller, and self-professed snake charmer. As Prohibition began, she took her wiles to Easton's Pine Street, already notorious for its bawdy houses, and snapped up properties. Clients arriving at her establishment could enjoy not only a $2, 30-minute service but also the famous Moetta's vivacious company and unfiltered conversation.

It's said that Moetta sent her girls via taxi for weekly medical checks. When they were arrested, she put up her property for bail. If charges were brought against her, she often managed to evade conviction, although there were occasional jail stints. Her generosity extended to police, for business purposes, but also to neighborhood families in need, who might discover that an angel bought a Scout uniform they couldn't afford, or a shipment of coal to heat the home.

Not that Moetta had a monopoly on the claim to colorful Easton madam. One careless competitor earned the immortal headline, "Underworld Woman Accidentally Shoots Herself While Drunk." And Moetta's $2 service wasn't the cheapest in town. That distinction belonged to Fifty-Cent Rosie, whose place was so "notoriously seedy" that even the 50-cent rate could be discounted.

With at least 64 Easton brothels to choose from, Moetta Newhart deployed a proven tactic to direct business her way. Gentlemen visitors debarking from the train would find boys jumping on the running boards of their taxis. These "runners," each employed by an Easton bawdy house, guided the visitors on "a tour of the carnal delights of Pine Street," as Troy explained it to me.

Moetta's runner was the entrepreneurial "Six Fingers" Sam Bruneo, who really did have six fingers.

"Pine Street is only about three blocks from the railroad station," Troy said. "You could have walked there. Sam would have them take a circuitous route and say what was available at each house. Every time the guy came back to town, he would look for Sam to get him back to the same place, and he worked for tips."

Taxi drivers, grateful for the roundabout fares, often kicked back a quarter or two to the runner.

The Brewpub Revolution: The rebels cowered in cellars, concealing their illicit acts. They defied federal taxation and restrictions until they were lifted. Emerging into the light, some defied state law that still banned their passion, gathering to teach each other their practices and talk a little treason.

They were fighters against an Evil Empire that threatened to crush a cherished way of life. They were the home brewers of America, taking a stand against Big Beer.

In 1879, Pennsylvania was home to 317 breweries, second only to New York. Then Prohibition killed many of them. Those that survived were engulfed in a wave of post-World War II consolidations. By the late 1970s, mass-market lagers dominated. Industry experts predicted a day when only five companies would be brewing beer in the U.S.

But a few hardy souls said, "Bleh." They longed for beer liberty ("libeerty," perhaps?) and experimented with restoring flavor to beer, but until 1978, federal law limited output and alcohol content. Today's breweries celebrate Prohibition Repeal Day, but maybe they should also mark the anniversary of Oct. 14, 1978, when President Jimmy Carter signed a bill repealing federal restrictions on home brewing. Finally, it was legal to brew beer of more than 0.5 percent alcohol (I mean, why bother?), and taxes on large quantities were lifted.

The shackles were off. Homebrewing flourished. Some took the leap into brewpubs even before their states legalized them, but there was no stopping this movement.

As the Brewers Association for Small and Independent Craft Brewers put it, the brewpubs were "serving their local communities a taste of full-flavored beer and old world European traditions; all with what was to become a uniquely American character." Craft brewers grew from eight nationwide in 1980 to more than 6,000 in 2018. Pennsylvania's breweries doubled to more than 200 from 2011 to 2016, and a search of any local news site shows more on the way.

Big Beer took notice. The corporate giants made their own crafty-sounding beers and bought hefty shares in actual craft breweries, but the Brewpub Revolution couldn't be quashed. Consumers have learned the difference between fizzy beer products and flavorful beer, and the uprising has matured into a social movement, where brewpubs anchor neighborhoods.

Sitting in the Two Rivers' Seven Spirits Club, I asked Troy if he feels like part of a revolt.

"Absolutely," he said. "Part of our goal is to be Easton's beer." While other brewers in town are multi-state operations, Two Rivers is "the only brewery brewing beer in downtown Easton."

It's also a matter of "building bridges in the community." Almost monthly, Two Rivers produces "Great Beer for Great Causes," naming a beer after a local person and, at the release party, donating a dollar per beer to that person's favorite charity. The first one was named after "The Easton Assassin," former world heavyweight boxing champion Larry Holmes. The second was named after Bob Freeman, who happens to be an old buddy of mine, and who, as the area's representative in the state House, has devoted his career to Easton and the revitalization of Main Streets throughout Pennsylvania.

But the not-so-well-known get their beers, too. Marishka Titus Michener is a businessperson, arts benefactor, and "downtown business evangelist," Troy said. "She's a person who makes our city better in small ways every day."

"Curt's the same way," Chef Jeremy interjected.

That's Curt Ely, known affectionately as "Man about Town."

"He's like Super Volunteer," Troy said. "He volunteers for everything. He's a financial planner who makes his own schedule. Instead of going home and watching *SportsCenter* at night, he spreads his day out so he can do a lot of volunteer work."

And in what Troy called "probably our biggest event so far"—Jeremy said, "There's no 'probably' about it"—they raised almost $1,300 to support the recovery of a Pennsylvania State Police trooper wounded in the line of duty.

It's about the pub connecting with the town.

"My vision wasn't just that we need to do X to make X amount of money," Troy said. "I wanted to create an institution, so when people think about Easton beer, they think about Two Rivers."

And that, I would say, is the town connecting with the pub, coming full circle to the days when taverns were social hubs, offering community experiences that equaled more than the sum of their food and their drinks.

SECTION III

Touch history

Like the rivers inspiring its name, Two Rivers is a confluence of two things—history, and things that taste really, really good.

The Zenith bar: In 1927, the world shrank like a deflating balloon. Americans living on the East and West coasts could hear the same news from New York or London *at the same time*. Eager to know the winner of the Tunney-Dempsey heavyweight fight? No need to wait for the morning paper. Turn a button, and you don't just know the results. You actually listen to the fight *as it happens*.

The radio. While Prohibition rocked communities, another revolution was upending our home lives. A piece of living room furniture was issuing news, music, and even short plays or funny Vaudeville-style sketches. In 1920, radios were science lab-looking contraptions with disarming, square antennas, appealing mostly to hobbyists. By 1929, the craze had put a radio in 100 million homes.

With that kind of heft, the look of the radio took on its own mystique. Radio buyers demanded décor worthy of family gatherings and envious guests, and radio designers found inspiration in Art Deco motifs and sleekly modern skyscrapers.

Sometimes, radio returned the favor to the world of design—as in, inspiring the look of a bar that made its way to a speakeasy on Northampton Street in Easton, Pennsylvania. The Zenith Radio bar at Two Rivers Brewing Company doesn't have a radio, but it has the look of one. Black skyscraper-style accents travel the length of the bar front. Art Deco insets punctuate the gracefully arching bar back.

And it all came through a catalog. The Mount Vernon Hotel owners reportedly found this beauty in a Sears, Roebuck catalog. In all likelihood, the entire bar came in a kit. After all, this is the Sears that sold build-your-own-home kits from 1908 to 1940. Sears would deliver your home in 30,000 pieces or so, minus the nails and screws, and you and your friends and family would assemble it. My own husband's aunt and uncle lived their lives in a sweet, humble, and sturdy Sears home on the family farm.

For Sears, a bar would have been small potatoes, but for Two Rivers Brewing Company, this bar stands as a testament to 20th-century ingenuity and craftsmanship.

Host station: In the bar, take a moment to check out the host station. It's normally the most functional (translation, "boring") spot in the room, a space for taking reservations and storing menus and a "Good evening, folks." Here, it's a time machine. This was the hotel front desk, that place we've seen in a million old movies where a guest register was flipped open on the counter, and a sullen clerk reached over his shoulder to pull the room key from a cubbyhole.

"The key cubbies are still there," Troy said, pointing to the slots that now hold notes and message pads and duct tape. Next to it, there's the old switchboard, with rows of plugs and a glass-fronted room indicator, numbered from 1 to 50. The curved glass case displaying t-shirts, hats, and 2RB decals? The old humidor, of course, because bars and hotels were once practically fueled on cigars.

Beer names: Why is Easton the right place for small-batch, handcrafted beers?

"It's always been ahead of the curve with craft beer," said brewer Josh. Just down the street, Porters' Pub "planted the flag." Since the days of canal and river transport, Easton has been a distribution hub for countless businesses, now including

Host station

A sampling of Two Rivers' beers

Weyerbacher Brewing Company and its multi-state availability. Easton has "always supported small-batch, interesting beers. Maybe it's that years ago it was a Colonial outpost."

Today, Easton has adopted an "artists' feel," Josh added. "People are into interesting and new. They're willing to try stuff."

"It's always been a progressive town," added Chef Jeremy.

"Quirky," agreed Josh.

Which prompted Troy to tell me that Josh calls one series of beer "our Dead Hooker series. So I pull names from brothels and madams that were around."

Hence, the cut-rate Rosie was immortalized with the Fifty Cent Rosie's Kriek, a Lambic-style bottled ale offering "huge cherry flavor and a pleasing funk" (and oh, my gosh, it was good). Sadie Green's Peach Juice honors the madam of the Delaware Inn, a brothel outside of town vulnerable to holdups by mobsters in a shakedown ring.

Other Easton characters show up in other brews. The entrepreneurial spirit of Sam Bruneo inspired Two Rivers' first run for bottling, the Six Fingers Sam saison ale. The notorious Mayor David "Blind Eye" Nevin showed up in the Nevin's Blind Eye Cervino. Whatever's in season, be sure to ask about the characters behind the names.

Any ghosts? Troy is "not a disbeliever," but he also infers some suggestibility at work. Creaky old building, you know. Still, when paranormals say that seven entities haunt the building, who can resist the temptation to give your speakeasy lounge the alliterative, dual-meaning name of the Seven Spirits Club?

Permanent guests here include Emma, a mischievous little girl heard running up the hall. Sometimes, she unties apron strings. One server in the Seven Spirits Club "had her hair lifted up," as if a hand pulled a ponytail, said Wendy Carroll. The same server was once cutting lemons, "and every time she left, the lemons were pushed off the cutting board."

"That was us messing with her," Josh joked. But then Wendy said, "There's a cat. That's a new one. On the fourth floor."

Josh was shocked. "What did they say??"

Wendy: "A cat."

Josh: "No way."

Josh, said Troy, "is a cat man."

Wendy hasn't had any personal experiences. "I like the building, so maybe it likes me and leaves me alone," she said.

Two Rivers' peanut butter bacon burger

The food: Did I get everything I needed? Chef Jeremy was asking as I sat at the bar. I told him I ordered the peanut butter bacon cheddar burger.

"Best in the Lehigh Valley!" he said.

As they say, it ain't bragging if you can prove it. Two Rivers' peanut butter bacon burger was named Lehigh Valley Live's 2017 "Best Burger in the Lehigh Valley."

Jeremy said he has "always been very comfortable in pubs and taverns," where he learned his trade. Even the rustic Italian restaurant where he once worked fit the vibe because the food "kind of goes hand in hand with pub fare because there are a lot of grilled meats." He has taught himself Southern cuisine. Seafood specials get creative—maybe mussels with garlic, bacon, celery, and Two Rivers' own Pine St. Blonde—and Jeremy's sauté cook gets to enjoy "a little playland" with the market fish.

"You can serve elevated cuisine but also serve a big cheesy mess on a plate with lots of meat," Jeremy said. "You can go one way or the other. That's what's fun about it."

He takes care to create dishes that complement Josh Bushey's beers. "You can take any of our beers and they would pair with at least five or six items," he said. "There's several beers that probably go with half the menu." The beers find their way into the dishes themselves, braising meats and mussels and such. "The stouts and porters are good for making reduction sauce," Jeremy said. "It's nice having a variety, so you can pick and choose."

Beers have even inspired such dishes as the New Year's Eve oysters, served in a traditional mignonette that included a Two Rivers saison. "Even for the cocktail sauce, I put in Eldorado hops and gin, and let those flavors develop and strained it," Jeremy said.

"He knows what he's doing," said Josh, his colleague and partner in crime.

I tried: The peanut butter bacon cheddar burger. Half-pound of grass-fed beef, topped with Lancaster County bacon, plus cheddar, peanut brittle dust, chili gastrique, and pickled red onions, all on a brioche bun. I had to approach it like eating an elephant, one bite at a time from any spot my teeth could grab. As juice dribbled down my hand, I checked my supply of napkins. The flavors unfolded with each bite. Even nibbling on the pepperoncini staked to the bun added a spicy element through the rich peanut butter taste. The guy beside me, eating the same thing, said, "I never had a burger with peanut butter before. It's good." How many times, I wondered, have I eaten a burger and had zero memory of its taste and feel by the time I was out the door? This one stays with you.

The beverage scene: I asked Josh what he brings to the flavor of his beers.

"Brewpubs have to have a wide variety of flavors," he said. "It's not like a production place where you make one beer 500 times a year. It has to, in some way, match up with the food. You can't have beer with too many sharp elbows to not complement what's coming out of the kitchen."

So, you'll always find 12 beers—four flagships, and eight rotating selections. The flagships are the Banker's brown ale, Colonel Left Eye IPA (named after Eastonian Colonel Charles Wikoff, who lost his life leading the charge up San Juan Hill that's long been credited to Theodore Roosevelt), Mount Vernon lager, and the Pine St. Blonde Belgian blond (do I detect a cheeky nod to the ladies who lived and worked in the alley behind the Mount Vernon?).

The flagships, Josh said, offer "something for everyone, including entry-level drinkers, and we can get a little weirder with some of the seasonals. People respond." So there might be a sour Belgian Lambic, or the Bourbon Barrel Aged Old Tilton's Barleywine, aged in a Four Roses bourbon barrel and named after an Easton police chief, decorated Civil War veteran, and resident of the Mount Vernon.

On my brewery tour, I saw some of those casks. Lined in a row, they include a Baltic porter and a hoppy Saison aging in a tequila barrel. A marsala wine barrel was coddling a Belgian dark strong.

Other barrels were waiting for their moment to produce a Two Rivers creation. "I've jammed our cellar full of oak barrels in spots I'm not sure they even fit," Josh said.

I tried: My bartender suggested the Banker's Brown Ale accompany my burger, for that peanut butter-chocolate vibe. Even before I sipped, I could smell the chocolate notes, complemented with coffee and caramel. There was not a hint of bitterness. Piping the brews straight from the tanks really does protect the freshness. And as we have learned, Easton brewers know all about pipes.

PLAN YOUR VISIT

Two Rivers Brewing Company
542 Northampton Street
Easton, PA 18042
www.tworiversbrewing.com, (610) 829-1131

WHAT'S NEARBY

Crayola Experience: Turn your picture into a coloring book page. Make spin art with melted crayons. Name and wrap your own Crayola crayon! I should borrow someone's kid just for an excuse to have all the Crayola Experience fun and recall the feeling of clutching a crayon on the way to reimagining the world. Crayola is now a Hallmark subsidiary manufacturing an array of art supplies, but its heart belongs to crayons. The company remains headquartered in and synonymous with Easton, the city of its birth in 1903. The Crayola Experience, considered one of the Lehigh Valley's top attractions, is less than a half-mile walk from Two Rivers Brewing Company. (www.crayolaexperience.com/easton)

Cosmic Cup Coffee Company: This is the place to pay homage to Troy Reynard's entrepreneurial and civic spirit. It's the coffee shop he founded before diving into another type of brewing, where the coffee is craft-roasted with the same care given to Two Rivers' beers. The fair-trade coffee served by highly trained baristas is personally selected by Troy on his travels to such coffee hotspots as Colombia and Costa Rica. (www.cosmiccupcoffee.com)

12.

HORSE INN

Lancaster, Pennsylvania

Knock three times and whisper low

Misbehavior makes history: The Horse Inn

■ An alley entrance with a sliding door. Narrow stairs rising to a hayloft. The perfect place for a speakeasy.

■ The law tried. They really did. But in "wide open" Lancaster, there was no keeping ahead of the booze piped straight from breweries to illegal joints like the Horse Inn.

■ Hooch inspired the opening of the Horse Inn, but post-Prohibition, it was food—to be specific, tips on toast—that transformed a speakeasy into a respectable restaurant.

■ The jukebox tells a story. The bar top tells a story. The piano tells a story. Every piece of décor and art is wrapped up in the history of Lancaster and its circles of friendships.

■ Today's scene: Cheeseburgers so good, even vegans eat them. Your handcrafted cocktail hearkens back to Prohibition days, without the rotgut.

Built: 19th century

Meet the owners

Matthew Russell calls the moment "surreal." He walked into the Horse Inn and knew immediately what to do with it. Concept, layout, cocktail program—all popped into his head fully formed.

He knew the Horse Inn, which might have helped. The long-time fixture on the Lancaster dining scene was part of his childhood. The atmospheric spot radiated mystique.

Horse Inn alley

"It meant a lot to people for special occasions," Matt said. People tell him, "I remember when I came here for my first date." Or "I came here for a celebration with my football team."

Funny thing is, I heard something like that, too. My husband's co-worker, told that I was coming here, said he once worked at an accounting firm and celebrated the end of tax season with an April 16 meal at the Horse Inn.

Matt and his wife, Starla Russell, bought the Horse Inn in 2014. They met at culinary school in Charleston, South Carolina. They were working in different restaurants owned by one family. He left town for a stint as a personal chef in New Hampshire. It lasted for two months.

"It paid well, but money's not everything," Matt said of that brief employment phase.

Returning to Charleston, he made a beeline for the old restaurant, hoping Starla still worked there.

How did he finally build the nerve to ask her out?

"I just went for it," Matt said. "She was kind of seeing someone else long distance. I didn't want to step on anybody's toes."

"I'm glad he stepped on 'em," Starla said.

Horse Inn owners Starla and Matthew Russell

They married in 2006. Their son arrived in 2012. From the beginning of their relationship, one thing was certain. "I always knew if I ever hooked up with him, I'd end up in Lancaster, because that's all he ever talked about," Starla said. "He just loved this place."

Now that she's here, the Southern girl loves the four seasons and the juxtaposition of the vibrant city against beautiful farmland. Matt remains madly in love with his hometown. He has worked in "some pretty respectable restaurants." For five and a half years, he honed his craft under Chef/Partner Sean Brock at Charleston's renowned, Michelin-starred McCrady's, now McCrady's Tavern (guaranteed to be a Well-Behaved Tavern if I ever write a South Carolina edition). Back home in Lancaster, Matt leveraged that experience with relationships among food vendors he built by prowling Lancaster City's famous Central Market, brimming with the bounty of the equally famous Lancaster County countryside.

"It's my love for Lancaster," Matt said. "It's a farmer's mecca here. I have an entire sleeve of tats of Lancaster on my arm." Sure enough, you can tour Lancaster on Matt's arm, from Lancaster Central Market, to a hot air balloon emblazoned with the Turkey

Hill logo, to a road sign pointing the ways to Intercourse, Blue Ball, and Bird in Hand.

Not that the road to the Horse Inn was smooth. Matt and Starla always knew they wanted to buy a restaurant in Lancaster. While planning the move, they had their eye on a "funky, speakeasy" kind of place on Cherry Street. The day they moved to town, Hurricane Sandy moved in along with them. U-Haul and all, they hunkered in his parents' home for a couple of days.

"Once we got everything unloaded and back together, Cherry Street went under contract," Matt said. "Back to the drawing board."

The search brought them to the Horse Inn, owned by Lancaster businessman Al Medved since 1972. The place with the built-in atmosphere that restaurateurs crave—and a former speakeasy, to boot—had everything the Russells wanted. Matt held his breath while the deal went through, his brain churning out ideas. He was "chomping at the bit," he told me. I don't think he intended the pun, but he's buying an inn named for horses, and he's "chomping at the bit." Meant to be.

The deal was sealed, and the real work began. Since there are always bills to pay, Starla bartended at an American Legion, the "perfect scenario," she said. "All they wanted was someone to talk to. Me being a Southern girl, sure, I'll talk all day." Matt stayed home and wrote the business plan while caring for their son, Kyuss. Matt admitted he "gained a few pounds" in those days.

Dad needs a bite of that mac and cheese, I said.

"Goldfish and mac and cheese," said Starla to her husband. "That was your diet for a while."

"And beer," he added.

So many things pointed to that meant-to-be aspect. The Russells bought the restaurant in 2014, the Chinese zodiac Year of the Horse. One year and a day after the January 6, 2014, settlement, a renovator found a newspaper wrapped around a pipe, dated January 7, 1933, the year Prohibition was repealed. The cross street is Marshall, the same name as Starla's grandfather's. Al Medved, the previous owner, was 38 years old when he bought the restaurant. Starla and Matt were 38.

"There were a lot of these things saying we were on the right path, and keep going," said Starla.

They almost changed the name to Horse Inn Tavern but decided to keep the Horse Inn name and just make the place "more

2014," Matt said. "We wanted a place where a guy covered in tattoos wearing a wife beater can talk to a guy in a three-piece suit, and he can have a can of beer, and the other guy can have a $70 pour of Pappy Van Winkle if he wants. You don't have to feel weird about what you're wearing. Just a casual, open place."

Which is, at heart, the history of American taverns, known as the commingling place for all levels of society. Early in the Russells' tenure, Matt and bartender/mixologist Benjamin Hash would close up for the night, but then they wouldn't leave. They would turn the lights on and just stare at their creation.

"Is this still here?" Matt would think. "Are we really doing this? Is this happening?"

Tour the Horse Inn
The Horse Inn is a team effort. When it's time to choose a house whiskey, a vendor brings selections to sample, and staffers vote on a favorite. A barrel of the winner is delivered, "and now we have bottles with our label, and it comes from a single barrel," Matt said. "You can't get it anywhere in the world, and our employees chose it."

As Starla put it, "You're with your employees more than you're with family, so you treat them like family."

Someday, the Horse Inn might sprawl across two levels, from the second-level speakeasy down into the cavernous basement. That basement was once filled with horse stalls but now is home to a motley collection of chairs and a disc golf basket, where employees come down to practice their strokes and blow off steam. For now, guests enjoy their Tom Collins and Horse Fries in the comfortable surroundings of the second floor.

Main bar/dining room: I had just met Matt when he introduced me to the bar.

"Where your knees hit is the original front door to Franklin & Marshall College," he said.

Really? I tilted my head and it came into view, sideways—the type of tall, elaborately carved door that ushered scholars into the hallowed halls of academia. This particular door landed in this particular spot in the early 1920s because the building's owner was a contractor. Built most of this section of East Lancaster in the 19th and early 20th centuries. He just had such things in his inventory, I suspect.

The mirrored bar back

This could also explain the mirrored bar back, dating to the late 1800s, hauled here from the nearby town of Columbia. Our generation certainly did not invent repurposing, and the thrifty people of Lancaster long ago raised it to an art form. As old buildings came down, the contractor—William Shaub, in business with his sons– made good use of salvage.

Their thrift, our delight. The décor here is gasp-worthy. In the early 1920s, it seems that much of the horse-related gear downstairs migrated to the hayloft. Everything needed for an atmospheric speakeasy made its way one flight up:

■ Wagon wheel chandeliers, sporting bare globes that still struggle to cut through the dim.

■ Booths formed from horse stall walls. If you're in one of the booths with individual chairs, turn one over and take a look. They are held together with an intricate intertwining of wires. "No screws," said Matt. "No nails."

■ Barstools fashioned from wagon hubs. Even the footrest is an antique wagon hitch.

■ Horseshoes nailed to posts as coat hooks.

Barstools fashioned from wagon hubs

Tables and chairs in the open dining area came with the place, too, purchased mid-20th century by a previous owner when the Toby Tavern, a Lancaster institution, closed its doors. My jaw dropped at every turn.

"It's like Cracker Barrel, but real," I told Matt and Starla.

And it was all here when they bought the place.

"People pay millions of dollars to make places look like this," Matt said. "Why mess it up?"

Friends were so enthused that they stepped up with their own contributions. A friend of Matt's father said the place needed a piano. A week later, the friend called from a huge Baltimore piano shop.

"Which one do you want?" he asked.

Matt was agog. "No way," he said. But it was true. The friend bought a piano and had it shipped. I try to imagine the effort it took to muscle it up the stairs, but that's why God made professional piano movers.

The piano inspired Matt to go out on a hunt for musicians. He found a jazz trio, approached the leader, and said he had a cool spot.

Dining room with wagon-wheel chandeliers

Booths formed from horse stall walls

"I was covered in tattoos, and he's looking at me like, 'Is this guy serious?'" Today, the Tom Pontz Trio appears Tuesday and Saturday nights, swinging the Horse Inn back to its roots with speakeasy jazz.

One thing that did change in this room was a bar overhang. Probably handy for speakeasy customers trying to fade into the woodwork, but for today's crowd, it only concealed that mirrored bar back. The Russells and staff were cleaning the space one day when Starla said, "You know what? Let's just knock that out."

So they did, and the angels sang. "You could see everything," she said. The vintage bar back was fully revealed. Reflections off the mirrors revealed corners that probably hadn't seen light since the Coolidge administration. On summer days now, open the skylight window, and "the light streams down on the bartender," Starla said. "It's like a halo."

Back bar: One thing to know about the Horse Inn is that they don't take reservations. Tables are first-come, first-served. Saturday nights can mean two-hour waits, but no one seems to mind.

It helps that the Russells converted a compact special-event space into a cozy bar adjoining the dining room. Matt had the idea for a sort of waiting room when his parents told him people used to line up around the block for their Horse Inn experiences.

While you're lingering over predinner drinks, take note of:

■ Rustic wood walls. In renovations, the old drywall peeled off like Colorforms, and behind were the former barn walls.

■ Flooring made from recycled tires. The original floor was beyond repair—"an ankle breaker," Matt said—so they found a local product typically used in horse stalls. It's the Horse Inn coming full circle.

■ Murals depicting Lancaster scenes in the four seasons. The Russells' friend Doug Panzone created them in spray paint. Yep. Spray paint, and they are astounding. Doug also created the mural inside the front entrance and on the side of the building.

■ Nate Rupp, the former Horse Inn bartender, creates a vivid scene in chalk beside the bar every three months. For 2018 Triple Crown season—the Horse Inn loves hosting the Derby, Preakness, and the other one (had to look up the Belmont Stakes)—he drew a racing scene with the familiar Churchill Downs grandstand in the background. "You have a bunch of talented friends to draw on," I told Matt and Starla.

■ Clawfoot tub behind the bar. Amish workers redoing the apartments next door were dragging out a tub when Matt said, "Where are you going with that? I'll take it." He has, of course, "been to a bunch of bars," and he once saw someone using a vintage tub for serving cold beer. So, every night, order a $2 mystery beer, watch as the bartender reaches into the ice, and you get "whatever you get." The occasional lucky customer gets a seasonal beer that's out of season, "so you get a pretty decent beer for two bucks."

This is a good place to mention yet another piece of serendipity attached to the Horse Inn. Directly across the street is a small building with a sloping drive leading to dock doors. The building was the warehouse of that original contractor. The Russells' contractor—yet another friend pulled into the job—arrived and pointed across the street. In that building, he and his dad had set up shop when they opened their business.

"You guys are one big circle of life," I told Matt and Starla.

"Seriously," said Starla.

"It's crazy," agreed Matt.

SECTION II

The history of the Horse Inn: Hide in plain sight

Meander down Marshall Street as if you're just out for some air. Glance around, and dart into the nameless alley. Approach the barn, staying alert to your surroundings. Check over your shoulder one last time and walk to the door. Give the secret knock—two taps, pause, one more tap. The door slides to the right, and you're in. Climb the steep, walled-in steps, and you've reached your destination—the dark bar in the hayloft. Your drink is waiting.

Okay, I made up the secret knock. But everything else is true. The vast hayloft in William Shaub's stables seemed tailor-made for a speakeasy. In the City of Lancaster, Pennsylvania, this is not as surprising as you might think.

Wide open town: The Shaub family bought this building on Fulton Street for its contracting business for $800 in 1911. There was no door fronting Fulton Street. Access came by an alleyway door. Horses and carriages in the first level. Hay in the second.

A perfectly respectable Lancaster business. Hold that thought.

There's a term called "wide open." In the upright horse-and-buggy age, it was slang for any town that was wide open to vice—usually the trinity of booze, prostitution, and gambling.

Welcome to "wide open" Lancaster. Do you want vice? A morality crusader found 44 brothels within six blocks of Penn Square, the city center. Minors were buying beer in dance halls citywide.

Even before beer was illegal, Lancaster had a nickname: "Munich of the U.S." German immigrants made Lancaster a brewing hub. Americans were loving their beers and ales and lagers, and Lancaster was producing 7 percent of them.

When the U.S. House approved the 18th Amendment in 1919, sending it to states for ratification, a Lancaster newspaper announced that Prohibition would have a "Silver Lining Even for Rummies." In bars, proprietors "moulded a pinched expression over their faces when they learned that even their regular patrons intended to back the dry movement to the limit."

Not so fast, Lancaster newspaper. One month into Prohibition, in September 1920, the first "wholesale batch" of indictments brought against Pennsylvania saloonkeepers included two in Lancaster, for "selling intoxicants, having possession of liquor illegally, and maintaining a nuisance."

In that round of charges, it was reported, "one of the surprises of the report by the grand jury was the ignoring of thirteen bills of indictment for liquor sales, nine against saloonkeepers and four against bartenders."

Indifference. A powerful weapon in the fight against an unpopular law.

People often wonder why the Horse Inn's dining room booths, here on the second floor, are made from horse stalls hauled up from the first level. My guess? It's the early 1920s. Automobiles and trucks are replacing horses and buggies. The Shaub family didn't need their horses, or stalls, or the hay in the vast hayloft.

But here in this "wide open" town, friends and neighbors sure could use a place for a drink and a friendly game of shuffleboard. Out goes the hay. In comes the bootleg liquor served to guests at the bar and in booths crafted from those obsolete stalls. Smart businesses keep ahead of the times.

Supply would have been easy to obtain. Some Lancaster breweries continued brewing, confident that police would turn a blind eye. Others went surreptitious, even constructing hidden breweries within their walls. Pipes that once brought in water now pumped out beer, to trucks waiting offsite and, possibly, right here to the Shaub speakeasy, nice and fresh.

When some pipes were discovered, the resourceful Reikert's Brewery ran a fire hose through the Lancaster sewer. One day, a sewer worker shouted to his boss on the street above, "There's a hose down here."

"No, there is no hose down there," said the boss, "and don't tell anyone you saw it."

Think about that for a minute. You didn't see the hose that's not down there. Makes me laugh every time.

Shaub's idea to turn the barn into a speakeasy was hardly an anomaly. In every block, it seemed, enterprising homeowners offered their houses as gin mills. One Lancaster dad taking regular drives to Rawlinsville, 13 miles south, would tell the kids to hop in the car. Any cop seeing the family outing would think, "Oh, he's okay." Back home at the family-run hotel, complete with bar, dining room, and slot machines, Dad would concoct homemade whiskey and gin from the pure alcohol carted back from Rawlinsville, with kids as cover.

Tunnels catacombed under Lancaster hotels, breweries, and streets. Matt Russell remembers seeing tunnels under the Pressroom Restaurant, once home to the Lancaster *Intelligencer.*

Well, yeah, I said. Had to keep the reporters supplied in liquor.

In a January 1928 raid of Lancaster's Wacker Brewing Company, the region's top Prohibition agent himself, Mr. Franklin S. Weaver, dropped through a cellar window. His raid yielded a whopping one arrest and nine half-barrels of "alleged high powered beer."

"Prohibition is in its infancy," Weaver had announced a few months prior. "It is here to stay and it will be enforced."

If Prohibition was in its infancy, it died awfully young. In the game of Prohibition cat and mouse, the "mouse" was a tight-knit network of saloonkeepers, bartenders, customers, and the law. Speakeasy operators paid off local police. Federal agents who informed local police in advance about raids usually found the building empty and the hooch scant.

In one day that will live in the annals of nearby Columbia— the original home of the Horse Inn's bar back—police raided the openly operating Columbia Brewery. The cops were supposed to pour kerosene into the vats. Inadvertently, or maybe not so inadvertently, they opened the taps, and 200,000 gallons of fresh beer gushed into the stormwater system.

Citizens of Columbia dove into the gutters and culverts with cups and buckets. Spectators cheered while parents sent their kids to retrieve the stuff from spots too compact for grown-up bodies.

Children were apparently handy things to have on hand during Prohibition.

Lancaster was not immune to Prohibition's tragic side. In 1927, one of the few honest cops on the Lancaster police force, Lt. Elwood Gainer, was seen getting into a large touring car. The next morning, his bullet-riddled body was found near Philadelphia, his hand holding an apple with one bite taken from it. "Philadelphia rum runners" were suspected. Two years later, police found a charred body in a Newark, New Jersey, dump. The victim, identified by dental records, was believed to be one of Gainer's slayers.

On Valentine's Day 1930, an anniversary of note in Prohibition history, the news came out that many of Lancaster's "prominent society women" were banding together "to effectively combat prohibition." They were followed closely "by the organization of a similar group of men."

Lancaster had had enough. Prohibition was a failure. The Horse Inn's speakeasy days would soon be over, but its food—and one dish in particular—would keep the doors open.

Tips on toast: At the Horse Inn, longtime regulars order the famous tips on toast. It's a Horse Inn fixture that Matt upgraded a bit. Sous Chef Russell Skiles told me it takes two days to make the veal stock.

"There's a ton of effort put into that," he said. Most other places, you'd be getting "some weird concentrated base that they're putting warm water in." Here, they "spend the time to do it right, and something seemingly very simple takes on a whole new life." The secret to tips-on-toast perfection, it seems, is preparing it with "a ton of love."

For the original, thank William Shaub's wife, Florence, for a stroke of genius. The speakeasy was attracting customers. Booze makes people hungry, and hungry people are a source of income. Florence started serving tips on toast. Customers came back for more. Word spread. The menu expanded. A five-piece band played swing jazz.

The Shaub place was no longer just a speakeasy. It was a full-fledged restaurant, horse-stall booths and all. In 1935, with Prohibition now history, the proprietor was Emily Shaub, daughter-in-law of William, and she gave the place a new name that wouldn't have been hard to dream up, given the décor: The Horse Inn.

SECTION III

Touch history

The Horse Inn is called the longest consecutively running restaurant in Lancaster City. The Russells are only its fourth owner. The history of the city and the restaurant's ties to the surrounding county are palpable here.

Hay door and beam: You have horses. Horses have to eat, so you need a place for the hay. The hay goes in the loft. The loft is the upper level where the hay stays fresh and free from moisture that could turn good hay into compost.

Here's the thing. Have you ever lifted a bale of hay? Fifty pounds of scratchy, balky, bulky hay? You wrap your work gloves around the twine, grunt, and hoist.

So how could anyone possibly fill that loft with a supply of hay to keep feeding the hungry horses below?

From the alley entrance of the Horse Inn, look up and to the right. A beam protrudes from above a kind of second-floor door. You've seen the same thing at other stables and carriage houses. Today, most of those beams are unadorned, like the Horse Inn's, but in its utilitarian day, a pulley hung from this post. A rope running through the pulley connected to another pulley, or better yet, a mean-looking grappling hook. That potentially lethal hook would snare the hay, loose or maybe baled by a circa-1870s contraption called a hay press, and hoist it into the loft. Happy horse. Happy horseman.

Inside the Horse Inn dining room, you can sit at a table beside that door and enjoy your tips on toast or shrimp and grits. Just be sure to watch out for swinging grappling hooks.

Sliding door: Starla assumes the Horse Inn's sliding door has "been there for*ever.*"

Yes, the Russells went to a great deal of trouble to add a front entrance. It's gorgeous, with wood-framed glass door with gold lettering done by yet another talented friend. The horse mural just inside the foyer is another astounding creation spray painted by Doug Panzone.

But for the full speakeasy experience, you must enter via the alley. The sliding door won't slide for you, unfortunately. It gets slid open in the morning and slid shut at night. But you can see a piece peeking from its slot, just behind the screen door.

Jukebox: Prospective buyers Matt and Starla were walking through the Horse Inn with seller Al Medved. Along one wall, a tarp covered something bulky.

"What's that?" they asked.

"It's an old jukebox," said Al. A 1961 Seeburg, to be exact. I talked to Al about this. Seems he also owned an amusement company, selling "anything you put coins in." A friend traded the jukebox for a slot machine. Al spent a couple of thousand dollars refurbishing, with all-new wiring.

The Russells asked if it could be part of the deal. Sure, Al said. He gave it to them. The music, too, about 3,000 45s his employees had brought back over the years from servicing other jukeboxes.

Today, there's no need to drop a nickel in the slot. This jukebox runs for free. Do your best air guitar with Jimi Hendrix's "Foxy Lady," rock out to Springsteen's "Born to Run," or best of all, give a nod to the Horse Inn speakeasy days with Glenn Frey's "Smuggler's Blues."

Back bar counter: Drop your elbows on the bar top, and let me tell you a story. There was a hotel built in 1900, in the Lancaster town of Pequea (I'm pronouncing it peck-way). By 2004, it was the Martic Forge Hotel, an out-of-the-way place with a bar and a few residents, including several elderly and one person with Down syndrome. One night, around 2 a.m., a police officer saw flames shooting from the old hotel. He called county dispatch and a fellow officer. He and his colleague ran into the burning building, rousing residents and kicking in doors when they got no answer. One resident had been overcome by smoke when the officers found him just in time. The hotel was a complete loss, but everyone in the building got out alive, thanks to Southern Regional Police Officers Tim Ferrell and Adam Cramer.

Take another look at the bar top. The contractor on the Horse Inn renovations had a cabinetmaker friend. In the friend's barn were salvaged floor joists from the Martic Forge Hotel. Those joists got turned into the bar holding up your elbows. Kind of gives you new respect for a simple bar, doesn't it?

Plus, the wood's history goes even deeper than a heroic rescue in an old hotel. Those floor joists were themselves repurposed, from the city trolley lines. Each dark spot is a stain from the oil where a workman swung a hammer and drove in a nail.

My favorite Lancaster trolley story is, well, the only Lancaster trolley story I know, but it's a good one, showing the bumpy journey from trolley tracks to hotel joists to bar top. It's 1932, and trolleys are obsolete. Workmen are pulling up the streetcar tracks of Conestoga Transportation's Lancaster-Manheim branch. They start at opposite ends, planning to meet in the middle, in the town of East Petersburg. Except that when they arrive, with the line torn up in both directions, a trolley car is still on the tracks—that last, disconnected stretch of tracks, holding a lonely, forgotten, five-ton streetcar. How they got themselves out of this pickle is lost to time, but as a news story on the dilemma put it, "further wrecking operations were called off while officials went into a huddle."

Signs of the Horse: On Marshall Street, perpendicular to the old horse barn, a sign pointed down the alley, toward the building's only entrance. "Horse Inn," it said. I have to assume the sign went up after Prohibition.

Anyway, the handmade sign of a horsehead cutout, hanging in what appears to be a yoke, no longer hangs outside. "If you touch it, it just disintegrates," said Starla. But you can still see it if you come through the new front entrance and look up. It's hanging high on the wall, protected from the weather. Maybe someday, they'll have a duplicate made and hang it outside.

There's another Horse Inn sign, this one in the alley over the back entrance with the sliding door and steep stairs. I asked, what about that one?

"That's another one that needs love," sighed Starla.

"It's been there for a long time," Matt said.

On the garage door along the front, an H is carved into the wood. The Russells just gave it a little paint to highlight it. They don't know its origins, but it's fun to look at.

And I'd like to add a sweet thing that former owner Al Medved said about his successors. He comes to the Horse Inn for music some Tuesday nights. It's nice to know, he told me, that the restaurant started in the 1920s and is "doing better than ever and is as popular as ever. It's like a child to me and I'm passing it on, and the new people adopted it, and they're doing fantastic."

Any ghosts? "Every minute I've been in this building, nothing," Matt said. "I spend a lot of time alone in here."

Bartender Ben Hash agreed. "I've been here late by myself more than enough times, and the only thing that ever bugs me is catching my reflection in the mirror."

There was the time, Matt admitted as he pointed to a dining room light fixture, "when somebody thought it'd be cool to mess with Starla and kept turning off this light."

Ben immediately defended himself. "I only did it one time!"

The food scene: Did you hear the one about the Brooklyn vegans who walked into a bar and asked for a cheeseburger?

No punchline. That's the joke. A real-life vegan couple travels from New York once a month just to eat the Horse Inn's cheeseburger. Starla asked them if she could make a t-shirt saying, "Even vegans eat our cheeseburgers."

"Yeah," they said. "But don't use our names."

Matt proudly lists his food purveyors on the Horse Inn's chalkboard and website. In the kitchen, Sous Chef Russell Skiles—slated to take over as chef one day—is "passionate about what he does," Matt told me. "Also pretty romantic about it." When he and Matt hike, Russell forages for mushrooms and wild berries that might show up in a Horse Inn cocktail or salad.

I grabbed a few minutes with Russell before the Horse Inn opened for the night. What does he bring to the food?

"Geez, at this point in my life, something honest," he said. "It's got to have the best possible ingredients. It's got to be from the heart. It has to make perfect sense in the particular establishment."

You don't come here for nouveau or avant-garde, he said. He's done with silly and gimmicky. Then again, "cool and creative" are certainly on tap, and Lancaster's mini-cosmopolitan vibe, with a blend of cultures, makes its way to the plates.

"We've all gone to places where the food was a completely different culture, but it still touched on those comfort foods," he said. "Have you ever tried something brand new to you, but for some reason it felt like you've been eating it your entire life?"

Russell grew up in Lancaster, in this neighborhood. His mother made the elegant leather binders holding the cocktail menus. He rattled off the cultures he grew up among—Puerto Rican, African-American, Vietnamese, Kamei. Some of his best friends are Cambodian, and he has tried some "really funky Southeast Asian, ultra-fermented stuff."

Cocktail menu

Cheeseburger

Then add Polish and Pennsylvania Dutch, Matt said. "We're not locked down to one cuisine. We can do basically what we want, but tavern style."

That's the common denominator, Russell said. "It's a tavern, and it's got to feel like the Horse Inn. That means hyper-quality ingredients, technically sound, consistent every time."

I tried: "That first cheeseburger order is probably mine," I told Russell. And it was so very, very good. Juicy and smoky, a blend of short rib, brisket, chuck, and 10 percent dry-aged beef, on a fresh roll from Alfred & Sam's Bakery of Lancaster. This is the type that stays in your hand because it's breaking into pieces as you eat, but that's okay because you can't wait for the next bite.

The women beside me ordered the banh mi, which looked perfectly at home on the bar, proving Russell's point that comfort food is cross-cultural. He also brought me a dish of the parmesan agrodolce he was testing out, a rich and heavenly baked parmesan pannacotta. If I were those people from Brooklyn, I wouldn't just drive here once a month. I would buy the house next door and never bother to use the kitchen because this is where I'd cozy up every night for dinner.

The beverage scene: "Mind if I work while we talk?" Beverage Manager Benjamin Hash asked.

No problem. He had a job to do, setting up for another night of miraculous cocktails. So how did he dream up his alchemy of mixology?

It starts with traditional cocktails, he said, "and in a weird way, understanding what the town was," working " backward and forwards at all time." They worked hard to get the classics right, the Sazeracs and Tom Collins that "for some reason, people tend to mess up."

"But at the same time, we had to move forward, so we looked at where we are," he said. "We're in Lancaster, so we have a lot of produce. We were working on getting cocktails that reflected the area, what we had available to us, going to market, and the way the kitchen was working the food."

For instance? Perhaps Matt brings back cantaloupe and watermelon from the Central Market that didn't work for the salad, "but maybe it'll work for a soda." Recently, they got some chervil–.

I interrupted. Chervil?

"It's used in herbs de Provence," Ben explained, pulling out a plastic clamshell of minuscule green leaves. "But as you can see

The Beverage Manager and bartender Benjamin Hash

they sent us these really, really tiny things. 'Well, it's waste.' Well, it can't be waste. You've got to find a way to use it." So it goes into a drink recipe.

Every juice in every drink is fresh squeezed, pressed for about an hour daily by bar staff. They make their own syrups, bitters, tinctures. The new batch of lavender grenadine involved "a serious process" of reducing the pomegranate juice and building it back up with sugar and orange blossom. I got a sniff. As bartender Tim Heege described it, "it smells a little boozy, but it's got an herbal kind of thing."

When he first bartended in a chain restaurant, Ben said he was "kind of a knucklehead bartender, to be honest with you. There comes a point where you've got to decide if it's what you want to do, and you want to do it right, or it's just something you're doing to get by."

He started entering cocktail-making competitions. Realized he was pretty good at it. Books on cocktails and spirits fill a bookshelf behind the bar. He stays on top of trends. American palates are moving toward bitter tastes, in cocktails and in beer. In the 1980s, he said, "it was glitter bombs. A lot of it was fruity and sweet."

"Fuzzy navels!" I said. "Wine coolers." It was like we were still drinking Hawaiian Punch, but spiked.

I had to ask Ben about his look, a sort of speakeasy bartender re-imagined for our age, with suspenders and thin tie and mobster-on-a-hit-job haircut.

Seems he was in a Philadelphia cocktail competition early on the first day he worked at the Horse Inn. No time to change between the two. At the Horse Inn, everyone loved the look. Now he was stuck, but that was okay.

"I do wear this because it's respectful bartender's apparel," Ben said. "Sloppy is not a term you would want to associate with food or drinks." And maybe it's a little "messed up" to say, but people often look at him and say, "He looks like a good bartender. I bet we can get a good cocktail from him."

How does he set his cocktail menu? He pulled out a handwritten, hand-sketched cocktail journal, one drink per page. Some recipes were X'd out, two or three on a page tried and rejected, until the final stood.

"We've got over 120 original cocktails," Ben said. "Some of them we have to manipulate a little bit."

The menu, laid out and drawn by Ben, is broken down by spirits, starting with my favorite—gin, or as it's known here, "botanicals." Maybe you want a tequila drink that's not a margarita. They have it. Maybe you feel like a vodka drink, but you know what? There's a gin cocktail you might like. Getting people to try new things is part of the fun.

"That Chantilly we did—it was like a strawberry Pop Tart, it was so good," said Ben. "It was mind-blowing."

Breakfast as cocktails. Now we're talking.

Pennsylvania spirits abound. Thistle Finch from Lancaster, produced in a National Register of Historic Places-listed tobacco warehouse. Heirloom grain-based Wigle from Pittsburgh, named after western Pennsylvania farmer Philip Wigle, whose resistance to the 1790s whiskey tax helped spark the Whiskey Rebellion and who barely escaped a date with the hangman. The popular Bluecoat from Philadelphia, whose gin and other spirits honor the "spirit" of revolutionary soldiers.

The Horse Inn also partners with local brewers. Working with Ephrata-based St. Boniface Brewing Co. to create the nitro Ace in the Hole was "probably our best move," Ben said. They also serve beers from Wacker Brewing Co., the successor to that Lancaster brewery once raided by the agent dropping through a basement window—finally put out of business by Big Beer in 1956, and revived in 2014. Maybe Wacker was served here during Prohibition. I call that coming full circle.

Ben certainly appreciates the symmetry.

"You get goosebumps sometimes when you think about the bartenders that have walked this floor," he said from behind the bar. "The cigarette burns on the back bar. The history you don't even pay attention to. All of a sudden, it jumps out at you. It can really get to you. It's really a privilege to be in a place like this. You could be in a sterile environment in a building that's 10 years old, that has no story to tell. This place—people joke that I probably just fade into the wall when the lights go out."

I tried: The St. Boniface Ace in the Hole delivered, a nicely balanced nitro with just enough fizz to cut through the heft of the burger. My pre-dinner cocktail was the Devine Sage (chosen from among such speakeasy-recalling names as Pistol Under the Pillow and Scofflaw). I watched Ben concoct my mixture of Bluecoat gin, apricot, Rothman & winter peach, lemon, orange bitters, and sage. Mad scientist-like, he would reach into this jar

Devine Sage drink

or that, and then add something with an eyedropper. My drink really was divine, smooth and refreshing, beautifully balanced. The sage, like all the spices, had been prepared from whole, fresh spices, but the taste was flavorful, not overwhelming. "You can't expect to cut corners and do it right," Ben said.

PLAN YOUR VISIT

The Horse Inn
540 E. Fulton Street
Lancaster, PA 17602
www.horseinnlancaster.com, (717) 392-5528

WHAT'S NEARBY

An artful night's sleep: You've enjoyed your evening immersed in the colorful past. This is not the time to spend your night in the sterile present. The Lancaster Arts Hotel, a five-minute drive from the Horse Inn, occupies a restored tobacco warehouse and is stocked with a museum-worthy collection of fine and local artworks. Each room beckons as a unique getaway, with brick walls, exposed posts and beams, and original decor that upends old notions of hotel art. (www.lancasterartshotel.com)

ACKNOWLEDGMENTS

"Hi. I'm a writer. I know this is your life's work and you devote 18 hours a day making sure your food is tasty and your very old building stays intact, but I'd like to drop in for an afternoon and learn about everything you do."

I sometimes worry about being a writer-leech, living off the life-blood of others, but then someone says they could never do what I do, and I figure I must offer something of value to the world. Still, there's no question that the tavern owners and proprietors gracious enough to share their time and knowledge made this book possible. They are: Walter Staib, City Tavern; Patrick J. Byrne, General Warren Historic Hospitality; Leah Kaithern Patterson, Blue Bell Inn; Jan Hench, McCoole's at the Historic Red Lion Inn; Brett Biggs, Tavern at the Sun Inn; Brandon Callihan, Jean Bonnet Tavern; Grant Ross, Black Bass Hotel; Jacqueline White, Dobbin House Tavern; Sarah Dull, Farnsworth House Inn and Sweney's Tavern; James T. Croley II, Wooden Keg Tavern; Troy Reynard, Two Rivers Brewing Company; and Matthew and Starla Russell, the Horse Inn.

Many others helped along the way. Aaron White scheduled me with the busy Chef Staib at City Tavern, and Chef's assistant Jonathan Jones was an entertaining tour guide. Seth Cornish introduced the cast of revolutionaries who visited the Sun Inn. Timothy H. Smith shared tales of the Farnsworth House's Gettysburg battle days, and of drinking with Sam Elliott. Black Bass Hotel Beverage Manager Clayton Deering kept conversations flowing, and Executive Chef John Barrett shared his culinary and historical knowledge. At Two Rivers, a sit-down with Executive Chef Jeremy Bialker, Head Brewer Josh Bushey, and Front of House and Banquet Manager Wendy Carroll provided a glimpse into the camaraderie crucial to a successful establishment. Horse Inn's stylish Beverage Manager Benjamin Hash and personable Sous Chef Russell Skiles opened my eyes to the difference that passion makes when it's an ingredient in your cocktail or dish.

Others? Gary Myers shared stories of his father's time as a speakeasy bartender and that epic day in Columbia, Pennsylvania,

ACKNOWLEDGMENTS

when the gutters flowed with beer. Jack Sherzer of Message Prose was thrilled to learn I was writing a book, never once asking if it would interfere with the jobs he was paying me to do. All my editors kept the jobs flowing. Publisher Lawrence Knorr heard a five-minute pitch and said it was right up Sunbury Press' alley, sparing me the folder full of rejection letters I thought was required to become an author.

Siblings Brian, Bob, Carol Maureen, and Sharyn, and all their spouses and kids, have been my cheerleaders at every step. Sharyn and Carol Mo—two-thirds of *Tres Hermanas*—squealed with delight when they learned I had a contract, and Sharyn has my eternal gratitude for blurting out what would become the title when I told them I was writing a book about taverns where rabble-rousers stirred up trouble.

Our mom, Margaret McCormick, inspires everything I do, showing how to live life with joy and cheer. If our dad, John P. McCormick, were with us, he'd be uncapping his highlighter to highlight my name on the cover.

My spirited and loving stepdaughters, Bryden McCurdy and Meaghan Farrell, and beautiful granddaughter Adria McGarry provided support, patience, listening ears, and much-needed laughs.

My husband, Marc Farrell, liked the idea when I got brave enough to tell him. That was all I needed—that and a year of his patience and putting food in front of me when I emerged from my writer's cave and occasionally ordering me out for a glass of wine. He tolerated his crazed wife and the cat-hair tumbleweeds. He is my biggest fan and my peerless reader, offering insights and ideas that made each chapter better.

SOURCES

Introduction

Adams, John. "The Works of John Adams, vol. 2 Diary, Notes of Debates, Autobiography) (1850), Online Library of Liberty, http://oll.libertyfund.org/titles/adams-the-works-of-john-adams-vol-2-diary-notes-of-debates-autobiography.

Chapter 1: City Tavern

Author interview with Walter Staib, City Tavern, Philadelphia, Pennsylvania, Presidents' Day, Feb. 19, 2018.

Adams, John. "The Works of John Adams, vol. 2 (Diary, Notes of Debates, Autobiography) (1850)," Online Library of Liberty, http://oll.libertyfund.org/titles/adams-the-works-of-john-adams-vol-2-diary-notes-of-debates-autobiography.
Anishanslin, Zara. "Dancing Assembly," The Encyclopedia of Greater Philadelphia, http://philadelphiaencyclopedia.org/archive/dancing-assembly/.
"City Tavern," USHistory.org, http://www.ushistory.org/tour/city-tavern.htm.
"11h. The French Alliance," USHistory.org, http://www.ushistory.org/us/11h.asp.
Gaines, James R. For Liberty and Glory: Washington, Lafayette, and Their Revolutions. New York: W.W. Norton & Company, 2007.
"George Washington and the Marquis de Lafayette," George Washington's Mount Vernon, http://www.mountvernon.org/digital-encyclopedia/article/george-washington-and-the-marquis-de-lafayette/.
Gold, William. "The City Tavern Restaurant—A Taste of Philadelphia History," Phila Place, http://www.philaplace.org/story/1209/.
Hendrix, Steve. "The epic bender to celebrate George Washington and the newly finished U.S. Constitution," Washington Post, Feb. 22, 2018, https://www.washingtonpost.com/news/retropolis/wp/2018/02/22/the-epic-bender-to-celebrate-george-washington-and-the-newly-finished-constitution/?utm_term=.35743845a22a.
Hines, Nick. "The Definitive History of Grog," Vinepair, https://vinepair.com/articles/the-definitive-history-of-grog/.
Independence Park National Register for Historic Places application, March 4, 1988, https://npgallery.nps.gov/pdfhost/docs/NRHP/Text/66000683.pdf.
Karsch, Carl G. "City Tavern: A Feast of Elegance," Carpenters' Hall, http://www.ushistory.org/carpentershall/history/feast.htm.
Lengel, Edward G. "The Battle of Brandywine," War Times Journal, http://www.wtj.com/articles/brandywine/.
NCC Staff, "On this day, the first Continental Congress meets in Philadelphia," National Constitution Center, Sept. 5, 2017, https://constitutioncenter.org/blog/the-first-congress-meets-in-philadelphia-240-years-ago-today/.
"Paul Revere," Museum of Fine Arts, Boston, http://www.mfa.org/collections/object/paul-revere-32401.
Raphael, Ray. "Paul Revere's Other Rides," Journal of the American Revolution, April 28, 2014, https://allthingsliberty.com/2014/04/paul-reveres-other-rides/.

Robinson, Martha K. "British Occupation of Philadelphia," The Encyclopedia of Greater Philadelphia, http://philadelphiaencyclopedia.org/archive/british-occupation-of-philadelphia/.

"Sons of Liberty dump British tea," The History Channel, https://www.history.com/this-day-in-history/sons-of-liberty-dump-british-tea.

Staib, Walter, and Paul Bauer. *The City Tavern Cookbook.* Philadelphia: Running Press, 2009.

"10e. Second Continental Congress," USHistory.org, http://www.ushistory.org/us/10e.asp.

"10g. The Declaration of Independence," USHistory.org, http://www.ushistory.org/us/10g.asp.

"Who served here? The Marquis de Lafayette," Historic Valley Forge, http://www.ushistory.org/valleyforge/served/lafayette.html.

Yun, Lawrence. "Largest Cities in the United States in 1776, And In 2076," Economists' Outlook Blog, July 3, 2012 http://economistsoutlook.blogs.realtor.org/2012/07/03/largest-cities-in-the-united-states-in-1776-and-in-2076/.

Chapter 2: General Warren Historic Hospitality

Author interview with Patrick J. Byrne, General Warren Historic Hospitality, Malvern, Pennsylvania, Nov. 3, 2017.

Author visit to Paoli Battlefield, Malvern, PA, Nov. 3, 2017.

Bruce, Robert. "The Historic Philadelphia-Pittsburgh Route," *Motor Travel,* June 1917.

Chester County Historic Preservation Office, "Pennsylvania Historical Resource Survey Form," 1988, General Warren Historic Hospitality binder.

"Colonial Taverns of Lower Merion," *The Pennsylvania Magazine,* 1928.

Darby, D. Weston, Jr., letter to Patrick Byrne, May 13, 1993, General Warren Historic Hospitality binder.

Editors of Encyclopaedia Britannica, "King George's War," Encyclopaedia Britannica, https://www.britannica.com/event/King-Georges-War.

Erickson, Winona C. "General Warren Inn," General Warren Historic Hospitality binder.

Gordon, Ronald J. "Conrad Beissel and his Communal Experiment," Church of the Brethren Network, revised March 2016, https://www.cob-net.org/cloister.htm.

Kerr, Richard D. "The Lancaster Road and Turnpike," Haverford Township Historical Society, revised Sept. 30, 2013, http://haverfordhistoricalsociety.org/wp-content/uploads/haverford_firsts/HTHS_06_The_Lancaster_Road_and_Turnpike.pdf.

Klein, Christopher. "10 Things You Should Know About Joseph Warren," The History Channel, Jan. 22, 2015, http://www.history.com/news/10-things-you-should-know-about-joseph-warren.

"Major John Andre," USHistory.org, http://www.ushistory.org/march/bio/andre.htm.

McGuire, Thomas J. *Battle of Paoli.* Mechanicsburg, PA: Stackpole Books, 2000.

McIntyre, James R. "Seven Years' War," The Encyclopedia of Greater Philadelphia, 2015, http://philadelphiaencyclopedia.org/archive/seven-years-war/.

"Petition of Charles Fahnestock for Licence," Aug. 2, 1825, General Warren Historic Hospitality binder.

"Siege of Louisbourg (1745)," Wikipedia, https://en.wikipedia.org/wiki/Siege_of_Louisbourg_(1745).

Twaddell, Meg Daley. *Inns, Tales, and Taverns of Chester County.* Country Publications, 1984.

"Who served here? Benedict Arnold," USHistory.org, http://www.ushistory.org/valleyforge/served/arnold.html.
"William Penn Landing Site," Wikipedia, https://en.wikipedia.org/wiki/William_Penn_Landing_Site.

Chapter 3: The Blue Bell Inn

Author interview with Leah Kaithern Patterson and Ronnie Scherf, The Blue Bell Inn, Blue Bell, Pennsylvania, Nov. 4, 2017.

"Adam Stephen," George Washington's Mount Vernon, http://www.mountvernon.org/digital-encyclopedia/article/adam-stephen/.
"Battle of Germantown," BritishBattles.com, https://www.britishbattles.com/war-of-the-revolution-1775-to-1783/battle-of-germantown/.
Bean, Theodore W., ed., *History of Montgomery County, Pennsylvania, Volume II.* Philadelphia: Everts & Peck, 1884.
Chernow, Ron. *Washington: A Life.* New York: Penguin Books, 2011.
Dickey, Mike. "Battle of Germantown," Skippack Historical Society, http://www.skippack.org/revwar_germantown.htm.
Fleming, Thomas. "The Enigma of General Howe," *American Heritage*, February 1964, https://www.americanheritage.com/content/enigma-general-howe.
"History of the Battle of Germantown," Cliveden, http://www.cliveden.org/revolutionary-germantown-festival/.
Kennedy, Joseph S. "A moral triumph in Montco," The Philadelphia *Inquirer*, Nov. 3, 1996, https://www.newspapers.com/image/178364051.
Lengel, Edward G. "The Battle of Brandywine," War Times Journal, http://www.wtj.com/articles/brandywine/.
Moon, Robert C., M.D.. *The Morris Family of Philadelphia* 1898. https://archive.org/stream/morrisfamilyofph02moon/morrisfamilyofph02moon_djvu.txt.
Philbrick, Nathaniel. *Valiant Ambition.* New York: Penguin Books, 2017.
"Waynesburg, county seat for Greene County," Greene County Government, http://www.co.greene.pa.us/secured/gc2/history/AnthonyWayne.htm.

Chapter 4: McCoole's at the Historic Red Lion Inn

Author interview with Jan Hench, McCoole's at the Historic Red Lion Inn, Quakertown, Pennsylvania, June 9, 2017.

"American hero rocks the cradle, saves Liberty Bell," The State Museum of Pennsylvania, Dec. 16, 2014, http://statemuseumpa.org/american-hero-rocks-cradle-saves-liberty-bell/.
"Approved markers," Pennsylvania Historical and Museum Commission, 2018, http://www.phmc.pa.gov/Preservation/Historical-Markers/Pages/Approved-Markers.aspx?View=%7B20fef81f-9644-4644-9879-65de96d254dd%7D&SortField=County&SortDir=Asc.
Cheney, Jim. "Visiting the Hiding Place of the Liberty Bell at Allentown's Liberty Bell Museum," https://uncoveringpa.com/liberty-bell-museum-allentown.
Chernow, Ron. *Grant.* New York: Penguin Press, 2017.
Colimore, Edward. "Little Known Peales' brother portrait returns to Philly," Philadelphia *Inquirer*, updated Dec. 5, 2016, http://www.philly.com/philly/news/20161205_Little_known_Peales_brother_portrait_returns_to_Philly.html.
The Editors of Encyclopaedia Britannica, "Philadelphia Centennial Exposition," https://www.britannica.com/event/Philadelphia-Centennial-Exposition.

SOURCES

The Editors of Leben. "The Mystery of America's Liberty Bell," WND, 2013, http://www.wnd.com/2013/06/the-mystery-of-americas-liberty-bell/.

"John Fries Rebellion," James Mann Art Farm, http://www.jamesmannartfarm.com/friesreb1.html.

"John Jacob Mickley, The Hopkin Thomas Project," http://himedo.net/TheHopkinThomasProject/FamilyTies/BiographicalData/ps09/ps09_160.htm.

"The Liberty Bell. Col. Thomas Polk's Overnight Bivouac," James Mann Art Farm, http://www.jamesmannartfarm.com/libbell.html.

Marshall, Jeffrey. "Historic Quakertown," Bucks County magazine, Sept. 11, 2013, http://www.buckscountymag.com/what-to-do/our-towns/historic-quaker town/.

Nash, Gary B. *The Liberty Bell*. New Haven, CT: Yale University Press, 2010.

Newman, John Douglas. *Fries's Rebellion: The Enduring Struggle for the American Revolution*. Philadelphia: University of Pennsylvania Press, 2004.

Snodgrass, Mary Ellen. "The Underground Railroad: An Encyclopedia of People, Places, and Operations." London and New York: Routledge, Taylor & Francis Group, 2015.

Thompson, Peter. *Rum Punch & Revolution: Taverngoing & Public Life in Eighteenth-Century Philadelphia*. Philadelphia: University of Pennsylvania Press, 1999.

Wartenberg, Steve. "Quakertown's historic Red Lion Inn back in business," Allentown *Morning Call*, Aug. 27, 2003, https://www.newspapers.com/image/284275807.

Whelan, Frank. "On the track to freedom," Allentown Morning Call, March 15, 1998, https://www.newspapers.com/image/277559793.

Chapter 5: Tavern at the Sun Inn

Author interview with Brett Biggs, Tavern at the Sun Inn, Bethlehem, Pennsylvania, March 9, 2018.

Author phone interview with Seth Cornish, March 30, 2018.

"General Pulaski Honored in Bethlehem," Lehigh Valley Ramblings, April 29, 2013, https://lehighvalleyramblings.blogspot.com/2013/04/general-pulaski-honored-in-bethlehem.html.

Grossman, Elliot."Bethlehem's Sun Inn celebrates 20 years of restoration," Allentown *Morning Call*, June 17, 1991, https://www.newspapers.com/image/284555380/?terms=Hughetta%2BBethlehem.

Historic Sites, Historic Bethlehem Museums & Sites, https://historicbethlehem.org/about/historic-sites/.

Huetter, Karen Zerbe. *John Adams' Bethlehem: "A Curious and Remarkable Town."* Bethlehem, Pennsylvania: Oaks Printing Company, 1976, http://bdhp.moravian.edu/visitors_accounts/books/johnadams/page12-13.html.

"Hughetta Bender, 89, Former President of Sun Inn Association," Allentown *Morning Call*, March 14, 1995, http://articles.mcall.com/1995-03-14/news/3016426_1_historic-preservation-historic-inn-sun-inn-preservation-association.

Jordan, John W. "Bethlehem During the Revolution," The Pennsylvania Magazine of History and Biography, Volume XIII, 1889.

Jordan, John Woolf. "The Military Hospitals of Bethlehem and Lititz, Penn'a, During the Revolutionary War," Pennsylvania Magazine of History and Biography, July 1896, https://ia800307.us.archive.org/31/items/militaryhospital00jord/militaryhospital00jord_bw.pdf.

Kovalenko, Anne. "Restoration Of Sun Inn On the Move," Allentown *Sunday Call-Chronicle*, Sept. 24, 1972, https://www.newspapers.com/image/275328063/?terms=Hughetta%2B%2B%2BBBethlehem.

Laux, James B. *Brother Albrecht's Secret Chamber*, 1910.

Nerl, Daryl. "Spirit maker attached to Sun Inn seeks to operate distillery in Hanover Township," Allentown *Morning Call*, July 27, 2017, http://www.mcall.com/news/local/bethlehem/mc-nws-hanover-sun-inn-distillery-20170726-story.html.

"Peekskill, New York," A Revolutionary Day Along Historic US Route 9, http://www.revolutionaryday.com/usroute9/peekskill/default.htm.

Procknow, Gene. "British Fascination with Ethan Allen," Journal of the American Revolution, March 11, 2014, https://allthingsliberty.com/2015/03/british-fascination-with-ethan-allen/.

———. "Ethan Allen: Patriot, Land Promoter or Turncoat?," Journal of the American Revolution, Nov. 5, 2013, https://allthingsliberty.com/2013/11/ethan-allen-patriot-land-promoter-turncoat/.

Radzievich, Nicole. "New spirits could occupy Bethlehem's Sun Inn," Allentown *Morning Call*, March 30, 2015, http://www.mcall.com/news/local/bethlehem/mc-bethlehem-sun-inn-distillery-20150330-.story.html.

Sheehan, Daniel Patrick. "Bethlehem honors a Polish war hero," Allentown *Morning Call*, April 29, 2013, http://articles.mcall.com/2013-04-28/news/mc-bethlehem-pulaski-celebration-20130428_1_pulaski-day-.

———. "With Broadway madness ongoing, could 'Hamilton Slept Here' be Bethlehem's next tourism catch phrase?," July 4, 2016, http://www.mcall.com/news/local/bethlehem/mc-alexander-hamilton-bethlehem-20160703-story.html.

69 News, "History's Headlines: Bethlehem played host to Revolutionary War hero Marquis de Lafayette in 1777," WFMZ.com, http://www.wfmz.com/features/historys-headlines/historys-headlines-bethlehem-played-host-to-revolutionary-war-hero-marquis-de-lafayette-in-1777/18500578.

Sunderland, Jean R., and Catherine S. Parzynski, eds. *The Lehigh Valley from Settlement to Steel*. Bethlehem, Pennsylvania: Lehigh University Press, 2008.

"The Works of John Adams, vol. 2 (Diary, Notes of Debates, Autobiography) (1850), Online Library of Liberty, http://oll.libertyfund.org/titles/adams-the-works-of-john-adams-vol-2-diary-notes-of-debates-autobiography.

Virgintino, Mike. "Preserving A Peekskill Revolutionary War Battle Site," Peekskill Patch, Oct. 16, 2016, https://patch.com/new-york/peekskill/preserving-peekskill-revolutionary-war-battle-site.

Weil, Lorna. "Sun Inn president honored," Allentown *Morning Call*, April 9, 1983, https://www.newspapers.com/image/284185490/?terms=Hughetta%2BBethlehem

Wenner, Cheryl. "Couch Potatoes march with ghouls," Allentown *Morning Call*, Oct. 17, 1988, https://www.newspapers.com/image/282676553/?terms=%22Hughetta%22%2B%2B%2B%22Marcincin%22.

"Who served here? General Nathanael Greene," USHistory.org, http://www.ushistory.org/valleyforge/served/greene.html.

Williamson, Lanie. "Marquis de Lafayette healed his wounds in Bethlehem," Allentown Morning Call, Sept. 13, 2007, http://articles.mcall.com/2007-09-13/opinion/3771279_1_single-sisters-house-marquis-lafayette.

Chapter 6: Jean Bonnet Tavern

Author interview with Brandon Callihan, Jean Bonnet Tavern, Bedford, Pennsylvania, Dec. 7, 2017.

"Behind the Marker," Bonnet Tavern Historical Marker, ExplorePAhistory.com, http://explorepahistory.com/hmarker.php?markerId=1-A-29B.

"Capt. Robert Callender," Smith Rebellion 1765, http://smithrebellion1765.com/?page_id=97.

SOURCES

Dunn, Walter S., Jr. *Frontier Profit and Loss: The British Army and the Fur Traders, 1760-1764.* Westport, CT: Greenwood Press, 1998.

———. *People of the American Frontier: The Coming of the American Revolution,* Westport, CT: Praeger Publishers, 2005.

Eicher, Kory. "Jean Bonnet Tavern," May 18, 2001, Bedford County Historical Society.

Frear, Ned. *The Whiskey Rebellion.* Bedford, PA: Gazette Publishing Co., 1999.

"From George Washington to Robert Callender, 20 October 1775," Founders Online, https://founders.archives.gov/documents/Washington/02-02-02-0125.

Grubbs, Patrick. "Whiskey Rebellion Trials," The Encyclopedia of Greater Philadelphia, 2015, https://philadelphiaencyclopedia.org/archive/whiskey-rebellion-trials/.

Hofstra, Warren R., ed. *Ulster to America: The Scots-Irish Migration Experience.* Knoxville, KY: University of Tennessee Press, 2012.

Ridner, Judith. *A Town In-Between: Carlisle, Pennsylvania, and the Early Mid-Atlantic Interior.* Philadelphia: University of Pennsylvania Press, 2010.

Veach, Elaine. "Feel the history at the Jean Bonnet Tavern," Mature Living.

Chapter 7: Black Bass Hotel

Author interview with Grant Ross, Black Bass Hotel, Lumberville, Pennsylvania, Feb. 9, 2018.

"An Era Rich in History and Culture," Delaware & Lehigh National Heritage Corridor, National Canal Museum, https://canals.org/learn/the-canal-era/.

Byrne, James P., Philip Coleman, and Jason King, eds. *Ireland and the Americas: Culture, Politics, and History, A Multidisciplinary Encyclopedia, Volume I.* Santa Barbara, CA: ABC-CLIO, Inc. 2008.

———. *Ireland and the Americas: Culture, Politics, and History, A Multidisciplinary Encyclopedia, Volume II.* Santa Barbara, CA: ABC-CLIO, Inc., 2008.

"Canals," Immigration to the United States, http://immigrationtounitedstates.org/403-canals.html.

Dale, Frank. *Bridges Over the Delaware River: A History of Crossings.* New Brunswick, NJ: Rutgers University Press, 2003.

Devlin, Frank. "Settlement not yet final in Black Bass Hotel suits," Allentown *Morning Call,* Oct. 31, 1992. https://www.newspapers.com/image/283513862/?terms=%22delaware%2Bcanal%22%2B%22Lumberville%22%2B%22Herbert%2BWard%22.

"'Drunken, Dirty' Irish Build Canal," Lockport *Free Press,* June 15, 1978, https://www.lewisu.edu/imcanal/johnlamb/section_17.pdf.

Frazier, Lynne McKenna. "Irish canal diggers built prosperity," Fort Wayne News-Sentinel, http://fwn-egen2.fortwayne.com/ns/projects/history/canel.php.

Gagnier, Mary. "Restaurant sues state over crumbling canal," Allentown *Morning Call,* Oct. 16, 1991, https://www.newspapers.com/image/283470763/?terms=%22delaware%2Bcanal%22%2B%22Lumberville%22%2B%22Herbert%2BWard%22.

Gauvreau, Emile. "An Inn Which Grew Up With The Nation," Black Bass Hotel.

Lumberville Historic District National Register for Historic Places application, Aug. 9, 1984, http://www.dot7.state.pa.us/CRGIS_Attachments/SiteResource/H079664_01H.pdf

McClellan, Robert J. *The Delaware Canal: A Picture Story.* New Brunswick, NJ: Rutgers University Press, 1967.

"Paid Notice: Deaths, Ward, Herbert Everard," New York Times, Jan. 21, 2004, https://www.nytimes.com/2004/01/21/classified/paid-notice-deaths-ward-herbert-everard.html.

"Pieces of Lumberville-Raven Rock Bridge donated to Roebling Museum," Hunterdon County *Democrat,* April 21, 2013, http://www.nj.com/hunterdon-county-democrat/index.ssf/2013/04/pieces_of_lumberville-raven_ro.html.

Rivinus, Willis M. *Lumberville: 300 Year Heritage*, 2006.

Strausbaugh, Joseph A. "The Influence of the Pennsylvania Mainline on Public Works," The Gettysburg Historical Journal, Volume 5, Article 4, 2006, http://cupola.gettysburg.edu/cgi/viewcontent.cgi?article=1063&context=ghj.

Way, Peter. *Common Labor: Workers and the Digging of North American Canals.* Baltimore, MD: The Johns Hopkins University Press, 1993.

Yoder, C.P. "Bill". *Delaware Canal Journal: A Definitive History of the Canal and the River Valley Through which it Flows.* Bethlehem, PA: Canal Press Incorporated, 1972.

Chapter 8: Dobbin House Inn

Author interview with Jacqueline White, Dobbin House Inn, Gettysburg, Pennsylvania, June 25, 2017.

Blight, David W. *Passages to Freedom: The Underground Railroad in History and Memory.* Washington, DC: Smithsonian Books, 2001.

Coco, Gregory A. *A Strange and Blighted Land. Gettysburg: The Aftermath of a Battle.* Gettysburg, PA: Thomas Publications, 1995.

Fisher, Sydney George. *The Making of Pennsylvania.* Philadelphia: J.B. Lippincott Company, 1908, https://library.si.edu/digital-library/book/makingofpennsyl00fish.

"Gettysburg National Cemetery, Gettysburg, Pennsylvania," National Park Service, https://www.nps.gov/nr/travel/national_cemeteries/pennsylvania/gettysburg_national_cemetery.html.

"History of the Soldiers' National Cemetery at Gettysburg," National Park Service, https://www.nps.gov/gett/planyourvisit/150th-anniversary-dedication-day-cemetery-history.htm.

"Remembering Frederick Douglass' escape from slavery," National Constitution Center, 2017, https://www.yahoo.com/news/remembering-frederick-douglass-escape-slavery-100000602.html

"Timeline: Civil War and National Cemeteries (1862)," National Park Service, https://www.cem.va.gov/cem/history/timeline/timeline-1862.asp.

Wertz, Hiram E., Esq. "The Underground Railroad." Kittochtinny Historical Society, Pennsylvania AHGP, 1911, http://paahgp.genealogyvillage.com/underground-railroad.html.

Chapter 9: Farnsworth House Inn and Sweney's Tavern

Author interview with Sarah Dull, Lorin Miller, and Timothy H. Smith, Farnsworth House Inn and Sweney's Tavern, Gettysburg, Pennsylvania, March 16, 2018.

"Battle of Gettysburg," HistoryNet, http://www.historynet.com/battle-of-gettysburg.

"Battle of Gettysburg: Union Cavalry Attacks," HistoryNet, http://www.historynet.com/battle-of-gettysburg-union-cavalry-attacks.htm.

Bloom, Rachel. "Gettysburg Remembrance Day Parade and Illumination 2017," Trip Savvy, updated Nov. 15, 2017, https://www.tripsavvy.com/gettysburg-remembrance-day-parade-illumination-1038446.

Bloom, Robert L. "'We Never Expected A Battle': The Civilians at Gettysburg, 1863," file:///C:/Users/Owner/Downloads/24708-24547-1-PB.pdf

"Brigadier General Elon J. Farnsworth," Military History of the Upper Great Lakes, http://ss.sites.mtu.edu/mhugl/2016/11/18/brigadier-general-elon-j-farnsworth-2/.

Custer, Andie. "Into the Mouth of Hell: Farnsworth's Charge Revisited," Blue & Gray Magazine, Volume XXIII, Issue #1, http://www.bluegraymagazine.com/farns/farns4.html.

SOURCES

Gilpin, Drew, and Ric Burns. "At Gettysburg, Death and Transformation," *Time*, July 3, 2013, http://newsfeed.time.com/2013/07/03/at-gettysburg-death-and-transformation/.

Greenspan, Jesse. "Remembering the Only Civilian to Die at Gettysburg," The History Channel, July 1, 2013, https://www.history.com/news/remem bering-the-only-civilian-to-die-at-gettysburg.

Larson, C. Kay. "The Horses of War," New York *Times*, Feb. 2, 2013, https:// opinionator.blogs.nytimes.com/2013/02/02/the-horses-of-war/.

"'Legends, Lore, Ghosts Galore' Gettysburg tour dates announced," Gettysburg *Times*, Aug. 9, 1994, https://www.newspapers.com/image/46864360/?terms=%22Far nsworth%22%2B%22Gettysburg%22%2B%22movie%22

Ringle, Ken. "'Gettysburg,'" Washington *Post*, Oct. 10, 1993, http://www. washingtonpost.com/wp-srv/style/longterm/movies/videos/gettysburg pgringle_a09e44.htm.

Smith, Timothy H. *In the Eye of the Storm: The Farnsworth House and the Battle of Gettysburg*. Farnsworth Military Impressions, 2008.

Chapter 10: Wooden Keg Tavern

Author interview with James T. Croley II, Wooden Keg Tavern, St. Clair, Pennsylvania, March 26, 2018.

Flaherty, Anne. "'The Stories Were All Lies': Pinkerton, McParlan and Sherlock Holmes Tell a Tale of the 'Molly Maguires,'" From John Kehoe's Cell, http:// mythofmollymaguires.blogspot.com/2011/07/.

"Give Them A Rifle Diet," BMWE *Journal*, Volume 106, Number 10, November 1997, https://www.bmwe.org/journal/1997/11NOV/05.htm.

"Immaculate Conception reopens to celebrate the Virgin Mary," Pottsville *Republican Herald*, http://republicanherald.com/news/immaculate-conception-reopens-to-celebrate-the-virgin-mary-1.1242784.

Kashatus, William C., III. "The Molly Maguires: Fighting for Justice," *Pennsylvania Heritage*, Pennsylvania Historical and Museum Commission, http://www.phmc. state.pa.us/portal/communities/pa-heritage/files/molly-maguires-fighting-for-justice.pdf.

Lewis, Arthur H. *Lament for the Molly Maguires*. New York: Harcourt, Brace & World, Inc., 1969.

Loy, Matt. "The Legend of the Molly Maguires," Pennsylvania Center for the Book, http://pabook2.libraries.psu.edu/palitmap/Mollies.html.

Moffett, Cleveland. "The Overthrow of the Molly Maguires," McClure's Magazine, Volume IV, December 1894 to May 1895. https://ehistory.osu.edu/exhibitions/gildedage/content/mollymaguires.

"The Molly Maguires (1970)," Lehigh University, http://www.lehigh.edu/~ineng/paw/paw-history.htm.

"'Molly Maguires' Records," Pennsylvania Historical and Museum Commission, http:// www.phmc.pa.gov/Archives/Research-Online/Pages/Molly-Maguires.aspx.

"Molly Maguires story echoes through new Mahanoy City statue," Pottsville *Republican Herald*, http://republicanherald.com/news/molly-maguires-story-echoes-through-new-mahanoy-city-statue-1.800170.

Schuylkill County, Pennsylvania; genealogy—family history—biography; containing historical sketches of old families and of representative and prominent citizens, past and present. J.H. Beers & Co., http://www.ebooksread.com/authors-eng/jh-beers--co/schuylkill-county-pennsylvania-genealogy--family-history--biography-containin-ebh/page-54-schuylkill-county-pennsylvania-genealogy--family-history--biography-containin-ebh.shtml.

Serfass, Donald R. "Area Irish mystery remains unsolved," Lehighton *Times News*, March 17, 2014, https://www.tnonline.com/2014/mar/17/area-irish-mystery-remains-unsolved.
Varonka, Steve. *Molly Justice*. Bloomsburg, PA: Coal Hole Productions, 2001.
Wallace, Anthony F.C. *St. Clair: A Nineteenth-Century Coal Town's Experience with a Disaster-Prone Industry*. New York: Alfred A. Knopf, 1987.

Chapter 11: Two Rivers Brewing Company

Author interview with Troy Reynard, Jeremy Bialker, Josh Bushey, and Wendy Carroll, Two Rivers Brewing Company, Easton, Pennsylvania, Jan. 12, 2018.

Acitelli, Tom. "When Brewpubs Started Booming," *All About Beer* magazine, Feb. 11, 2015, http://allaboutbeer.com/when-brewpubs-started-booming/.
Allen, Sarah. "10 Minutes with Troy Reynard," *Barista* magazine, April 12, 2014, http://www.baristamagazine.com/10-minutes-with-troy-reynard/.
"Beer History," Craftbeer.com, https://www.craftbeer.com/beer/beer-history.
Flowers, Jeff. "The History of Homebrewing: How Beer-Making Has Evolved Over the Years," Kegerator.com, Feb. 7, 2014, https://learn.kegerator.com/history-of-homebrewing/.
"History of Craft Brewing," Brewers Association, https://www.brewersassociation.org/brewers-association/history/history-of-craft-brewing/.
Hope, Richard F. *The Little Apple: Easton, PA During Prohibition*. Lulu Press, 2013.
Martin, Clive. "Why the radio is one of history's most important inventions," CNN, July 27, 2017, https://www.cnn.com/style/article/history-of-radios-cooper-hewitt-museum/index.html.
Olanoff, Lynn. "West Bethlehem speakeasy part of Historic Bethlehem Partnership Rooms to View tour," Lehigh Valley Live, June 3, 2011, http://www.lehighvalleylive.com/bethlehem/index.ssf/2011/06/west_bethlehem_speakeasy_part.html.
"Our Coffee," The Cosmic Cup Coffee Co., http://www.cosmiccupcoffee.com/our_coffee.htm.
"Our History," NBCUniversal, http://www.nbcuniversal.com/our-history#decade_1.
"Truckload of Seized Booze Topples into the Delaware Canal," Allentown *Morning Call*, Aug. 26, 1922, https://www.newspapers.com/image/281245636.
Wills, Warren. "The State of American Craft Beer—Pennsylvania," American Craft Beer, May 11, 2017, http://www.americancraftbeer.com/state-american-craft-beer-pennsylvania/.

Chapter 12: Horse Inn

Author interview with Matthew and Starla Russell, Benjamin Hash, and Russell Skiles, Horse Inn, Lancaster, Pennsylvania, Feb. 1, 2018.

International News Service, "Forgotten Trolley Found in Lancaster After Tracks are Removed," Harrisburg *Evening News*, Oct. 8, 1932, https://www.newspapers.com/image/58038695/?terms=%22Conestoga%2BTransportation%22.
Modern Machinery, July 1899.
"Prohibition Will Be Enforced Says New Agent Here," Harrisburg Telegraph, Oct. 24, 1927, https://www.newspapers.com/image/41471245/.
Robinson, Ryan. "Police officers save residents as Martic Forge Hotel burns," Lancaster Online, June 14, 2004, http://lancasteronline.com/news/police-officers-save-residents-as-martic-forge-hotel-burns/article_25e1fd29-2231-5ec2-bb98-0094ee3b1983.html.

About the Author

M. Diane McCormick found her love of history in her parents' stories of Pennsylvania's anthracite region. Her mother's antique shop at a York County, Pennsylvania, crossroads stocked weird and wonderful things that felt like keys to other eras. She and her husband, Marc Farrell, spend their time prowling pubs and restoring their circa-1910 Harrisburg home, where they sit on the front porch during rainstorms, and enjoy their green backyard sanctuary on summer evenings.

Diane walked off the day-job cliff and into freelance writing on Jan. 2, 2005. For *TheBurg* newspaper in Harrisburg, Pennsylvania, she explores city life and issues, winning a 2017 first-place Keystone Press Award. As Harrisburg magazine's "Adventure Chick," she handled a python and drove a Ferrari, among other wild and crazy doings. She is a regular contributor to Susquehanna Style and varied industry magazines.

Diane has been a journalist for the Harrisburg *Patriot-News*/Pennlive.com, where she had a regular column, and the Hanover, Pennsylvania, *Evening Sun*. She served 10 years as a press secretary in the Pennsylvania House of Representatives and is former communications director for the policy advocacy organization Pennsylvania Partnerships for Children.

She holds a bachelor's degree in journalism from Indiana University of Pennsylvania, and master's degrees from Penn State University in American studies, and from Goucher College in creative nonfiction.

"Nobody lived in the past," says David McCullough. "They lived in the present. It is their present, not our present, and they don't know how it's going to come out." Diane agrees but couldn't resist criss-crossing past and present as she wrote *Well-Behaved Taverns Seldom Make History*. Someday, she will write a history keeping her characters within their realms of understanding, but for now, another McCullough quote explains her approach to her first book: "No harm's done to history by making it something someone would want to read."

46585485R00187

Made in the USA
Middletown, DE
03 June 2019